Dangerous to Know

Dangerous to Know

*Women, Crime, and Notoriety
in the Early Republic*

Susan Branson

PENN

UNIVERSITY OF PENNSYLVANIA PRESS

PHILADELPHIA

Copyright © 2008 University of Pennsylvania Press

All rights reserved. Except for brief quotations used for purposes of review or scholarly citation, none of this book may be reproduced in any form by any means without written permission from the publisher.

Published by
University of Pennsylvania Press
Philadelphia, Pennsylvania 19104-4112

Printed in the United States of America on acid-free paper

10 9 8 7 6 5 4 3 2 1

Library of Congress Cataloging-in-Publication Data

Branson, Susan.
Dangerous to know : women, crime, and notoriety in the early republic / Susan Branson.
p. cm.
Includes bibliographical references and index.
ISBN: 978-0-8122-4088-7 (alk. paper)
1. Carson, Ann Baker. 2. Clarke Mary, fl. 1815–1838. 3. Women—Pennsylvania—Philadelphia—Biography. 4. Female offenders—Pennsylvania—Philadelphia—Biography. 5. Women authors, American—19th century—Biography. 6. Philadelphia (Pa.)—Social conditions—19th century. 7. Sex role—United States—History—19th century. 8. Crime—Social aspects—United States—History—19th century. 9. Fame—Social aspects—United States—History—19th century. 10. Social status—United States—History—19th century. 1. Title.

HQ1439.P5B73 2008
305.48′9623092274811—dc22
2008009040

For Kaitlin

Contents

PREFACE ix

1. TWO WORKING WOMEN 1

2. MARRIAGE, MANHOOD, AND MURDER 24

3. THE "ENRAGED TYGRESS" 46

4. COURTING NOTORIETY 69

5. AN UNSUITABLE JOB FOR A WOMAN 90

6. BETRAYAL AND REVENGE 105

AFTERWORD 135

NOTES 141

INDEX 175

ACKNOWLEDGMENTS 181

Preface

In the early spring of 1822 two women, just released from Philadelphia's Walnut Street prison on a robbery charge, hailed a passing carriage. They drove from boardinghouse to boardinghouse throughout the city. Though the women had sufficient money to rent a room, they were denied admittance everywhere. In a final attempt to find lodging for his passengers, the coachman took them to a brothel. But even the madam of a house of prostitution refused them entry. The worried coachman declared, "They must be a pair of she devils when even a brothel refused them admittance." Finally, someone did agree to take the infamous Ann Carson and her companion, Mrs. Stoops: Captain Parrish, who ran a gambling house on South Third Street. Even there, Carson was admitted only because Parrish cared more for her money than for his reputation; she and the more affluent Mrs. Stoops paid for a week's lodging in advance, ordered oysters and punch, and conspicuously displayed their cash. Shortly after this episode, Ann Carson contacted Mary Clarke, a respectable woman who earned her living by her pen. She asked Clarke to ghostwrite her autobiography. Clarke not only agreed to write Carson's book, she also invited Ann Carson to live in her home. Seven months later, *The History of the Celebrated Mrs. Ann Carson* rattled Philadelphia society and became one of the most scandalous, and eagerly read, memoirs of the age. This gripping yarn told the story of a woman who tried to rescue her lover from the gallows (by blowing up the Walnut Street prison, if necessary), attempted to kidnap the governor of Pennsylvania, and chose a life of crime over one of genteel poverty. It entertained readers with accounts of love, murder, and criminal daring.

Dangerous to Know is a paired history of Carson and Clarke. An intertwined biography relates episodes in each woman's life that highlight the strategies these women used to succeed in a society that constrained women's activities and ambitions.

Ann Baker was married at age fifteen because her parents were too impoverished to keep her. For twelve years, she led a tumultuous life with John Carson, an irresponsible sea captain whose unreliable income forced her to seek work. She opened a small shop, which brought her success. And John's long absences gave her a measure of personal independence; unfettered by her husband's authority, Ann Carson sought pleasure in several adulterous relationships. But a murder one cold January night in 1816 propelled Ann Carson irrevocably into the criminal underworld of robbers, counterfeiters, and conmen. She embraced this dangerous life; though it was rife with tenuous alliances and ever-present risk, Carson found the economic and personal freedom that had previously eluded her.

Carson's ghostwriter was no less daring. Mary Clarke pursued dangerous associations and wrote scandalous exposés based on her experiences. Like Carson, Clarke was forced to become her family's breadwinner. Also like Carson, she found respectable work—as a playwright and journalist. But Clarke walked a fine line between respectability and notoriety. Her collaboration with Carson was just the beginning of a series of publications that supplied readers with sex, scandal, and murder. Clarke immersed herself in the world of criminals and disreputable actors, and she used her acquaintance with this demimonde to shape a career as a sensationalist writer.

The activities of Mary Clarke and Ann Carson seem far removed from prescribed female behavior in early nineteenth-century America. Both women deliberately violated gender conventions and courted publicity. Why would Clarke jeopardize her reputation, and hence her livelihood, through associations with a criminal? And why would Carson, already on a downward social and economic spiral, wish to publicize her infamy rather than disguise it? The answers lie in the two major sources for this study: *The History of the Celebrated Mrs. Ann Carson* (1822) and *The Memoirs of the Celebrated and Beautiful Mrs. Ann Carson* (1838). The first is Carson's autobiography (written with Mary Clarke). The second is Clarke's continuation of Carson's life story. The books relate actual events in both women's lives—their family circumstances, work, and Carson's trials and incarcerations. But Carson and Clarke are unreliable narrators. Ann Carson and Mary Clarke used their writings, and manipulated their readers, to further their own ends.

Few people know the histories of these two women, who did extraordinary things for their time. Yet their circumstances must have been familiar to a large group of people: middling women, fallen on hard times, who struggled to keep themselves afloat. Of course, none used the methods that Ann Carson did. And few women were in a position to be a professional author like Clarke. These two women were highly conscious (and critical) of the social norms of their time. They had an accurate sense of what was possible, what was not, and how they could get what they wanted given the constraints under which they lived. Both women deliberately challenged gender conventions because they could not afford to abide by them; both women devised ways to do what they wanted *despite* social norms. For Carson, this meant open violation of convention. Clarke, however, worked within the system to circumvent it. Regardless of their methods, each woman was dangerous to know: Carson because she got other people into trouble as well as herself and Clarke because she wrote scandalous accounts of the lives of acquaintances and friends. David C. McCullough has remarked that "no harm's done to history by making it something someone would want to read." My hope is that readers will find the unique experiences of these two women intriguing, and at the same time come away with a more nuanced perspective on the ideas, assumptions, and prejudices about American women in the early nineteenth century.

I
Two Working Women

NEITHER MARY CLARKE nor Ann Carson expected to work outside the home, let alone become the sole breadwinner for her family. Necessity propelled them into the marketplace; illness, disability, and subsequent financial hardship forced both women to become economically resourceful (and, in the case of Clarke, creative). Although legal restrictions kept most women under feme covert status, many, like Carson and Clarke, crossed the boundary of domestic space into the public world of paid work.[1] They were not alone. The early nineteenth century was an era of increased manufacturing and capitalization in the economic sector, but these advances were accompanied by an atmosphere of uncertainty and financial peril. First the embargo in 1807, then three years of war from 1812 to 1815, followed by the panic of 1819, all contributed to this insecurity. More women ventured into the marketplace as wage-earners and entrepreneurs. They did so in a complex, fluid, and risk-filled environment. These were the conditions under which Clarke and Carson made their economic choices.

The type of work Ann Carson chose was determined by her education and her social status. Carson's father, Thomas Baker, had served on a privateer during the Revolutionary War and was held prisoner on the infamous *Jersey* prison ship in New York harbor. By the time of Ann's birth in 1785, he was a ship's captain employed by a Philadelphia shipping firm. Baker was able to keep his family in genteel comfort: he and his family lived in a style "suitable to his rank and fortune; the first being highly respectable, and the latter easy."[2] Affluence meant the Bakers enjoyed, as Ann recalled, "the luxuries of the West Indies" as well as "the delicacies of our plentiful city." Ann described her childhood and youth as "scenes of perfect happiness unalloyed."[3]

The Baker daughters received an education typical for young women of means in the late eighteenth century. Ann attended, by her own admission, "the best seminaries Philadelphia then afforded."[4] Though she did

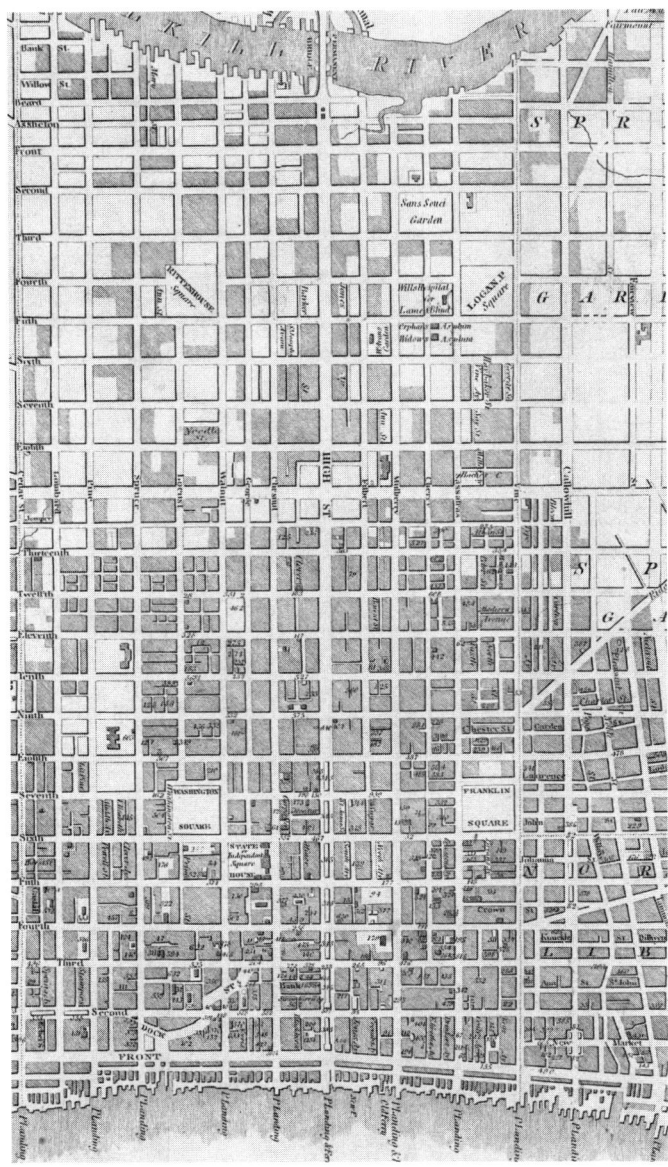

Figure 1. Map of Philadelphia. Most of the places Ann Carson and Mary Clarke lived and worked were in central Philadelphia. Carson's china store was at Dock and Second streets, near the Delaware River. The two women later shared a house in the western part of the city, near the Schuylkill River. Detail of *Map of the City of Philadelphia*, drawn by J. Simons, published by C. P. Fessenden, 1834. Courtesy of the Library Company of Philadelphia.

not specify which these were, the most famous school for young women, the Young Ladies' Academy of Philadelphia, was not among them. Ann went to a coeducational school, and later condemned the practice of throwing the sexes together during their impressionable years. Ann became "complete mistress of my needle, and excelled in plain sewing and fancy work."[5] These attainments were expected of, and needed by, a middle-class woman who did not work outside the home. Ann, like her mother, was trained to run a household: supervise what few servants they could afford, perform some of the household work, keep accounts, educate children, and socialize with other men and women of her class. Like many seaport families whose fortunes were tied to commercial shipping in the late eighteenth century, the Baker family's troubles began during the undeclared war with France, called the Quasi-War, in the 1790s. This conflict stemmed from the Jay Treaty; it stabilized commercial relations between the United States and Britain but it threw American relations with France into a tailspin. The Proclamation of Neutrality of 1793, intended to protect American ships from both the French and the British, was not honored by the British. Even worse, the British negotiated a truce with Portugal, which allowed the Algerian pirates free access to the Atlantic and enabled them to prey on American ships after 1793. The United States did not recognize these bandits as a legitimate power and refused to pay them tribute money. Thus, by the end of 1793, over 250 American ships had been seized. Philadelphia was one of the hardest hit ports, in part because of its trade with the French West Indies. All these incidents brought pressure to bear on the U.S. government to find a solution to ease the strain on commerce. But the Jay Treaty created as much controversy as it attempted to settle.[6]

Thomas Baker, employed as a ship's captain for Philadelphia merchants, was detained in France for eighteen months between 1794 and 1796. After his return to Philadelphia, Baker did not work for the next three years. Whether this was by choice or because of the difficulties with American shipping is unclear, though Carson suggested that her father may have declined to work, having "contracted a habit of indolence and a disgust to his profession."[7]

Without a salary, the family lived on their accumulated savings, which were soon exhausted. When Baker finally resumed his career with the navy, he sailed to the West Indies, leaving behind a letter to his wife in which he informed her of their financial embarrassments. Jane Baker learned that they no longer owned the house they were living in. It was mortgaged to a Captain Davis, from whom Thomas Baker had borrowed money. Thomas Baker's appointment as captain of the frigate *Delaware* secured the family a decent income, but only just. With no safety net and several debts to pay, the Bakers completely depended on Thomas's earnings to keep them afloat. This security came to an end within a year. Baker, on assignment near Curacao in January 1800, contracted yellow fever. The disease (or perhaps the treatment for it) so affected Baker's health that he retired from the navy in 1801. His memory was so compromised by his illness that, according to Ann Carson, he never again was capable of conducting any kind of business. The Bakers' only source of income was Captain Baker's pension.[8]

The Baker family, with five daughters and two sons, was considerably poorer than they had been a decade before. Ann and her mother and sisters, accustomed to a protected, privileged life free from money worries, now faced an uncomfortable truth: no male head of the household would support them and they were unprepared to provide for themselves. Ann lamented that her father's pride, and his sense of what was proper for women of the upper reaches of the middle class, prevented his wife from contributing to the family income: "Had he permitted my mother to keep a shoe, grocery or grog shop, how at this time our family might have been opulent, and some of its [male] members probably lawyers, doctors, and even clergymen. The parents of numbers of our various professional characters were then of that class of society."[9]

Ann Carson may have been thinking specifically about a family with whom she had uncomfortably close encounters on several occasions in the late 1810s. The fortunes of the Merediths exemplified the rapid economic and, equally important, domestic transformations that eluded the Baker family. Jonathan Meredith, a successful tanner, began his career in the 1770s living above his shop. By the time he retired at the turn of the century, he had moved his residence away from the tannery and built several new homes in the city as rental income and investment properties. And rather than training under their father in preparation to take over his business, Meredith's sons attended university and became professional men. Jonathan's wife, unlike Jane Baker, contributed to the family's affluence, which in turn created the opportunity for their children to become professionals and entrepreneurs. Elizabeth Meredith kept the tannery books, supervised apprentices, and cared for boarders and her household. Her economic activity enabled her daughters to attend the Philadelphia Young Ladies' Academy and to socialize with other young men and women from middling and elite families. It also meant that the Merediths, should they have needed it, had a financial safety net that the Bakers lacked.[10]

With hindsight, Ann knew that her mother should have been similarly occupied. The problem lay with Captain Baker's social aspirations. A sea captain was on a par economically with a successful currier or shipbuilder, not a merchant or a lawyer. But Thomas Baker believed his family was socially on a level with families above the Bakers in terms of wealth. He also believed it was inappropriate for his daughters to work. Ann recalled that her father's pride forbade "the idea of his daughters' learning any trade."[11] The Bakers lived up to, and beyond, their means with no way of recovering when financial disaster struck. Ann's wishful thinking may have been prompted by the fact that as a child and an adult she was surrounded by economically unreliable men: her father, her husband, and even two of her brothers-in-law, Thomas Abbott and Joseph Hutton. Ann saw in her mother's life, her own life, and her sisters' lives the consequences for women of overdependence on male breadwinners. Thus, in her autobiography, Ann advocated, like her contemporary Judith Sargent Murray, that young women be more than just ornamental.[12] They needed skills to enable them to contribute to the family income.

The Baker family moved from Philadelphia to New Castle, Delaware, during Thomas's West Indian employment. When he was invalided out of the navy in 1801, the family remained in New Castle for a time. There, Ann, fifteen years old, and her elder sister Eliza, seventeen, attracted the attention of several eligible naval officers. Eliza soon became engaged to a Captain Hillyard, commander of the sloop of war *Pickering*. Ann drew the attention of the *Pickering*'s purser, Mr. Willock, who asked Ann's parents for permission to marry her. With such precarious finances, her parents readily agreed: "He was rich, and his situation lucrative, which at once conciliated [Jane Baker's] good will; nor had my father any objection to make to the proposed alliance. Mr. Willock was therefore received as my destined husband by the family."[13] Unfortunately, Ann's and Eliza's happiness was cut short when the *Pickering* was lost at sea with all hands. Soon after this tragedy the Bakers moved back to Philadelphia. Despite Captain Baker's desire to keep his wife from working, Jane Baker took eight boarders into their home on Dock Street.[14]

This reversal of the family's fortunes in the late 1790s made marrying off their oldest daughters an attractive proposition. Eliza, after mourning the loss of Captain Hillyard, became engaged to John Hutton, the eldest son of a neighboring family. Ann, after her introduction to male society in

New Castle, and her flirtation with Willock, attracted the attention of another naval officer, John Carson. The twenty-four-year-old Carson had been second lieutenant under Baker on the *Delaware* (Carson had also contracted yellow fever on the disastrous voyage to Curacao). Perhaps out of financial desperation, the prospect of removing two children from the Baker household compelled Thomas Baker to listen to John Carson's request to marry fifteen-year-old Ann. As Ann understood it, her father's affectionate attachment to Carson, whom he "loved . . . as a son, having participated in each other's afflictions, and endured the dark hour of adversity together," combined with Baker's "imbecility of mind," persuaded Baker to agree to the marriage. As to Ann's feelings about this life-changing event, she described Carson in the following terms: "He was ever uniformly allowed to be a handsome man, his natural advantages were increased by his naval uniform, and a certain air of command which I had ever admired, as well as his dashing appearance."[15] As to Ann's emotions at the prospect of marriage, she later claimed that "to the tender affection that ought to be the basis of all matrimonial engagements, my heart was an entire stranger."[16] This is hardly surprising given her age and her minimal contact with someone who was her father's colleague, an adult nine years her senior.

What attracted Carson to a fifteen-year-old girl? Ann described herself as taller than the average woman and physically mature by the age of fourteen. Though, as she admitted, "This rapid growth gave me the appearance of womanhood, before age justified the idea, or my understanding was sufficiently cultivated to render me a suitable companion for gentlemen of my father's standing in society and profession."[17] Ann, as the daughter of a sailor, could readily adapt to the peripatetic lifestyle of a spouse who would be away from home for long periods of time. The Bakers' residence in New Castle after her father's illness was Ann's first introduction to male society. There she was "surrounded by gay, gallant, dissipated officers from all the states in the union, some of whom vied with each other to gain my approbation and favour. Thus were the seeds of vanity and the love of conquest cherished in my heart."[18]

By her own admission, Ann found naval men more attractive than those of any other profession: "Sea-faring men are generally possessed of strong minds and extended ideas; their profession carrying them to every quarter of the globe, and the extensive intercourse they have with persons of all ranks of society, gives a liberality to their minds which few, if any other class of men ever acquire. This, united to their education and habits of command, gives them a superiority over landmen."[19] John Carson was such a man. He was handsome, came from a good family (his father had been a prominent Philadelphia physician), and he was a college-educated naval officer on the fast track to promotion and financial success. John Carson's income and social background could restore Ann to her comfortable middle-class world.

Ann Baker married John Carson in June 1801. The following month, John departed for India, working as chief officer on the ship *China*. John Carson may have chosen to leave the navy at this time to earn a larger income in the private sector. Whatever his reason, he sought work as a master on merchant ships in both the East India and China trade for the next six years. Ann moved in with her parents. When John came back from the East Indies, the couple set up a house, "furnished in a genteel manner," at 47 George Street in Southwark, a few blocks from the river.[20] Ann later returned to her parents' home when she was pregnant with her first child. This was her pattern over the next several years: residing with her husband between voyages and staying with her parents during John's absences.

In 1804, John Carson assumed command of the *Pennsylvania Packet*, owned by Joshua and Thomas Gilpin. Carson made voyages to Madras and Calcutta in May of that year and then sailed to Canton in June 1805.[21] Ann Carson was materially well cared for during these years. Her time was spent rearing a growing family (they had three sons between 1803 and 1811). Financially, John's position as a ship captain provided the Carsons with a comfortable income. Moreover, and of importance to Ann's economic future, John took advantage of his visits to the East to purchase quantities of porcelain—an investment as well as an enhancement to the family's lifestyle.

But Captain Carson's trip to China was not without incident. The *Pennsylvania Packet* arrived in Canton loaded with ginseng, a commodity much in demand by the Chinese. According to Ann's account of the misadventure that followed, John, against his better judgment, was persuaded by an unnamed gentleman—probably the supercargo—to sell some of the shipment illegally. Disaster ensued. John Carson himself was only indirectly involved, as the laws of the port of Canton required foreign ships to anchor at Whampoa, four miles down the Pearl River from the city. Only small boats that ferried the cargo into Canton were allowed back and forth between the sailing ships and the warehouses on the docks.[22] The *Pennsylvania Packet*'s supercargo was responsible for conducting business in the city while the captain remained on the ship. The authorities arrested the supercargo and seized the *Pennsylvania Packet*. Carson and his crew spent the next three months trapped in the harbor. This delay meant sailing home without benefit of the seasonal trade winds. After enduring a hurricane off the Cape of Good Hope and a puncture to the hull (caused by a swordfish), the crew bailed water around the clock until the ship reached Philadelphia. The *Pennsylvania Packet* limped home with an exhausted crew and a "dissipated and intoxicated" captain.[23]

Ann marked this particular voyage as the beginning of her husband's twin struggles with steady work and sobriety. Ann Carson may have known of her husband's alcoholic habits. She later acknowledged that John's drinking was "peculiar to all his family."[24] Carson tendered his resignation to the Gilpins. Not surprisingly, as Ann recalled, the "disasters of the last voyage had injured him in the estimation of the merchants."[25] Carson made sporadic attempts to seek employment. At one point he traveled to Baltimore, taking half the family savings with him, and stayed drunk for four weeks. Later he went to Charleston, South Carolina, going so far as to disguise his name (he used Hunter, his mother's family name). Perhaps he feared that his reputation had preceded him: maritime circles were small enough that Carson's failings may have been common knowledge on the waterfronts up and down the coast. In Charleston, he found work for a few months on a gunboat. But after more than a year of unemployment, Ann's confidence in John's ability to retain a job was low. With the family's financial resources almost gone and two children to provide for, Ann Carson decided to take command of their economic fortunes.

In 1807, Ann Carson moved to a house at 184 South Second Street, complete with an existing shop on the ground floor in "a part of the city well calculated for business," and began to sell china, queensware, and glassware. Rent was $500 a year. Here she lived with her two children, her parents, and at least four of her younger siblings. Ann Carson confronted several obstacles in her effort to earn a living. The most personal of her obstacles was the opposition of her mother, who feared that Ann's lack of experience was likely to lead to failure. But Ann was confident of her abilities and scornful of her mother's fears: "My mind, ever active and enterprising, was not to be intimidated by her imbecile doubts and false pride. Independence was my idol."[26]

Few business opportunities were available for women in the early nineteenth century. Professions and crafts were exclusively male, though many of these occupations relied on the participation of female family members. Some women, married or single, ran taverns, boardinghouses, small shops, or schools. Ann's sister, Sarah, ran a school from 1807 until at least 1811.[27]

For married women, their legal status as feme covert could impede economic pursuits; without the ability to make contracts, it was difficult to conduct business. Many towns and cities, including Philadelphia, made provisions for this situation by issuing feme sole trader licenses. Carson received such a license, thus guaranteeing her creditors and customers that she was responsible for her business.[28]

The disintegration of Ann Carson's financial and familial stability occurred against a background of national economic and diplomatic crises. By 1806, trouble with the British over blockades, impressments of American sailors, and confrontations between British and American naval vessels resulted in the Nonimportation Act. This act barred the export of British goods to the United States, and it was quickly followed by the Embargo Act at the end of 1807, which closed American ports. For more than a year, all shipping-related businesses were shut down.[29]

Carson's decision to open a china shop rather than seek to earn a living with her needle (which was the only trade she possessed any training for) was based on the desire to physically combine home and work and the need to earn enough to support her family: Carson and her servants could tend to the shop without neglecting domestic responsibilities. The millinary trade was dominated by women who put their needlework skills to economic use. Ann Carson may have realized that selling her needlework skills in a saturated market would not guarantee a sufficient income. However, imported china, as Ann Carson well knew, was a scarce commodity in Philadelphia and elsewhere. Wholesalers' stock was low and few retail shops were competing with her business. Moreover, consumers in this era were increasingly interested in spending money on tableware, despite the trade restrictions that limited supply. The wealthy purchased high-end Chinese porcelain. Middle- and lower-class consumers bought the British-manufactured pearlware and creamware that Carson sold.[30]

Carson found the cash to open her shop by selling some of her furniture. Jane Baker also lent her money to help with the shop. Carson's initial stock was her own accumulation of chinaware that John had brought home between 1801 and 1805. She augmented this supply with purchases from wholesalers in Philadelphia. When she exhausted her credit with Philadelphia merchants, Carson traveled to New York and Boston. Her business was steady. In 1811, she asked merchant Stephen Girard for a loan to purchase stock to make good on a contract she had with a shipping firm to outfit its ship.[31]

The opening of trade with China in the late eighteenth century created a consumer demand for elegant porcelain dinnerware, textiles, and lacquerware. Wealthy Philadelphians, such as Girard, dined off delicate porcelain plates embellished with bridges, cherry blossoms, cranes, or special-order, one-of-a-kind family crests and initials. Newspaper advertisements alerted Philadelphia consumers and china sellers when new shipments arrived from Canton. John Carson may have purchased Chinese porcelain (and during his ill-fated voyage to Canton in 1805 he certainly had enough time to do so). But Ann Carson had neither the means nor probably the inclination to restock her shop with these rare and expensive items. Instead, she, like the other small china sellers in Philadelphia and elsewhere, catered to Philadelphians' quotidian plate, bowl, cup, and dishware needs. She stocked the modestly priced, creamy-white British queensware popular in the early nineteenth century.[32]

In taking the initiative, Ann Carson managed to provide for herself, her children, and the Baker family. By combining households and resources, the house on Second Street became a family home and a business. Carson, her younger sister Sarah, as well as two of Carson's servants, Temperance Barkley and Sarah White, worked in the household and waited in the shop when needed. Thus Carson was able to care for her three young children and run a business. When she needed to be away from home, such as when she made her trips to Boston and New York, her mother cared for her sons.

Despite the absence of the "ease elegance and retirement" that she had come to expect from her upbringing, Carson was proud of her talents as a working woman. She took satisfaction in being "a useful and active member of society." She described herself at this period in her life as valuing the financial independence her work brought her. Through her own efforts she "daily increased [her] little capital, and added to [her] stock in trade." Her achievements were even more remarkable considering the problems John Carson continued to cause his family.[33]

John returned to Philadelphia after several months of work in South Carolina. With increased confrontations between the Americans and the British at sea, the U.S. government reversed the downsizing policy begun under President Jefferson. Carson reentered the navy in the summer of 1808 but failed to get his lieutenancy back. Instead he was given a commission as sailing master with orders to join the *Wasp* at Philadelphia. Carson sailed with the *Wasp* to Gloucester Point, a few miles down river from Philadelphia. Ann must have been relieved at the prospect of her husband once again contributing to the family income. But a week later a midshipman called at the house inquiring for him. Once out of Philadelphia (and out of Ann's sight), John left the ship and went on a drinking spree. He finally returned to the house "dressed in a round jacket and sailors' trowsers, with a small bundle tied up in a pocket handercheif [*sic*] in his hand." Ann learned that John "had been to the Yellow Springs on a frolic," where he had sold his clothes. He had also sold a watch belonging to his wife—one that she had hoped to save for their eldest son.[34]

Despite his dereliction of duty, John Carson stayed with the *Wasp* on its voyage to France, but when it returned to New York in the spring of 1809, Carson again left the ship without permission, returning to Philadelphia. Ann may not have known that her spouse was absent without leave until Lieutenant Cassin, sent by his commanding officer, tracked down John Carson at his home. This time, John resigned (or was made to resign) his commission. Not surprisingly, his behavior "precluded [him] from all hope of employment in the public service."[35]

Yet John Carson's disgrace with the navy did not prevent him from obtaining work on private vessels. He may, when sober, have been very good at his job. Alternatively, navy recruitment might have put a pinch on private shipping, forcing merchants to scramble for both masters and crew. In 1810, Carson signed on to one of Stephen Girard's ships heading for India. Though Carson was hired to be first mate, he was given the wages and status of a captain. This bonus pay may have reflected the scarcity of available labor. But while in harbor preparing for the voyage, Carson again disappeared, returning home after a few days "squalid and dirty." Girard quickly hired a replacement.

Again Carson's network of support, or the demand for workers, came to his rescue. A Captain McKibbin asked him to be his first mate, and Carson was again paid captain's wages. To Ann's surprise, John sailed on the *Phoenix*'s voyage to Cádiz in October 1811. In the early spring of 1812, Ann read a notice of the ship's arrival in a Philadelphia newspaper. The *Phoenix* was anchored a hundred miles south of Philadelphia in the Delaware River, waiting for ice to clear. Ann sought out Captain McKibbin, who had come ashore in advance of the ship's docking, to ask after John. The news was good: John was sober and industrious. A week later, Ann encountered McKibbin again. This time she learned that John had left the ship when it docked in Philadelphia, but he had not returned home. Once again, John Carson was off on a drinking spree.

Ann tracked her husband down to a disreputable boardinghouse where the landlady, a Mrs. Payne, freely supplied John with the means and opportunity to indulge himself. Ann went to the house, retrieved her husband, who was in a drunken stupor, had him carried back home, and, as she recalled, "enforce[d] my first resolution, and no longer consider[ed] Capt. C. as a husband." Ann Carson refused John "all the privileges of a husband as regarded myself, but the house was at his service—all, save my person, and chamber, which were sacred."[36] John Carson became just another mouth to feed and another one of Ann's responsibilities.

This latest demonstration of John's weakness was the final straw—and a personal turning point for Ann Carson. Saddled with a spouse who could not hold a job, or his liquor, she again sought to find him employment on a ship. By now she had no expectations that John would provide an income for the family. Ann's disgust, registered in her recollections of these years, more than hints that she was probably seeking to get him out of the way. Both Carsons traveled to New York City in the spring of 1812. For three weeks Ann remained there, trying to find John a job. She did not succeed. She returned to Philadelphia alone—to her business and her children. Shortly after her return, John sent his wife a letter that told her he had found work and was about to take ship for Europe. For Ann, this must have been welcome news. Though still legally married, she was in practice a single woman with a successful business, answering to no one. As she put it, "My own spirit had emancipated me from thralldom . . . delicacy forbade me my declaring my infranchisement [sic], but I did not the less enjoy it."[37] Ann Carson's newfound security was short lived. As relations between the United States and Britain devolved into full-scale warfare, the precarious import trade diminished even further. Carson was again bereft of sufficient stock to supply her customers. To supplement her shrinking income, she and her mother became part of the legion of uniform suppliers of the U.S. Quartermaster Corps. Both women put their needle skills to work. Enterprising as always, they subcontracted the actual sewing of garments out to other women while Carson and her mother cut out material and then passed it on to "the females that depended on us for bread, and the support of their families."[38] Jane Baker was the one who contracted with the Purveyor of Public Supplies at the Schuylkill Arsenal. She benefited from the Quartermaster's use of uniform production as a form of financial aid to soldiers' widows (or, in this case, the spouse of an invalided officer). Carson and her mother were only two of the several thousand workers employed to turn out as many as three thousand uniforms every week at the height of the war.[39]

Though the conflict with Britain curtailed her supply of imported tableware for a time, income from the uniforms kept the Bakers and the Carsons financially afloat. Carson kept her shop going and purchased new supplies when they became available. And she was rid, at least for a time, of her troublesome spouse. She had succeeded, of necessity, in entering the marketplace. Without experience but with a great deal of energy and incentive, Carson developed a business that suited her family circumstances and catered to an important consumer market.

Mary Clarke's work life was also created out of necessity. Like Ann Carson, Mary Clarke was an educated middle-class woman who needed to earn a living. Unlike Carson, Clarke did not write an autobiography. But her publications contain important clues to the personal circumstances that compelled her to become the primary earner for her family. In December 1814, Mary Clarke placed an announcement in a Philadelphia newspaper, the *United States Gazette*, that she proposed to publish a "Weekly Miscellaneous Paper."[40] To attract readers, Clarke offered a free subscription to anyone who obtained twelve subscribers for her. She left subscription papers in many of the bookshops and circulating libraries in the center of the city. Though she admitted to a fear that the prospect of a woman undertaking to publish and edit a magazine would "excite the scoffs and censure of the malignant part of mankind," Clarke nevertheless intended to pursue her scheme because, as she told readers, "A Mother will brave death for the support of her children, and she has five who look up to her for support and protection; and by patronizing this work each subscriber will contribute their mite towards assisting her with her family.[41]

It is unclear what immediate circumstances prompted Clarke to begin the *Intellectual Regale, or Ladies Tea Tray*. In her proposal, she says she had considered publishing a magazine for four years. By 1814, there were no magazines catering directly to women, in either Philadelphia or New York City. (Samuel White's *Weekly Visitor or Ladies' Miscellany*, after a ten-year run, ended in 1812.) Even the long-lived British *Lady's Magazine* (London, 1770–1811) had ceased publication. Clarke's *Tea Tray* met a local, and perhaps even regional, need. Like Ann Carson, Mary Clarke sought to cater to an existing market rather than face the challenge of creating a demand for her product. But Clarke's entry into the publishing trade set her apart: no American woman had ever edited and published a magazine for women. Moreover, Clarke's personal situation, amply documented in the pages of the *Tea Tray*, is vivid evidence of the challenges faced by women during a time when very few were able to support themselves through writing of any kind.

Little is known about Clarke's personal circumstances beyond what she revealed about herself in biographies and ghostwritten memoirs of other people that she penned in the 1820s and 1830s. Born sometime in the early 1780s, she was married with several children by the time she began to publish the *Tea Tray*. Whether her husband or family was involved in printing or publishing is not known, but Clarke undertook, as she informed her *Tea Tray* readers, to edit, publish, and for a time print the magazine herself. From her subsequent statements, her husband was probably serving with the American military, leaving Clarke the sole provider for herself and her five children. Though married, Clarke, like Carson, held feme sole status that enabled her to claim proprietorship of the magazine. As she discovered, this legal identity was a double-edged sword: it conveyed economic freedom, which was unusual for married women, but also made her responsible for her debts.[42]

Clarke, who must have known the risks involved, chose to create a magazine by herself in 1814, during the war with Great Britain. Editors and owners, often the same person, were responsible for seeking financial backers, quickly establishing a subscriber list large enough to support the magazine, and handling submissions and advertising. Moreover, quixotic subscribers and difficulties with printers and distributors made magazine publication a precarious undertaking. Clarke did this not only at a time of great economic uncertainty but also during an era when financial autonomy was often difficult for women to achieve. Few possessed the necessary skills and fortitude to enter the very public (and therefore male-defined) printing and publishing trade.[43]

Clarke was quick to dismiss the notion that she courted literary fame, a tactic that she may have thought necessary to quell any criticisms of her entry into a male province. She emphasized that necessity to feed her children compelled her to start her publication. She candidly stated in the preface to the first issue of the *Tea Tray* that she "wanted employment, to drive away distressing reflections, and money for necessary purposes. Therefore I issued proposals for the paper, and fairly invited everybody that chose to pay six and a quarter cents, to my *Tea Tray*."[44] Thus Clarke provided subscribers with the double satisfaction of giving charity to a deserving family and enjoying literary entertainment. Clarke cast her net over both sexes: she relied on "the liberality and known philanthropy of the females of Philadelphia," to subscribe to the magazine, but she also asked for the "protection" of the gentlemen.[45]

In turn, Clarke extended aid to other disadvantaged women. In her proposal she offered to place free advertisements for "females of good character wanting employment, and widows who keep boarding houses." Although Clarke's entry into the marketplace was an economic enterprise, she clothed her activities within an acceptable rhetorical framework: dependency and maternal responsibility. This language of sentiment fit well with the tone of the magazine's content and with the predilections of the era. Clarke offered readers predisposed to shed a tear for fictional characters a chance to extend their sympathies to one of their real-life neighbors while fostering a sisterhood of interdependence and mutual aid.[46]

This culture of sensibility evoked by Clarke had a long and transatlantic career that began in the late eighteenth century and continued into the nineteenth century. H. C. Lewis, who published the *Ladies Literary Museum* (Philadelphia) shortly after the demise of the *Tea Tray*, also expressed his dependence on the benevolence of readers to help support his wife and children. And Sarah J. Hale, like Clarke, in the prospectus for the *American Ladies' Magazine*, used "a language of support" to inform the public of her financial need. The prose and verse in the *Tea Tray* embraced this literary style and content. It also presaged the coming of a more public, active benevolence on the part of middle-class and elite women.[47]

Clarke's magazine also reveals the origins of the ideas and attitudes identified by scholars in the works of later authors such as Catharine Maria Sedgwick and Lydia Maria Child. Like Clarke, these writers preserved a delicate balance between gender conventions and women's entry into a public economic sphere. Sedgwick published her first book, *A New England Tale*, in 1822. Child started her magazine, the *Juvenile Miscellany*, in 1826. Like these better-known "literary domestics," as Mary Kelley terms them, Mary Clarke faced the challenge of maintaining a public presence and fulfilling private responsibilities and roles. Unlike Sedgwick and Child, however, Clarke chose to capitalize on her domestic predicament in a profoundly public way. Though Clarke did fashion her magazine after others of its kind, what sets the *Tea Tray* apart is Clarke's deliberate exploitation of early nineteenth-century gender conventions and her enlistment of readers' sympathies to make her magazine succeed. Similar periodicals of the time included editorial comments to subscribers and readers, but in none of them was the editor a character or persona as Clarke was in the *Tea Tray*. Nor did editors deliberately manipulate the emotions of readers, taking advantage of gender conventions to elicit sympathy (and sales) as Clarke did.[48]

The *Tea Tray* was also part of a developing American print medium in which women played an increasingly important role both as authors and as readers. Coincident with the rise of academies for young ladies and the proliferation of texts, both prescriptive and recreational, aimed at women, was a developing readership and authorship that fit well with a republican ideology that encouraged women's intellectual pursuits and fostered their active participation in the civic life of the nation.[49]

Clarke may also have based her appeal at least tacitly on the fact that she and her readers shared these values and aspirations. Clarke's ability to write, her knowledge of literature, and her frequent literary allusions indicated her social and educational background. But without the support of a spouse, Clarke found it necessary to enter the marketplace—a situation her financially secure female patrons did not share.[50]

The geography of Philadelphia helped Clarke attract readers and contributors. The city was still relatively compact in the early nineteenth century; Philadelphia's population in 1810 was slightly less than fifty-four thousand. Most inhabitants still lived between the Delaware and the Schuylkill rivers, an area approximately twenty-two blocks square. Most of the *Tea Tray*'s subscribers lived within walking distance of Clarke's office and residence near Arch and Second streets. Contributors dropped off their writing at the *Tea Tray* office, where many may have had at least a nodding acquaintance with the editor. All of these factors added to the sense of intimacy and sympathy that Clarke sought to instill.[51]

The title of Clarke's magazine set the tone for its content. Like the conversations of women around the tea table, her publication discussed the fabric of women's lives. The stories and poetry, whether set in fanciful, far-off castles or genteel homes of the early republic, involved loves lost or won and virtue challenged and rewarded. Much of the short fiction imitated popular novels such as *The Coquette, The Power of Sympathy*, and *Charlotte Temple* in subject matter and style. In this regard, the *Tea Tray* was much like many other magazines of the time, whether specifically addressed to a female readership or not. In the proposal for the *Tea Tray*, Clarke announced that the magazine would include "A portion of History, Chronology, Biography, Geography, Morality, Botany, Anecdote, and a variety of useful information; with a retrospection of the News of the week; and singular Occurrences, marriages and deaths.... The Fashions, if they can be ascertained—any new songs worth publishing—poetry—a List of new publications—an occasional theatrical criticism—and a Review of the different novels extant.... A Monthly account of the variations in the market prices of provisions and clothing."[52] This miscellany of news, fashion, literature, and instruction succeeded in attracting a large number of subscribers. Over six hundred individuals signed on as readers. At least 40 percent of these subscribers were women. They were the wives and daughters of merchants and professional men, shopkeepers, and craftsmen. Some women were themselves proprietors—milliners, seamstresses, a bonnet maker, a printer, and two owners of circulating libraries.[53]

Clarke intended the *Tea Tray* as a venue for original poetry and fiction provided by readers as well as a vehicle for publishing her own work. But problems plagued the enterprise from the start. Though Clarke solicited contributions, she never received enough to fill an issue. This was despite her claim that "as some ill-disposed persons have predicted that the *Tea Tray* will not stand long, the editress assures the public, that she has a stock of solid matter to fill its pages for *five years*, all the productions of her own pen." She defiantly proclaimed that "while her friendly correspondents continue their assistance, and she retains her life and faculties, it shall stand, and smile derision to malevolence."[54] Her ambition to publish the magazine weekly, which was common at the time, made her task more difficult. To encourage submissions, she gently chided her authors: "Why does the Muse of Editha slumber? Methinks we miss Anna's gentle effusions, and Apollo's notes. Mary will amply atone for Rosa's desertion." Some contributions had to be turned away. She noted, for example, that "the piece in a female hand signed 'C.' is too personal for the *Tea Tray*."[55] On another occasion, she informed "Mortimer," if he "will reperuse [*sic*] his last communication carefully, he will agree with us in thinking that its publication would neither be creditable to himself nor honourable to us."[56]

Because sufficient acceptable contributions were not forthcoming, Clarke herself may have written a significant proportion of the anonymous and pseudonymous fiction and plays in the magazine, drawing from her boasted "stock of solid matter." Two plays for which she did claim authorship, *Lake Champlain, or The American Tars on the Borders of Canada* and *Venture It: A Comedy in Five Acts*, were both serialized in the magazine. Her separately published play, *The Fair Americans*, performed in Philadelphia in January 1815 under the title *The Return from Camp*, was prominently advertised there.[57]

Although the content of the *Tea Tray* was not particularly unique, Clarke's editorial intrusions were. She inserted frequent comments, apologies, and announcements in the *Tea Tray*. Clarke framed her personal and professional trials and tribulations almost as though they were another of the *Tea Tray*'s serial stories. Each issue revealed the difficulties she faced in collecting money, assembling material, and gathering the necessary printing supplies. For example, she apologized for the inferior quality of paper used in several issues, "but the difficulty she has found in procuring it has been great."[58] At one point, she announced that her ill health had prevented timely publication. This circumstance, compounded by the absence of "some friends on whose judgment and assistance I placed implicit confidence," Clarke explained, meant that she found herself "deserted." As a consequence, "a heavy depression has hung on my spirits for some weeks past."[59] Clarke made sure her readers understood that she depended entirely on their sympathy to support her not only economically but emotionally as well. And she conveyed this information in a way guaranteed to appeal to their sensibilities. Other magazine editors from time to time announced delayed publication or some other mishap, but their tone was straightforward, with little explanation of the circumstances. The *Port Folio*, for example, the most successful early nineteenth-century Philadelphia publication, suffered similar difficulties. Like Clarke, editor Joseph Dennie apologized to his readers for the scarcity of supplies and complained of the delinquency of subscribers' payments."[60] Clarke informed her readers not only of her financial difficulties but also of her emotional state. She drew readers into her life: she expected sympathy and comfort in the form of patience and continued subscriptions as she struggled to make ends meet. Thus Clarke positioned her editorial identity both as an authority in control of the magazine's content and as the magazine's protagonist to whom things happened. Unlike other editors of the time, Clarke revealed the very personal process of producing the *Tea Tray*, thus providing a layer of complexity and intimacy to the experience of reading. Clarke added something distinct and new to what has been described as a polyphonic, participatory, and dialogic medium: she gratified expectations of acquaintance, or even friendship.[61]

Though Clarke expressed optimism about the magazine's prospects and gratitude to her supporters, in the first issue she announced that the *Tea Tray*'s two hundred subscriptions were insufficient to ensure its success. The subscriber list she printed at the conclusion of volume one contained more than six hundred names, but her frequent reminders to subscribers that prompt payment was necessary to the survival of the publication suggest that many supporters did not fulfill their pledge.[62]

Without sufficient funds, the magazine suffered. Clarke apologized that "the title page and index to the first volume would have been given before this time, but the payments are so bad, that pecuniary considerations retarded it; and we again request the distant subscribers to discharge their arrears, and printing and paper requires ready money." When a reader criticized her writing style, Clarke responded by sharing more of her personal difficulties: "I am fully conscious of the faults you point out: but failure of payments on the part of many of my subscribers, and meanness in others, has involved me in pecuniary difficulties. These you must allow, are unfavorable to playful fancy." Clarke was not hesitant to criticize wrongdoing in those from whom she sought, and expected, cooperation.[63]

To compound the financial difficulties caused by the magazine's unreliable clientele, her employees seem to have been untrustworthy and perhaps even unsavory. She announced to her readers in early 1816 that "a black fellow named John Lowry, has gone round, taking the *Tea Trays* to be bound, in her name,—This is to inform those persons who may have committed their papers to his care, that he was discharged two weeks ago for dishonesty." That same month, she offered to those who "find it disagreeable to pay the carriers," the alternative of being called on "by a girl, of eleven years old, if they desire it."[64] She moved her office three times, presumably because of her pecuniary difficulties. These moves only exacerbated her editorial problems. And whether because of disagreements with printer Dennis Heartt or Clarke's inability to pay him for his services, by April 1815 Clarke had hired another printer. She apologized to her subscribers for the untidy state of recent issues, "which was occasioned by the taking of the printing into her own hands, and the confusion incident to a new establishment." Clarke assured her readers that "nothing of the kind shall occur in future." This was a promise she could not keep.[65]

What she did not tell her readers was that by early April 1815 she was running the *Tea Tray* from debtor's prison. Though Clarke produced the magazine as a way out of her financial difficulties, it only exacerbated them. She was arrested at the demand of Jacob Risley, to whom she owed eleven dollars and fifty-six cents for unspecified goods or services. Risley was only one among many businesspeople who called in Clarke's debts. She owed money to her printer, Dennis Heartt, but she also owed rent to several landlords—suggesting that her difficulties had been going on for some time. The schedule of property she submitted to satisfy her creditors included a list of *Tea Tray* subscribers who still owed Clarke money. The list included two of her more prominent readers, Major Manigold and General Gaines. A local printer, Thomas Smith, came to Clarke's rescue. In exchange for two hundred and fifty dollars—enough to pay her debts—Clarke assigned to him all of "my right title property and interest in the establishment of said paper together with the printing press, types, printing apparatus, paper and all diverse other things and things of every kind & description appertaining to the said establishment & prop." But the *Tea Tray*'s supplies and apparatus did not cover the entire amount of her debt, so in addition to these business-related goods, Clarke was forced to sign over "all the goods, household & kitchen furniture, implements of household, & all other goods whatsoever belonging to me." Her tables, chairs, beds, bedding, china, crockery, and curtains went to Smith in exchange for Clarke's liberty and a fresh start.[66]

Clarke had used her situation as a woman without a male provider and as a mother with five children dependent on her sole efforts for their support to attract subscribers. Yet her insolvency and imprisonment, proof of her desperate financial state, went unmentioned in her *Tea Tray* comments. Clarke could have had any number of reasons for this silence. It may have been unnecessary for her to announce her plight: the size and familiarity of the Philadelphia community may have meant that her readers knew she was in the Prune Street debtor's apartments. The nature of Pennsylvania's debtor's law forced Clarke to publicly advertise her debts in the city's newspapers. More important, Smith's purchase of Clarke's rights in the *Tea Tray* meant that she was no longer the proprietor. His bailout rescued Clarke from financial catastrophe but, at the same time, robbed her of an important asset: she could no longer claim the identity of an independent businesswoman. She had used her maverick status as a woman attempting to do a man's job as capital that she drew on to sustain a readership, solicit contributions, and collect subscription fees. But legally Clarke was no longer the proprietress of the *Tea Tray*. She was now employed by Smith. This new situation placed her back into a more traditional gendered framework of dependence, one perhaps less likely to elicit the same level of sympathy.

Clarke's direct communication with her readers provides a unique view of her chaotic financial and domestic arrangements and the responsibilities she shouldered. She apologized to her contributors for the number of typographical errors afflicting several issues. This, she informed them, was a result of sickness.[67] Her various moves from one residence to another, which she candidly explained were the result of her lack of funds, increased the chaotic state of her files.[68] Clarke informed contributors that "in the confusion of moving, several communications have been lost, the one signed by G. I have never seen, and 'Narcissa to Mr. Fennell' is also gone."[69] A notice in a June 1815 issue read, "We have to beg pardon from Miss E. B. and our friend S. for not presenting theirs earlier: but they unfortunately fell behind a bureau, from whence they were this week rescued."[70] Two weeks later another note stated, "The editress is mortified to be obliged to present Edgar's answer to William imperfect. But a part of the copy was carried out of the window by the wind, and was not missed till too late to be replaced."[71] We can imagine Clarke's household, complete with five small children and a distracted mother, as untidy, noisy, and disorganized. The combination of domestic arrangements with professional ambitions was not a felicitous one.

Despite these difficulties, Clarke's situation had improved a month later when she informed her readers that as her health returned, she felt "her prospects brighten, a ray of hope seems breaking through the darkness of the future." Contributing to this rise in spirit was the fact that she now had assistance with the *Tea Tray*: "Several literary gentlemen, (subject to the inspection of the Editress) have more immediately undertaken the Editorial, whilst her attention will be principally employed in superintending the typographical department of the work. From this union, she looks forward for the happiest effects; confiding in the justice of her subscribers to enable her to prosecute her views with advantage to both."[72] Even so, apparently her subscribers' lack of confidence in Clarke's ability to manage the magazine prompted her to issue a defiant announcement four months later: "Some ill-disposed persons endeavoring to injure the TEA-TRAY, have circulated several reports to the disadvantage of the paper, all of which are falsehoods, dark as the hearts of their authors.— The establishment never was more flourishing—nor will any change take place except Improvement in Printing, Matter and Regularity; and all the editress expects from her Subscribers is punctuality in their payments to enable her to meet the demands which the business makes on her."[73] Clarke's assertion to the contrary, the reports may have had some foundation. On the same page as the announcement, she requested her subscribers to *The Fair Americans* to call at the office for their copy; Clarke was unable to deliver it because "several subscription papers have been lost and the names forgot."[74] Despite her confrontational tone and spirited assertion of competence, Clarke's dependence on "literary gentlemen" implied that she found editing and producing the magazine too much to handle. Her answer to the rumors circulated by unnamed "ill-disposed persons" suggests that Clarke's strategy of revealing her personal circumstances to readers to gain business had backfired. Clarke's acknowledged dependence on the kindness of strangers to support herself and her children, though calculated to elicit sympathy, had also produced doubt in the minds of her clients. Candor about the problems she encountered running the magazine may have worked against her rather than for her. With one trouble following another, her magazine struggled until December 1816.[75]

The *Tea Tray* is Clarke's first surviving publication. Before her collaboration with Ann Carson in 1821, Clarke briefly edited another magazine, the *Parterre*, wrote songs and poetry, penned two pamphlets on the local Catholic schism, and wrote a trial transcript.[76] The most remarkable aspect of Clarke's efforts to make a living by her pen is her ability to turn her situation from a liability to an asset. Clarke took advantage of early nineteenth-century gender conventions and attitudes and used the fact that she was a woman to her professional advantage. Rather than hiding the problems that afflicted her business, Clarke paraded them in full view of her customers. As editor, Clarke imposed herself as a visible entity, standing between readers and the text, thus making readers conscious of her presence. Clarke's magazine was truly a "social text" that drew writers, readers, and editors into a relationship with each other. This editorial persona later became a common practice, notably in the *American Ladies' Magazine* where Sarah J. Hale regularly communicated with readers regarding submissions and suggestions in a section titled "To Our Correspondents" (which quickly changed to the more intimate "To Our Friends"). But these sidebars, though cloaked in the language of friendship, lacked the intimacy and immediacy of Clarke's editorial voice. Clarke was a professional journalist several decades before it was a common occupation for women. The stature that Hale and other women gained in the literary world was a result, at least in part, of the strategies Clarke used.[77]

Ann Carson and Mary Clarke were two of the many American women who found ways to support themselves and their families. For both women, this was an unexpected and unwelcome situation. Carson expected to live out her life working within her household, not in the public marketplace. Mary Clarke may have published her plays and stories even if her spouse had provided a sufficient income, but as primary earner for their family she was compelled to make her writing pay. Both women used their education and their skills to develop businesses that suited their family circumstances, their abilities, and the social and economic conditions of the times. Ann Carson exchanged her comfortable middle-class domestic status for that of an independent working woman. Her occupation, selling china, would not have struck anyone as unsuitable for a female. Mary Clarke, however, stepped across the invisible boundary of the gendered division of labor to become the first American woman to edit a woman's magazine. Yet she did so in such a way as to gain acceptance (if insufficient support) from her readers and subscribers. When her magazine failed, she turned to other writing to support her family. Ann Carson's china shop limped along during the war years, forcing her to supplement her earnings with money from overseeing the production of military uniforms. She expected to increase her china profits when the war ended and the economy stabilized. But Carson's success as a businesswoman depended as much on a quiet household (and an absent husband) as it did on economic circumstances. Unfortunately, her hopes for domestic peace were short lived.

2

Marriage, Manhood, and Murder

ON THE EVENING of January 20, 1816, Ann Carson returned to her home on the corner of Second and Dock streets. She walked through the china shop on the first floor and went upstairs to the family parlor on the second floor above it. There, her parents, Thomas and Jane Baker, were in earnest conversation with Captain John Carson. Moments later, Ann's brother-in-law Thomas Abbott entered the room, his face of a "deadly paleness." Close behind him followed Lieutenant Richard Smith. Smith strode into the room, flung his hat on the sofa, and sat down. Captain Carson rose and confronted Smith, saying, "By God out of this house you must go." As Carson made an effort to grab Smith by the collar, Smith pulled a pistol from his coat and fired at Carson's face. Carson fell to the floor, and Smith dashed down the stairs with Thomas Baker in hot pursuit. Ann Carson flung open a window and shouted, "Murder" into the street below.

These events, which took only a few moments, precipitated two deaths and three court trials, all of which turned Ann Carson into the most well-known and, in some quarters, most vilified, woman in Pennsylvania. All Ann Carson's subsequent troubles stemmed from one moment—when Richard Smith fired a pistol at close range into John Carson's face. Without that instant of dreadful violence, we would know little of a woman named Ann Carson. There would have been no memoir. But because Smith fired that pistol, the law turned a spotlight on her life. This chapter examines two court trials involving Ann Carson: Richard Smith's trial for the murder of John Carson and Ann Carson's trial as accessory to her husband's murder. Both trials illuminate the dynamics of the married state and the conflicting priorities of legal and affective ties in the early nineteenth century.

The Events

In the early spring of 1812, John Carson sailed to Europe. That was the last his wife heard from him, or of him, for almost four years. By the time

John departed, Ann Carson was already an independent woman. Because of John's problems with alcohol, he repeatedly failed to find steady work. To all intents and purposes Ann Carson was the head of the family. It was her income and her steady presence that kept her three children clothed, fed, and cared for. At the time of John's departure, Ann and the children were still living with her parents on the corner of Dock and Second streets, with a shop on the ground floor where Ann sold her china.[1] With their combined families and incomes, Ann and her parents lived a cramped existence (the house had at most four small bedrooms on the third floor). Although the War of 1812 curtailed the importation of chinaware, Ann's business had revived enough by the spring of 1814 that she could afford the house rent on her own. Thomas and Jane Baker and their two youngest sons went to live with their youngest daughter, Mary Abbott, and her husband, a currier, on South Front Street (between Spruce and Pine streets) a few blocks away.

Sometime in the late fall of 1814 or early spring of 1815 (Carson said that her husband had been gone "near three years") she visited Thomas Armstrong, "one of the judges of the court, then a practitioner at the bar," to ask him if it was possible to have her marriage annulled because of John's continued absence and his lack of maintenance. Ann had already heard a rumor from a returning sailor that John had died in a hospital in Russia, but with no hard evidence of his death she wanted legal confirmation that she was a free woman. Judge Armstrong told Ann Carson two things that had a significant impact on her future: (1) she should assume John Carson to be dead and (2) no legal proceedings were necessary. She could consider herself a widow. This reassured Ann, who had no wish "to expose myself and family in a court of law." At age twenty-nine, Ann Carson controlled her own destiny. She had independence; financial security; and, according to her, a certain amount of beauty which attracted "many professed admirers."[2]

One of these admirers was a young lieutenant, Richard Smith. Smith had recently left the army after serving along the Great Lakes, where he had attained distinction at the Battle of Sacketts Harbor. Smith resided at Elliott's Hotel on North Fourth Street. For some months prior to meeting Ann Carson, Smith had daily passed by her door, exchanging glances without speaking. Smith persuaded a mutual acquaintance (whom Carson names only as Mr. G——n in her *History*) to introduce him to Carson. Four days after their first meeting, Carson agreed to ride with Smith a few miles out of town and to dine at a tavern. Despite their short acquaintance and, notwithstanding her disinterest in matters of the heart, Lieutenant Smith proposed marriage. Carson "declined his offered hand, in terms the most decided and unequivocal." Smith seemed to accept this refusal and they made their way back to Philadelphia. But at their last stop on the road, at Haines' Tavern in Frankford, the Sign of the Jolly Post, Smith led Carson into a private parlor where a clergyman waited to perform a marriage ceremony.[3] Carson recounted this improbable situation (and marriage): as she entered the room and the clergyman began reciting the vows, Carson froze into stillness and silence. "Indeed the first thing that roused me from my lethargic stupor, was the clergyman pronouncing us man and wife, and Lieut. Smith taking the accustomed salute from my lips."[4]

What are we to make of this unlikely occurrence? Certainly Smith may have been smitten with Carson and may have heard (and seen) enough about her in the previous months to form an opinion about her virtues and charms. Why would she have agreed, however passively, to marry Smith? She described him as handsome, charming, young (twenty-three), brave, and passionately devoted to her. However "accidental" this marriage may have been, Ann Carson chose a partner who in almost all respects was the opposite of John Carson. As proof, Carson described Smith's transformation within a few shorts weeks from "a gallant, gay, dissipated man of pleasure," into "a calm domestic family man, a kind father to my children, and a rational companion to myself."[5] This domestic tranquility lasted a mere two months. Rumors of Captain Carson's return began to circulate in the city. These rumors were confirmed one day when Ann's sister Mary told her that a Captain Milligan, recently arrived from Liverpool, had met Captain Carson there. One day, as Ann starched her muslins in the second-floor kitchen of her home, her youngest son, Joseph, ran into the room with cakes in his hand. They had been given to him by a gentleman (whom Joseph did not recognize) who asked after Ann, her parents, and her two older sons. It was John Carson. He did not meet with Ann. Instead, he went to the Bakers' home on Front Street. There Jane Baker received him as her "dearly beloved son." Trouble was just around the corner.[6]

John laid daily siege to his Ann. Despite her assurances to him that she was lawfully married to Smith and intended to remain that way, John Carson continued to urge her to leave Smith and accept him back as her husband. He expected Ann to welcome him as a long-lost, beloved mate. But Ann Carson had other ideas. When the topic of the children came up, Ann suggested that if John "would give me assurances that he would do his duty as a father by them, he might take them all or one, as he chose.

To this he replied by asking me what he should do with them. 'Maintain and educate them,' said I, 'as I have done for eight years.'" Ann was in no mood to be conciliatory or sympathetic. Nor was she willing to give back property that John had deeded her on their marriage. John was a wastrel, a spendthrift, and utterly unreliable (which makes one wonder why she was willing to let him have the children). She pointed out to him that she had housed, fed, and educated his children. And during the nearly four years he was away, John had been paid $100 a month salary, "five tons privilege" (to carry goods), free living expenses on ship, and "considerable remittances from his family in Scotland." He returned with only six dollars in his pocket.[7]

After more than a week of unsuccessful persuasion and firm evidence that Smith would stand his ground and defend his claim as Ann's husband, John Carson petitioned for a divorce. Ann was served with notice of his intention. The language of the petition may have come as a surprise, given John's recent expressions of love and devotion: "the said Ann, regardless of her matrimonial obligations, has entered into a second marriage with a certain Richard Smith, on or about the fifteenth of October last; and has also committed adultery, with the said Richard Smith, and divers [*sic*] other persons, whose names are unknown to your petitioner." This was nasty revenge on John's part. By law, he had to prove grounds for divorce. Ann's marriage to Smith was sufficient for this. But John went further, determined to defame his former wife, though without providing any evidence.[8]

John Carson's frame of mind is unclear. Despite the divorce petition, he continued to visit Ann's house and he did not try to avoid Richard Smith. Carson seems to have gone out of his way to irritate, annoy, and, finally, threaten Smith. Several days after Ann was served with the divorce subpoena, John showed up at her door one morning before breakfast. He stayed through the lunch hour and was still there when Smith, who had left the house to avoid him, returned for dinner in the afternoon. John, who had been drinking brandy all morning, was drunk and looking to pick a fight. He got one. Words between the two men became heated. Their exchange ended with a challenge by Carson, which Smith readily accepted. Like dogs fighting over a bone, Carson and Smith claimed possession of Ann. They agreed that the survivor of their duel would "take her." The situation was defused by Ann stating firmly that if they pursued their folly not only would she call in the law, but she would refuse to live with either of the surviving parties. Amazingly, all three then sat down to dinner. But John, as Ann recalled, "seemed determined on mischief." John Carson and Richard Smith continued to exchange insults. Finally, according to Ann, John rose with rage, picked up a knife from the table and tried to stab Smith. Smith ran from the room, down to the shop, and out of the house. Carson pursued him as far as the shop, growling, "Where is that damned son of a bitch?" He lingered there long enough for Ann to come downstairs. He then delivered a parting insult to her: "'Madam, hang out a flag at your door, with this inscription on it, here lives a woman that will marry any man.'"9

Richard Smith took John Carson's threat seriously. He sought legal advice from his friend, lawyer Jonathan Smith, who counseled Richard to have John Carson bound over to keep the peace. In the meantime, Jonathan Smith also gave his friend two pistols—just in case.10 Ann worried about the pistols, especially because Richard insisted on having them by him continuously, even going so far as to place them under his pillow at night. His behavior made Ann "tremb[le] with terror, lest the pistols should by accident go off in the night."11 This uncomfortable (and dangerous) situation may have prompted Ann and Richard's decision that he should leave Philadelphia for the time being. Smith planned to travel to Lexington, Kentucky, and await the arrival of Ann and her children.

On the morning of Saturday, January 20, 1814, Captain Carson once again showed up at Ann's house. He renewed his pleas that she return to him. Ann refused. She also informed John that Smith was leaving Philadelphia for his own safety (she did not tell him that she intended to follow Smith).12 Once more, Ann assumed that she had put an end to John's entreaties. But within hours he was back in her house, more insistent and annoying than ever. Here is Ann's account of that evening encounter:

He then renewed the former subject so hackneyed before, that I wondered he was not as much fatigued with it as myself. My replies were invariably the same on every point. I would never live with him, begged him to hasten a divorce, and permit me to enjoy again the peace he had thus barbarously interrupted. He continued to talk and I to listen; the watchman's voice announced the hour of ten, when I observed it was time for him to go home. "Home, madam," said he emphatically, "this is my home." I replied, "I believe not, Sir; this is my home, and all here is mine, the fruits of my own industry, besides the support of my children; while you have been you best know where, and doing you best know what, but nothing for either my children or me; besides sir, I have not an apartment to offer you, as all my chambers are occupied by myself and family." "Madam your chamber is mine, and there I design to sleep this night." "And where sir, am I to sleep?" said I. "With me unquestionably," was his answer.13

Faced with this threat to her home, her livelihood, and her body, Ann tried to leave the room, but John restrained her. The noise they made as she struggled and he barred her exit brought the servants to her aid. Ann then fled the house in search of Smith.

She found Smith on Dock Street on his way back to the house. Ann told him what had just occurred and suggested they find lodging for the night rather than return to confront an angry, and possibly dangerous, man. Smith objected; he did not wish to leave Captain Carson in possession of the house. So Ann and Richard turned to Jonathan Smith for advice. Despite the lateness of the hour (it was past ten o'clock), the lawyer answered his door, welcomed the couple, and suggested they seek out Alderman Badger or one of the other justices of the peace to have Captain Carson forcibly removed from the house. Richard left to do as Jonathan Smith suggested. Ann returned to her house to see if John was still there. He was, as were both her parents, whom John had summoned to support him. Challenged by this family resistance, Ann returned to Jonathan Smith's office to wait for Richard. On her way back to the lawyer's office, Ann met her brother-in-law Thomas Abbott (in whose house her parents now lived). He accompanied Ann to Smith's office. Richard Smith returned sometime later. All the justices, it seemed, had retired for the night. Jonathan Smith's next suggestion was that Ann and Richard should return to her house, go directly to the bedroom, and stay there until Monday morning when Ann could legally expel Captain Carson.[14]

Ann, Richard, and Thomas Abbott returned to the house. Smith and Abbott waited downstairs in the shop while Ann went up to the parlor. As soon as she entered, John and her mother began to insult Smith. Jane Baker castigated her daughter for choosing to live in sin with Smith, "that villain," and for denying her rightful spouse, John, his place in their home. Ann listened to this rant for some minutes until Abbott came up the stairs, pale and worried. What Ann did not know, and what accounted for Abbott's countenance, was that while she went to the parlor, Smith had gone upstairs to their third-floor bedroom and taken the pistols that Ann had made him put away earlier in the day. Smith entered the room soon after Abbott, proceeded to the couch and sat down. John Carson demanded that Smith leave. Smith then turned to Ann and asked, "Shall I go?" She said no. Smith stood up as John Carson pressed close to him. Abbott and the Bakers stood between Smith and the door. As Carson made a grab at Smith, Smith pulled a pistol from his coat and fired it at Carson's face.[15]

Smith ran down the stairs and through the china shop—the sound of crashing china testifying to his speed—where he was captured by Thomas Baker, who had followed him from the upstairs room. Captain Baker hustled him into the street, where a crowd, who had heard Ann Carson's cry of murder, repeatedly hit and punched Smith. The watchman soon arrived, stopped the vigilante violence, and carried Smith off to jail. Doctors were summoned for John Carson. Family, neighbors, and strangers began to swarm Ann's house. John's injuries were such that the doctors feared moving him. They set up a bed in the parlor where he lingered, in great pain, for the next nine days. An hour after Carson's death, Richard Smith was charged with murder. The following day, Constable John Hart issued a warrant for Ann Carson's arrest on a charge of accessory to murder.[16]

News traveled quickly. Papers in Philadelphia, New Jersey, and New York reported Carson's shooting. Though the editor of the Philadelphia *True American* claimed to have been on the spot when Smith was apprehended, most of the reports got the details wrong. At least two papers reprinted the same mistaken report, claiming that as soon as John Carson landed at Philadelphia, he returned to his home where he encountered Ann Carson and Richard Smith, who, without provocation, shot him.[17]

John Carson's funeral was also announced in the papers. *Relf's Philadelphia Gazette and Daily Advertiser*, *Poulson's American Daily Advertiser*, and the *United States Gazette* all printed a notice on the day of his funeral (February 6) announcing its time and location and encouraging "friends, as well as the shipmates and officers of the navy, now in the city" to come. The Captain's Society was particularly invited to participate. Perhaps because of this advance notice, Carson's funeral was well attended. *Relf's Philadelphia Gazette and Daily Advertiser* reported that "an immense concourse of citizens, who appeared deeply penetrated with sorrow for his untimely exit," accompanied Carson's remains to their final resting place. Ann Carson remembered that "some thousands," attended the funeral.[18]

Meanwhile, both Ann Carson and Richard Smith waited in the Walnut Street prison for their trials to begin. They had a long wait: the next Court of Common Pleas session was three and a half months away.

The Trials

Richard Smith's trial began on May 23 in the Court of Common Pleas with Judge Jacob Rush presiding. It took place in what is now the main room on the first floor of Independence Hall. The courtroom was packed. Public interest had not waned in the four months since the shooting. One of the spectators, hired by printer Robert Desilver, took down every word that was spoken for a transcript Desilver planned to publish as soon as the trial was over.[19] Because Smith was charged with a capital offense, the attorney general of Pennsylvania, Jared Ingersoll, led the prosecution. To counter such a formidable legal force, Smith had a first-class defense team composed of prominent Philadelphia lawyers, including William Rawle, a former attorney general and an experienced trial lawyer.

At first glance, Smith's trial on a charge of first-degree murder appears straightforward: the task of the prosecution was to prove, as they charged, that Smith was guilty of the specific crime of first-degree murder (as opposed to either of the two lesser crimes of second-degree murder or manslaughter).[20] Eyewitness accounts agreed that Smith fired the gun. The accounts also agreed about the sequence of events that led to the shooting. But the interpretation of those events was far from settled. What both the prosecution and the defense intended to establish during Smith's trial was the motivation and (as the defense argued) justification for his actions: was the shooting a deliberate, willful act of murder or was it an act of self-defense? But this question could not be answered without first answering several others. Central to the argument about justification was the question of who was the injured party. And what was the injury? Was it to property (real—the china shop, and personal—wife and family)? Was it to a marriage? If so, was it to an emotional bond or to a legal entitlement to wifely affections? The events of January 20 required the prosecution and the defense to explore fundamental relationships. What constituted a marriage? Who was Ann's husband? Who possessed rights that were to be defended or protected? Who had obligations toward Ann? To establish the facts about what happened was complicated; determining what happened depended on the identity of the people involved. Two witnesses may have agreed that Smith shot Carson. But they may have disagreed about Smith's guilt in the matter, or they might have disagreed about what action Smith performed when he shot Carson. Everything depended on how the witnesses answered the questions just posed.

Attorney General Ingersoll opened the case for the state. Ingersoll addressed the jury, telling them that his duty was to give them "a particular recital of the events, as they occurred." But Ingersoll's task as prosecutor was to prove Smith guilty of first-degree murder. Therefore the attorney general's recital of the circumstances and actions leading to Carson's shooting was based on the assumption that Smith was an interloper, an aggressor, and a deliberate murderer. For example, Ingersoll said that when Captain Carson returned to the house on Second Street, he found "the stranger, Richard Smith." By calling Smith a stranger, Ingersoll implied Carson's right to be there and Smith's intrusion. Ingersoll also described John Carson's actions on the night of the shooting as his having taken "peaceable possession" of the house. To further underscore Carson's right not only to be in the house but his position as a member of the family, Ingersoll painted for the jury a verbal picture of the scene in the parlor just before Smith arrived: "Captain Carson was sitting in the parlor, at the fire, with his youngest child on his knee; Captain Baker and Mrs. Baker his wife, sitting near, forming the family circle." Ingersoll used Carson's own words to further underline Smith's offense: "Captain Carson on his death-bed declared he had received the fatal wound from the prisoner, who had acted as a midnight assassin."[21]

Ingersoll reinforced Captain Carson's alleged rightful reintroduction to his home and family by telling the jury that John and Ann had agreed to reconcile, that they "were to live together in harmony," and that Smith had declared his intention to leave the city and abandon his claim to be Ann's lawful spouse. According to Ingersoll, Smith's entry into the parlor that night was a violent disruption in a peaceful family gathering, where "not a blow nor angry word proceeded from either side, until the prisoner drew his pistol, presented it to the mouth of Captain Carson, and fired." Ingersoll's scenario depicted John Carson, from start to finish, as the injured party.

Having asserted John Carson's innocence and Richard Smith's guilt, Ingersoll addressed three issues to argue his case: the status of Ann Carson's marriage to Richard Smith, John Carson's character, and Richard Smith's character. Ingersoll intended to show that Ann Carson had no good grounds on which to assume John Carson was dead and therefore was not at liberty to marry again. This argument rested on the criteria for divorce detailed in the Pennsylvania Statute:

That if any husband or wife, upon false rumor, in appearance well founded, of the death of the other (where such other has been absent for the space of two whole years) hath married, or shall marry again, he or she shall not be liable to the pains of adultery; but it shall be in the election of the party remaining unmarried, at his or her return, to insist to have his or her former wife or husband restored, or to have his or her own marriage dissolved, and the other party to remain with the second husband or wife; and in any suit or action instituted for this purpose, within one year after such return, the court may and shall sentence and decree accordingly.[22]

It was true that Ann Carson had not heard from John for more than two years, but the prosecution insisted that rumors of John Carson's death were not "well founded." Ingersoll said that Ann Carson had never heard that her husband had "died at a *particular* town, or *place*, was *shipwrecked*, or *lost* his life in some way."[23] He dismissed Jane Baker's testimony that a sailor returning to Philadelphia claimed to have heard that Carson died in Russia as "loose evidence," far below the standard required by law. Most troubling to the defense was Ingersoll's interpretation of the divorce law. He argued that John Carson's petition for divorce was not legally binding. He was free to change his mind, and, as his subsequent actions showed, that was exactly what Carson did (though he never withdrew the divorce petition). The prosecution contended that until the moment a divorce became law, a husband and wife were still married. As Ingersoll told the jury, "We are therefore clearly of the opinion that on the twentieth of January last, Ann Carson was the wife of John Carson, and that he had a right to settle his differences with his wife, and to receive her again into his arms."[24]

If John Carson were still married to Ann, then, as Judge Jacob Rush explained, John Carson was in rightful possession of his wife and home. Therefore Richard Smith was an intruder who "had acquired unlawful possession of the wife, of the house, and of the goods and chattels of John Carson."[25] Captain Carson's violent behavior toward Smith, especially his attempt to stab Smith with the dinner knife, was deemed reasonable; Carson's attorney testified that the captain had told him he acted the way he did (trying to stab Smith) because he was irritated at seeing Smith "assuming the command over the servants and children at the dinner table."[26] Smith was a usurper: ordering the servants about and sitting at the head of the table rubbed Carson's nose in the fact that Smith claimed rights (including the possession of Ann) to which he was not entitled.

Moreover, the prosecution took pains to demonstrate John Carson's peaceful nature. Ingersoll questioned the eyewitnesses present at the shooting to show that John Carson had given Smith no cause to shoot him. Thomas Abbott and Jane Baker both testified that Smith's exit from the parlor was not blocked. He had been free to leave at any time. When Ingersoll asked Jane Baker if Captain Carson had behaved in a threatening manner, she answered by repeating Carson's words to Smith: "My hands are tied, I will not raise the weight of my little finger against you." Baker also repeated Carson's phrase, uttered on his deathbed, that Smith came in "like a midnight assassin and like a coward shot him."[27]

Ingersoll also told the jury of the caring, tender affection John had for his wife. Jane Baker testified to John's concern for Ann: as he lay dying from his wound, John repeatedly asked for Ann "in the most tender, affectionate manner any one could do, and when he heard she was unwell, he advised her to go out and take the air, so much confinement would injure her. His children would come to the bed-side, and he would converse with them all."[28] Baker's description of this domestic scene, complete with a loving husband and father, juxtaposed with Smith's violent action, served to emphasize Carson's innocence and Smith's guilt. The prosecution created a sympathetic portrait of John Carson: a man who simply wanted, after a long absence, to reclaim his rightful place in his home, a man who wished to return to the arms of his loving wife and children and to live at peace with the world. But Richard Smith had robbed John Carson: "He took from him his wife; he took from him his life; and his vengeance is not satiated unless he can conclude by taking from him his character."[29]

Character was the heart of the argument for the defense. Attorney Peter Browne recited for the jury Richard Smith's early history and military service in the War of 1812. Browne portrayed Smith as an unfortunate orphan, "launched into life without an oar."[30] Smith was born in Ireland and sent to Philadelphia in 1803 because his widowed mother remarried. Four years later, Smith was adopted by his maternal uncle, Daniel Clark, and went to live with Clark in New Orleans. Browne conceded that the young Smith had behaved as well as he could, but he disappointed his uncle on several occasions. Browne placed Smith's disagreements with his uncle in a positive light, arguing that Clark put unrealistic demands on the teenaged Smith. Smith had a good war record, despite rumors that he had disgraced himself by fighting a duel. He served with distinction at the Battle of Sackett's Harbor.[31] Browne called one of Smith's commanding officers to testify to Smith's virtues. Colonel James R. Mullany, the quartermaster general, asserted that Smith, who served under him in his infantry regiment until the conclusion of the war, was an "active, intelligent, useful officer." Attorney Browne also informed the jury that Smith had come to the attention, and commendation, of General Gaines, who wrote to Mullany to express his satisfaction with Smith's performance of his duties.[32]

In 1814, this young man, with a sterling war record but no financial prospects (Clark, disappointed in Smith's earlier behavior, died without leaving Smith any money), returned to Philadelphia, where he met and married Ann Carson. Browne sketched a pathetic picture of Smith at this period of his life: "Educated to no profession, with no relations, few friends, and slender means of gaining an honest and honourable livelihood, he was reduced to a distressing situation."[33] Browne hastened to explain that Smith's decision to marry Ann Carson, despite the prosecution's portrayal of it as foolish and hasty, was made with forethought: "Considering his inexperience and situation suffice it, that he was assured that she was free from any pre-engagement."[34]

The defense relied on the same divorce law that the prosecution cited. In contrast to the prosecution's conclusions, however, the defense argued that the circumstances of John Carson's absence, combined with the actions he took on his return, all validated Smith's marriage to Ann. John Carson had been away at least two years. Ann had information that Carson was dead. There was no question but that Smith was looked on as "master of the family." Even Jane Baker acknowledged Smith as her son-in-law and, furthermore, "gave the strongest testimony of her approbation of the match." According to the defense, "She saluted him, called him her dear son, and wished him joy."[35] Once legally married to Ann, Smith took lawful possession of her house "and other property."[36] These facts, William Rawle told the jury, "placed Richard Smith upon the same protected ground the law gives to every father of a family, and to every husband; I mean the legal right of the defending of his family."[37]

The defense asked the jury to reconsider the prosecution's portrayal of the character and actions of John Carson to understand why Smith, not Carson, was the injured party. Smith acted in self-defense, not from a willful desire to murder John Carson. The prosecution gave the defense some assistance in their case against John Carson. Under Attorney General Ingersoll's questioning, Jane Baker admitted that Carson had left home because "his conduct here in Philadelphia was not what it should have been."[38] Ingersoll also asked Baker what resources John Carson had left his wife when he departed—house, property, and so on. Jane Baker confessed that her son-in-law had left nothing for his family to live on except for their own labor. Baker's answer confirmed what the defense sought to show: Carson left his wife and family to fend for themselves. Although Ingersoll assured the jury that Jane and Thomas Baker provided a safety net for Ann and her children, there was no denying that John Carson had left his family high and dry.

Jane Baker's comment that Carson's behavior was "not what it should have been" was the opening the defense needed to expose Carson's shortcomings as a husband and father. Under cross-examination, Baker admitted that on one occasion when John returned from a voyage Ann retrieved him, considerably the worse for liquor, from a boardinghouse. Browne carefully chose his questions to emphasize that John Carson had not lived up to his family responsibilities: "He left nothing then to maintain the children or her?" Jane Baker answered, "No sir; nothing; she has four children she clothed, educated and supported." The defense also established that John had no hand in starting or maintaining the china shop. First Ann's parents and then Ann herself paid the rent on the house at Dock and Second streets. According to Baker, John did not pay "one cent of it."[39]

Between voyages, John lived with his wife and in-laws, relying on all three for support. Ann Carson not only paid the rent and other expenses "in her own name," she also paid off John's debts. This included his dues to the Captain's Society and forty-five dollars to a joiner named Connolly (presumably for furniture).[40] The Bakers were, as Ingersoll pointed out, a safety net for their daughter. When she moved in with her parents, she sold some of her furniture to raise capital for the china store. The Bakers also lent her more money to purchase stock. Jane Baker said, "I would tell Ann—Ann, my dear, if you see a bargain buy it, and if you want one hundred or two hundred dollars let me know. When I wanted the money back again, Mrs. Carson would repay me." The defense, eager to emphasize John Carson's faults, asked if he ever repaid Baker: "No: when Captain Carson returned this last time, all the money he brought with him was six hard dollars and eighty cents, which I sold at Fletcher and Gardner's, and received six dollars fifty for."[41]

Browne also elicited from Baker the fact that her daughter, as a feme sole trader, had been imprisoned for debt. John Carson left his wife so unprotected financially that she spent time in the Prune Street apartments (the debtor's section of the Walnut Street jail) sometime between 1812 and 1815.[42] Carson was also careless with (what remained of) his wife's property. Baker, at Browne's request, told the jury about the time Carson pawned Ann's watch and went on a two-week drinking spree:

He took up a watch of her's to the Yellow-springs and pledged it, which was never redeemed. . . . In the morning he took a bundle, as we supposed, to go to the *Wasp*, at the Navy-yard. For two weeks or ten days we did not hear of him. I myself went to every stage-office, and as far as Darby, to see if I could find any tidings of him. I could hear none, until Mr. Tatem, the merchant, returned from the Yellow-springs, and told us he was there; which was the time he pledged the watch and returned home with a sailor's round-about jacket and trowsers.[43]

Here was a negative picture of John Carson: irresponsible, uncaring, and drunk. Jane Baker hesitated to put too much weight on Carson's drinking (she said that after his return in January she only twice saw him "a little gay"). Nor had it worried her that prior to his marriage to her daughter she had witnessed him drunk: "I have seen him intoxicated before his marriage, and Captain Baker also, but I did not suppose he was habituated to it." The defense sought to prove that Carson was not only a habitual drunk but a badly behaved one. Redwood Fisher, who sailed with Carson on the *Pennsylvania Packet*, testified that Carson was an "irritable man." When asked how irritable, Fisher said, "When he was intoxicated he was so particularly."[44]

The defense was satisfied that it had established that John Carson was not, at the time of his return, the legal spouse of Ann Carson. Furthermore, John abnegated his role as master of the household long before he physically absented himself from the family. The case turned on this point for both the prosecution and the defense. The identity of Ann's legal husband determined property ownership (even though Ann had been a feme sole trader, once she married Smith, her property became his). Moreover, as Ann's husband, Richard Smith was entitled, indeed he was obligated, to protect her, her property interests, and himself against the physical threats of violence by John Carson.[45]

But the defense also sought to emphasize the necessity of Smith's self-defense. Further testimony from Jane Baker about Carson's "wicked design" to seriously injure, if not kill Richard Smith, helped his case. Attorney Browne asked if she had heard Carson talk of his desire to injure Smith. Baker admitted that Carson said he would "take a big stick and beat him" like they did in Scotland. On another occasion, Carson said he wanted to knock Smith's "blue eyes into black ones."[46] Jane Baker's testimony helped Smith's attorney characterize Carson as a violent man, intent on evil-doing. In colorful, evocative language, Browne told the jury that John Carson was as "a man of Herculean make" who "with one blow of his athletic fist, could have felled [Richard Smith] to the earth." Carson deliberately stalked Smith, watching his movements. Ann's servant,

Temperance Barkley, recalled that she saw Captain Carson hide behind a poplar tree near the house. Browne asked rhetorically, "With what intent was he there? This was a lying in wait for Richard Smith; for no other intent at that time of night could he have been there, than to fall on Smith, when he should issue out upon his business."[47] Browne again related to the jury the knife attack. Carson chased Smith down the stairs and out of the house, Carson's "countenance enraged, his eyes starting out of his head and, when asked whether he intended to murder, he answers, 'Murder! Yes.'"[48]

Browne argued that Carson's behavior and acknowledged intentions "to revenge himself upon the person of Smith at all hazards" made it reasonable for Smith to take precautions. Under such inducement, it was no wonder that Smith armed himself. Browne reminded the jury that Smith was not the only target of Carson's wrath. John Carson's bill for divorce deliberately maligned Ann Carson's virtue, claiming she engaged in adulterous behavior with Smith and "diverse other persons."[49] Yet Carson's intention when he returned to the house on that momentous evening was to possess not only the house but his former wife as well. The defense claimed that Carson, with "the blackest malignity in his heart," had threatened Ann's person "with violation."[50] Despite his "crocodile tears," Carson's actions revealed his "evil intentions."

John Carson's behavior, according to the defense, more than justified Smith's response. Smith acted in self-defense after a long series of threats, intimidation and abuse of both himself and Ann Carson, and actual physical violence. John Carson was malignant and vindictive and held an "utter contempt for the law." He abandoned his responsibilities toward his wife, children, and society. Equally important, Smith behaved as men were expected to behave: Smith was the injured party, but he was not a helpless victim. His former military commander testified to his valor. His friends testified to his sense of responsibility and steadiness. Browne argued that Smith was a hero, not a coward: "It is said he could fly, and ought to have fled. What! Fly from his wife—from his home, without one manly feeling of resistance or of shame."[51] In standing his ground, Smith embodied the virtues of manliness. John Carson, in contrast, was a bully, a coward, and incapable of living up to his personal or professional obligations. By the standards of the day, such weakness and dependence confirmed him as unmanly.

On the morning of Tuesday, May 28, the fifth day of the trial, Smith's lead attorney William Rawle spoke one last time on his client's behalf. Then Jared Ingersoll concluded the prosecution's case by reminding the jury why the state sought to prove murder in the first degree—Smith had with *willful intent* planned and carried out the shooting of John Carson. With his final words to the jury, Ingersoll assured them that Smith would be "followed in all the windings of his unexampled turpitude; and his accumulated crimes, stripped of the false coloring bestowed by eloquence, shall be exhibited to your view in all their naked horror and deformity."[52] It was then up to Judge Jacob Rush to summarize the case for the jurymen, and to explain their task. Judge Rush began by reminding his listeners that Ann Carson could not be Smith's legal spouse if her marriage to John Carson was valid. He reminded them that there was no well-founded evidence of John Carson's death at the time that Ann married Smith. Rush explained what the law meant by well-founded: "a general report, that a man died at a *particular* town, or *place*, was *shipwrecked*, or *lost* his life in some way, which the *report* specifies."[53] Jane Baker's testimony of hearsay from a sailor, Rush told the jury, was not "the evidence the law requires, to justify a wife's marrying in the absence of her husband. There must be a general report of his death, and of the *place* and *manner* of it."[54] Therefore, Ann Carson's marriage to Richard Smith was null and void. The defense's argument that Smith was her legal spouse at the time of the shooting fell to pieces. With the argument went Smith's claims to defense of his rightful property. "It being universally understood and known, that the property of the wife, is the property of the husband, and that *he alone* has the control over it, the consequence is, that John Carson had an undoubted right to take possession of the house and goods which belonged to his wife, on his return in January last, to this city and to his family. It follows, that Richard Smith, the prisoner, was an intruder, and had acquired unlawful possession of the wife, of the house, and of the goods and chattels of John Carson."[55]

With this premise as his starting point, Judge Rush argued that John Carson's aggressive behavior was justified. Carson's knife attack on Smith at dinner was prompted by the sight of Smith acting as master of the house: "John Carson got into a rage, at seeing the prisoner assume the direction of his children, and his servants." In other words, Carson had been provoked into aggression. Although Carson sought violent means in a moment of passion to alleviate his feelings, it was Smith, not Carson, who willfully and deliberately carried out a fatal attack. As Rush described the scene in Ann's parlor on the night of January 20, Smith encountered a man of peace, who made no motion to attack Smith. Rush reminded the jury that all the witnesses agreed that Carson did not provoke Smith: "Much has been said of the principle of self-defense, as applied to the prisoner, but with what propriety, we are at a loss to discover. Who laid hands on him? Who attacked him? Who threatened him? Who touched him? He went voluntarily into the room, chose his station, and fired when he pleased. He was not dragged into the room, and there detained against his will. On the contrary, he *only* was armed, and under restraint from no person."[56] Furthermore, Smith's flight after the shooting, according to Rush, demonstrated his guilt. Rush left John Carson's dying words in the jury's mind: "the prisoner had come in like a midnight assassin, and had shot him like a coward."[57]

Rush believed that his recitation of the events "accords very much with the representation of it given by the witnesses." Rush did not weigh the evidence and arguments presented by the prosecution and the defense. Rush's presentation of the case to the jury was simply the prosecution's interpretation. Nor did Rush instruct the jury to weigh in their minds the validity of all they had heard; he instructed the jury to find Smith guilty of first-degree murder: "What is the case before you in substance, and in a few words? It is this—The prisoner having by colour and forms of laws acquired unlawful possession of the house of CARSON, of his goods and chattels, of his wife and children, deliberately shot him, afterwards, in his OWN house, in the very ACT of peaceably demanding restitution of all that was dear to him." At six in the evening, the jury retired to consider their verdict. Three hours later, they returned to the courtroom. Smith was convicted of first-degree murder.[58]

The press quickly conveyed the news to Philadelphia readers. *Relf's Philadelphia Gazette and Daily Advertiser*, perhaps with a hint of sympathy in its reportage, noted that Smith's defense attorney, William Rawle delivered "a very ingenious and able speech for the prisoner." The *United States Gazette* was more blunt in its reportage: "The interesting trial which has been pending for a week before the Court of Oyer and Terminer, in the case of RICHARD SMITH, for the Murder of Captain JAMES [*sic*] CARSON, was concluded last evening, with the Jury returning a Verdict of Guilty of Murder in the first degree—which, by the Law of this Commonwealth, is DEATH."[59] According to one of the defense attorneys, Sampson Levy, Smith's trial had "drawn multitudes."[60] Newspapers printed daily updates of the trial. Robert Desilver hurried into print the trial transcript—published in two parts "in consequence of the anxious desire of the public" to read it as soon as possible.[61] Citizens of

Philadelphia were not just curious, they were also disposed to be biased against both Richard Smith and Ann Carson. Attorney Browne cited the public's "indignation" against Smith. Sampson Levy heard reports that Ann Carson was "a lady of the utmost violence of conduct." At the beginning of the trial, Browne expressed his confidence that the jurors would "abandon every idle story you have heard out of doors." The jurors may have done so, but at least some of the spectators retained their prejudices. During Saturday morning's adjournment, as a crowd inside the courthouse "pressed upon the prisoner," someone took a swing at Smith.[62]

While Philadelphians waited for Judge Rush to pass sentence on Richard Smith, Ann Carson's trial proceeded. Jacob Rush again served as the presiding judge. The prosecutor was another Ingersoll, Jared's brother and law partner, Edward. Smith's defense attorney, Sampson Levy, was joined by Joseph Ingersoll (the attorney general's son) to defend Carson. Prosecutor Ingersoll, in his opening remarks to the jury, acknowledged that many of them had observed Smith's trial. As a consequence, they might have already made up their minds about Ann Carson's guilt or innocence. This circumstance did not perturb him. Indeed, Edward Ingersoll may have assumed that Smith's guilty verdict would help to make a case against Carson.

He told the jury that the state aimed to prove Ann Carson was guilty as an accessory on three counts: first, by aiding and abetting the murder with "expressions calculated to call forth the courage and the act, which caused the fatal event"; second, by telling Smith where he could find the gun; and, third, by deliberately seeking Smith and taking him back to the house to confront John Carson. The prosecution's case rested on proof that Ann Carson had deliberately manipulated Smith into killing John Carson. But the witnesses Ingersoll called did not confirm his allegations. Instead, both Thomas Abbott, Ann's brother-in-law, and Temperance Barkley, her servant, testified to the contrary. Ingersoll hoped to show that Ann had instructed John Carson to come to the house at a time that she knew Smith would be there. What Barkley said, however, was that Ann told John to arrive between eight and nine o'clock in the evening. He chose to ignore her instructions and show up at seven. Ingersoll also asked Barkley if she had ever heard Ann talk with Smith about a pistol or about shooting John Carson. Barkley denied hearing any such conversations.[63] Nor could she confirm the prosecutor's allegation that Ann Carson staged the meeting between the two men. On the contrary, Barkley

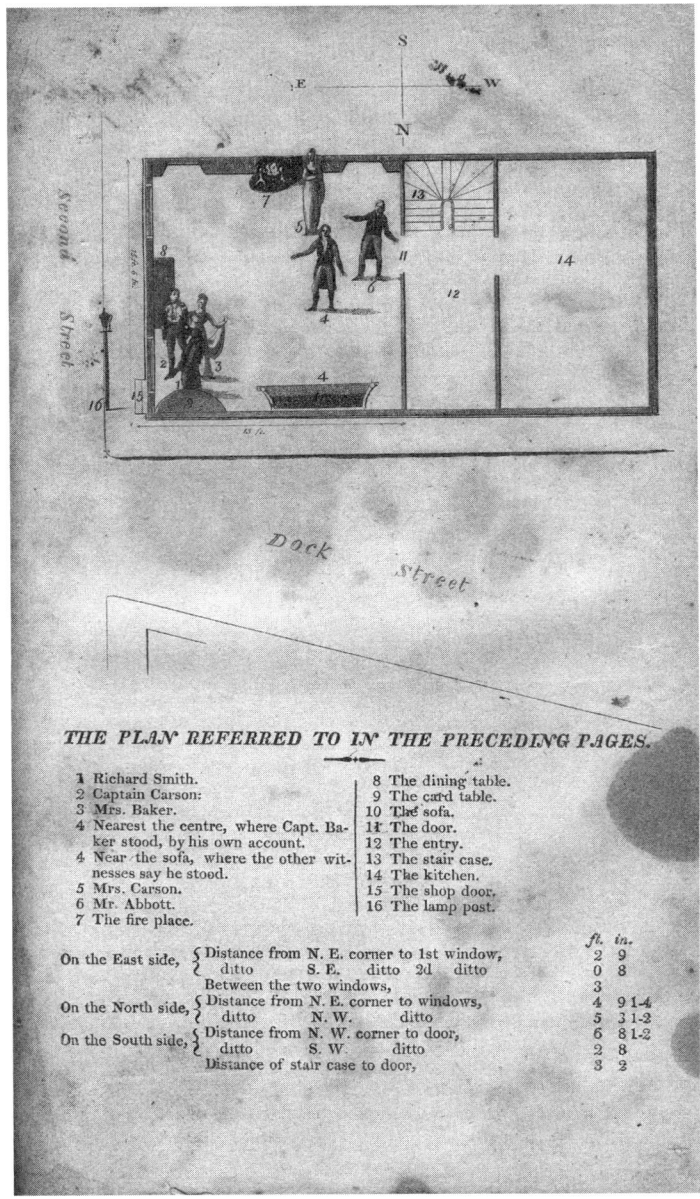

Figure 2. Trial diagram. This is one of the first uses of a diagram in a trial transcript. The plan was exhibited during Smith's murder trial to locate where he, John Carson, and Ann Carson stood at the moment Smith fired his pistol. *The Trials of Richard Smith . . . as Principal, and Ann Carson, alias Ann Smith, as accessory, for the Murder of Captain John Carson* (Philadelphia: Desilver, 1816).

witnessed Ann in the parlor trying to persuade John to leave the house. Fortunately for Ann Carson, Temperance Barkley, who took care of the younger children, cooked the family meals, and tended the shop when necessary, had her eyes and ears in all the right places at all the right times. She overheard things: she listened as John Carson read aloud Ann's letter telling him when to come to the house. From the kitchen, across the hall from the parlor, she witnessed the order of arrival of John Carson, her mistress, and Richard Smith on January 20.[64]

Barkley verified that Ann Carson intended to keep Smith and the captain away from each other that night. After failing to get John out of the house, Ann went to Barkley, asked for a hat and coat, then went to the kitchen where Barkley saw her take some money "out of a little red box, and put it in her reticule." Carson told Barkley not to be alarmed if she did not return until morning.[65] Ingersoll's questioning of Thomas Abbott revealed that it was Smith's attorney, Jonathan B. Smith, who counseled Smith and Carson to return to the house. And, finally, John Carson's own words and actions exonerated Ann. Ingersoll asked Jane Baker if, as Carson lay dying, he ever blamed or implicated her daughter. Baker replied, "No, sir—never. He would ask for her twenty times a day." Ann's sister, Sarah Hutton, confirmed her mother's testimony; she told the jury that John Carson spoke of Ann only with kindness and concern.

The prosecution admitted defeat. In his address to the jury, Edward Ingersoll said, "I believe the prisoner at the bar has committed crimes; but however [I] am obliged to acknowledge, that after all possible pains taken to procure information of the truth, I do not think the evidence on the part of the prosecution, is such as will justify me in urging her conviction." Judge Rush then informed the jury that neither the facts nor law would authorize a conviction. Although, "the prisoner was a bad woman," the proper verdict was acquittal. Without retiring from the box, the jury returned a verdict of not guilty on all counts.[66]

Ann Carson's acquittal was small consolation to her. John Carson was dead. Richard Smith was condemned to die. She had exhausted her money on lawyers for herself and Smith. And, once acquitted, she faced a bigamy charge (because Smith's case had determined that she was still John's wife when she married Smith). Ann Carson was able to post bail for herself, but she no longer had an income to support her family. As Joseph Ingersoll said at her trial, "It should seem as if the arch fiend of hell, had woven his blackest web, to display in one dismal perspective, the most complicated group of human wretchedness."[67]

Richard Smith's trial addressed the circumstances of one man caught up in a tangled set of personal relations. But his trial, and particularly the arguments and assumptions of both the prosecution and the defense, also illustrates what early nineteenth-century Americans believed about marriage relations and the rights of husbands (and, conversely, the lack of rights of wives). Smith's trial asked and answered a series of important questions: Who was Ann's husband? John Carson. Who possessed rights that were to be defended or protected? Carson again. What was a marriage? It was a relationship in which property and legal, rather than affective, ties took precedence. Who had obligations in a marriage? Husbands and wives both had obligations; but a husband's failure to fulfill his obligations was not enough to override his legal standing. The prosecution based its arguments for Smith's guilt on John Carson's identity as Ann's husband. As her spouse, John had a right to behave the way he did. The defense, however, tried to show that John Carson had abnegated his role as husband—not just in his prolonged absence but in his almost decade-long shirking of his financial and emotional support for his wife and family. But these failures could not, and did not, strip John Carson of his legal identity and possessions.

Nor did it matter that John Carson no longer wished to be Ann's spouse. On the night of the shooting, he was still her husband. It did not matter that John Carson was a bully, a drunk, and out to harm (either physically or emotionally) both Richard Smith and Ann Carson. And Smith could not claim self-defense because there was nothing for him to defend—Ann was not his wife. The shop was not his property.

Were these assumptions alone enough for the jury to render a guilty verdict? A number of factors may have contributed to their decision. Some of the jurors lived in the same part of town as Smith and Carson. Francis Douglass, a bricklayer on South Eleventh Street, or John Wilkins, a carpenter on Christian Street; David Seegar, a flour merchant on South Seventh Street; or George Thompson, a baker on Sixth Street near Fitzwater, may have passed Carson's china shop, may even have been her customers. They may have known the Baker family or remembered John Carson from former years. They may have assumed John Carson was still alive. After all, even before his departure in 1812 he had been absent more than he had been home; that was the nature of a sailor's life. Richard Smith had lived with Ann less than three months before John Carson returned; neighbors and customers may never have seen him. Under these circumstances it would be easy to view him as an interloper.[68]

The jurors may also have found Attorney General Jared Ingersoll's rhetorical performance and demeanor persuasive. Ingersoll was described by his peers as dignified and serious: "When you saw him walk in the street, or pace the floor of the court-room, it was difficult to resist the impression that in early life he had received a military training; and the dress of the pre-democratic age, a full suit of black, or of light brown or drab in the warm season, with knee breeches and shoes, and long after others had abandoned the usage, hair-powder and a cue, very much assisted the impression."[69] The sixty-seven-year-old may have affected the jurors much as President Washington did his acquaintances: austere, authoritative, and in command. William Rawle, Peter Browne, and Jonathan B. Smith, however, looked less impressive, but they used vivid imagery to describe John Carson's malicious behavior and Richard Smith's heroism. Their rhetorical strategy depended much more on winning the jury's sympathy with evocative descriptions than with their personal demeanor.[70]

How much did Smith's ethnicity (Irish), religion (Catholic), age (twenty-three) and background (his spendthrift youth, disinheritance by his uncle, and the duel he fought while in the army) influence the decision? Did it matter that neither Smith nor Ann Carson testified? All of the witnesses to the shooting who did testify were biased against Smith. The Bakers had repeatedly tried to persuade their daughter to take John Carson back. Thomas Abbott welcomed the captain into his home (where the Bakers were also living). Would it have made a difference if Ann Carson had told the jury her version of what happened in the room? She believed that John had physically threatened Richard Smith: his words "I cannot lift a finger against you" were spoken with sarcasm as he towered over the much-smaller Smith, an inch from his nose.[71] Moreover, as Ann Carson later explained, she had not agreed to reconcile with John. Richard Smith's departure from the city was only a temporary retreat to avoid further entanglements with Captain Carson. Ann planned to follow Smith to Kentucky as soon as she could.[72]

The jury never heard this information. And it may not have changed the outcome if they had. Their decision shattered Ann Carson's life. Her reputation and her means of earning a living were gone. With little to lose and much to gain, her determination to save Richard Smith's life became the dominant force in her own: it dictated her actions and it determined her future.

3

The "Enraged Tygress"

ON THE EVENING of July 10, 1816, Pennsylvania Governor Simon Snyder received an urgent letter from his close friend, Philadelphia newspaper editor John Binns. The note must have alarmed Snyder considerably: "A desperate attempt is planned to rescue [Richard] Smith from jail. Measures are taken to prevent its success. It cannot succeed. So far I am quite satisfied. The unhappy man knows nothing of what is intended. The infernal Fiend who has caused the murder of her husband and the violent death of him she called her husband is raging with madness and has put all upon the cast of the die. She is now dressed in man's attire and has got three ruffians desperate as herself and she contemplates to seize your person and compel you to sign a Pardon for Smith." Binns suggested that Snyder should leave his home at Selinsgrove and return to the capital in Harrisburg, urging him to "Do this or do anything else your judgment may direct to guard you against this enraged Tygress.... I beseech you to guard against all the machinations of this Fiend of Hell for a little while and all will be over." The "Tygress" whom Binns warned his friend against was Ann Carson. Her rage had been provoked by the sentence of death imposed on Richard Smith.[1]

Released from prison after a jury declared her not guilty on the accessory to murder charge, Ann Carson returned to her house on Second Street a defeated woman. She had been away from her children and her business for four months. The Bakers moved into her house after the shooting and remained there throughout Ann's imprisonment. Jane Baker kept the china shop open, but she did not replenish its stock. As the goods for sale dwindled, customers declined. By the time Carson returned, it was no longer a going concern. Nor was she emotionally in a position to improve it. "Spiritless and depressed," Carson took opiates to dull her grief. Gradually she roused herself, but she still did not take an active role in running the shop.[2]

Warned that she might be re-arrested on the outstanding bigamy charge, despite having posted bail, Carson fled Philadelphia. Her hope was to avoid another trial altogether.³ She set off in the mail coach to Burlington, New Jersey, at two o'clock one morning accompanied by her brother. Carson's intent was to remain in Burlington "incog," as she said, until "an amicable adjustment could be made."⁴ Carson had little hope of remaining anonymous, however. She was recognized by another passenger in the mail coach, who warned her that Burlington was not a safe destination. According to this helpful gentleman, "That part of Jersey was strongly prejudiced against me, being generally ignorant, consequently inquisitive, weak, credulous people, among whom concealment would be impossible."⁵ The anonymous passenger's assessment of Burlington's denizens was confirmed for Carson during a dinner-table conversation later that day. A farmer who had attended Carson's trial, and yet seemed not to recognize her, declared that Ann Carson was "a very bad woman, and guilty of all she is accused of." Affronted by his "ignorant" opinion of the matter, Carson suggested that the farmer should read the recently published trial transcript and "inform himself more correctly."⁶ Carson stayed in Burlington until the day before her scheduled trial. She then caught the steamboat at Bristol back to Philadelphia in time for a ten o'clock court appearance where she learned that her bigamy trial was postponed. She was again free to remain in Philadelphia without fear of imprisonment.⁷

With her personal concerns settled for the moment, Carson again turned her attention to Richard Smith. Smith's lawyers applied to the Pennsylvania Supreme Court for a writ of error, arguing that proper procedures in pretrial paperwork had not been followed: signatures were missing, and lists of potential jurors had not been provided. In addition, according to Carson, "hundreds" of individuals petitioned the governor to pardon Smith outright. Even the jury members petitioned for him, arguing that "their ignorance of the law" caused the jury to pronounce Smith guilty.⁸ But Snyder declined to grant a pardon. The newspapers were critical of Snyder's decision, citing the disquiet his refusal stirred up.⁹ Driven by grief and anger, Carson believed that Governor Snyder and his associates conspired to ensure that Smith would be executed. She contended that Snyder's motives were political: "Richard was sacrificed on the shrine of interest; from motives of policy he withheld a pardon which he feared would injure him in the estimation of the public."¹⁰ Carson also claimed that Smith's lawyer, Peter Browne, was barred from practicing law for a year because he defended Smith too vigorously and later attempted to obtain Smith a pardon.

Carson did not wait to find out if the Supreme Court would approve the writ of error and possibly grant Smith a new trial. With almost all lawful means of saving Smith exhausted, Carson was determined to liberate him from the Walnut Street jail. And she did not have to do it on her own. Either the publicity of Smith's case and his denied appeals or Carson's vocalization of her determination to save Smith from the gallows elicited offers of aid from "the fraternity of desperadoes, who keep civilized society in bodily fear for either life or property."[11] Carson was approached by Elijah Bowen, who offered to free Smith. Bowen told Carson that he had been an officer in Smith's regiment; Bowen's regard for his fellow officer and the injustice of Smith's sentence prompted his desire to liberate Smith. Bowen was also a former convict and inhabitant of the Walnut Street prison; his inside knowledge of the building's layout would help him devise an escape plan. Carson readily accepted his offer, and Bowen, along with Henry Willis and several others, paid her a visit to discuss ways and means.[12] However much concern Elijah Bowen expressed for Smith's welfare, Bowen and his associates made it clear to Carson that their services were not free. But Carson was broke; she needed the assistance of someone with both cash and an interest in saving Smith's life. Fortunately, Smith's first cousin, Sarah Jane Campbell of Lexington, Kentucky, was in the city. She and her husband journeyed to Philadelphia when they first heard of Smith's arrest. Carson believed that Campbell was a sympathetic ally and, most important, a wealthy one. Because Campbell held the purse strings, any plan had to be approved by her.

A number of proposals were suggested. The first plan was for Bowen and his associates to climb over the prison wall and retrieve Smith from his cell. Smith would identify his window with a white flag and would saw through the bars of his window with a tool smuggled to him. With the aid of Bowen and company, Smith would then make his escape by climbing a rope up and over the wall and enter a waiting carriage. But Campbell vetoed this plan, arguing that her cousin was not physically capable of making such an escape.[13] Undaunted, Carson's plotters suggested an alternative that did not rely on Smith's strength. His rescuers would enter the prison yard, then enter the prison itself and make their way to Smith's cell (he was held in solitary confinement, an area separate from the rest of the prison population). They would open doors with their own made-up keys or tools, release Smith, and make their way out of the prison.[14] This second plan was more daring, and less certain, than the first. Campbell vetoed it. Nor did she agree to a third plan for one of the men to feign intoxication, get himself arrested, and be taken to prison. The others would then rush in, overpower the keepers, and liberate Smith. Ann Carson even resolved to participate in this plan herself, "to accompany the men in disguise, share their danger, and unite in bearing my beloved Richard from this den of horror, in triumph, to a place of safety."[15] But Campbell proved adamant in her fear that none of the plans would succeed. By this time, Carson suspected that Campbell was not sincerely interested in Smith's liberation, and that she might betray Carson and her confederates. Her suspicions of Campbell's duplicity were strengthened when Campbell insisted on Carson meeting with her representative, a Mr. Armour of Germantown, who asked Carson if she was pregnant with Smith's heir. Carson answered that she was not pregnant. Her reply, Carson believed, "sealed my husband's doom for probably, had there been a living heir, his family might have taken more active steps for the preservation of his life."[16] She also suspected that Campbell and Smith were to be joint inheritors of the wealth that Daniel Clark had passed on to his mother—their grandmother. Without Smith, or Smith's heir, Campbell would inherit everything.

Despite her growing suspicions, Carson persuaded Campbell that a scheme to bribe the prison's keeper would work. So Carson approached Ferman Black. He refused to cooperate but promised to keep Carson's plans a secret. Carson then sent her mother to another keeper, Mr. Geise. He also refused. But unlike Black, Geise alerted the prison inspectors about the bribe and they placed a guard on Smith. Resigned to the inevitability of Smith's death, Carson resolved "to blow up the cells with gunpowder" to spare Smith the "ignominious death" of a public execution.[17]

Carson decided to make one final effort to save her husband from the gallows. She planned to kidnap Governor Snyder and keep him in custody "till he signed Richard's pardon, and he was released from the walls that immured him." She was convinced that her scheme could work. Her back-up plan, in the event that Snyder was unavailable, was to capture one of the governor's children. Failing that, Carson planned to kidnap one of John Binns's children because "it was well known he had influence sufficient to induce Simon Snyder to pardon Richard Smith." Because Carson knew that Binns's children often freely roamed the streets of Philadelphia, they would be easy prey for Carson's men.[18] Years later, Binns recounted how "I had, at that time, a son, who had been christened Snyder, after the then governor. This boy was about five years old, and went daily to school. . . . [Ann Carson] determined to order those men to seize and secrete the above child, in the expectation that the governor would, from his attachment to me, grant a pardon for Smith, in order to insure the liberation of my child."[19]

In contrast to Carson's account, John Binns remembered that his child, not the governor, was the primary target of Carson's plan. Binns claimed that it was only after this first attempt failed that Carson decided to kidnap the governor. According to Binns, it was his refusal to help Carson obtain Smith's pardon that caused her to seek out his son: "She and her mother and other relations, called on me more than once, and labored, with singular earnestness, to enlist my feelings and induce me to use whatever influence I had with the governor, to step between Smith and death. As I could not be prevailed upon to give any satisfactory promise to that effect, it was resolved, by this desperate and devoted woman, to coerce me into her measures." In the more than thirty years between the events and his recounting of them in his autobiography, Binns had mellowed considerably. No longer was Carson a "fiend from hell" but just a "desperate and devoted woman."[20]

Carson did not believe that liberating Smith from prison through direct or coercive means was either extreme or unrealistic. Excluded from "decent" society because of her trial and the circumstances of Captain Carson's death, her reputation in tatters, Carson had nothing to lose. She was confident that Governor Snyder would agree to her demands once he was captured because, according to some of his friends, Snyder "would have suffered death rather than commit an act derogatory to his dignity as governor; but those persons, should have remembered that he was of mean spirit, and low origin." These characteristics, Carson believed, would encourage Snyder's ready agreement to her demands; she assumed that the governor's fear for his own safety would overcome both his pride and his sense of responsibility.[21]

Carson chose to take personal command of the enterprise. Otherwise, she feared, "the governor might either outbid me, or intimidate the men by threats of future punishment." Armed with the dueling pistol Smith had used to kill John Carson, accompanied by Elijah Bowen and Henry Willis, Ann Carson left Philadelphia at five in the morning on July 16. They headed to Selinsgrove, forty-seven miles north of Harrisburg, where the Snyder family lived. Carson kept rough company. Both Willis and Bowen were convicted felons. A third man, Henry Way, who traveled separately from Carson's group, planned to meet them near Selinsgrove. But en route to the rendezvous, Way robbed a drover. He was quickly captured and taken to the Lancaster jail, where he escaped, nearly killing his jailor in the process. Way was never apprehended.[22] With her two remaining accomplices, Carson planned to lie in wait for Snyder on the road to his home. Once kidnapped, Carson planned to take the governor by boat south on the Susquehanna and hold him at an isolated house until he agreed to sign a pardon. After Smith was freed, Carson, Smith, and her accomplices planned to release Snyder and quickly make their way to Canada.[23]

At Harrisburg, the two men left Carson at the Golden Fleece Inn while they retrieved a horse in Middletown, twelve miles to the south. Carson, calling herself Miss Jones, joined other travelers at dinner, where the conversation generally revolved around Smith's case.[24] The male guests made several comments at the table that suggested to Carson they suspected her true identity. One guest, Henry Antes, who proved to be related to Governor Snyder by marriage, discomposed Carson with a comment that Smith was almost certain to be executed. Her suspicions grew that someone—probably Mrs. Campbell—had betrayed the conspiracy back in Philadelphia.[25] When Bowen and Willis returned to the inn, Carson shared her concerns and suggested that they should give up the scheme. But the men dismissed her "womanish fears" and they continued on their way toward Snyder's home. On learning that the governor was in Harrisburg, Carson changed her plan. They would continue on to Selinsgrove and capture one of Snyder's children. She had no doubt that Snyder would bow to their demands once they held one of his children as a bargaining chip: "Who that knows the doating [*sic*] fondness of an old man for the child of his age, will question his compromising for its return on any terms?"[26]

Ten miles north of Harrisburg, they stopped for the night at Armstrong's Ferry. After spending a restless night, during which she tried to suppress a conviction that their plot had been uncovered, Carson's fears were confirmed when three officers of the law rode up to the inn early in the morning with a warrant for the arrest of Carson, Bowen, and Willis.[27] This moment could not have been completely unexpected. Carson had left a trail of evidence behind her in Philadelphia. Despite her resolve to leave Mrs. Campbell out of her plans, Carson had approached Smith's cousin for money to pay Bowen, Willis, and Way. Carson had met with Campbell in the presence of both Armour and Campbell's servant Mary Connellin. Connellin, an Irish Catholic like her mistress, told her priest, the Reverend Michael Hurly, pastor at St. Augustine's, about Ann Carson's plans.

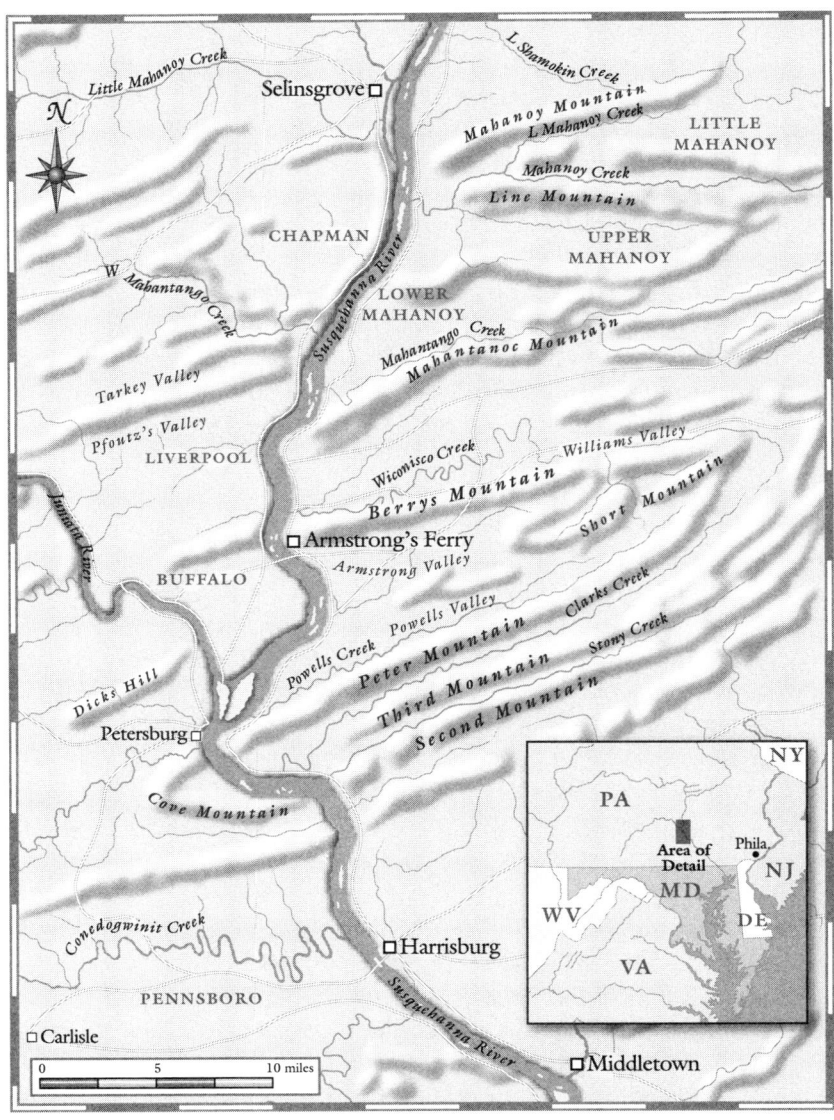

Figure 3. Carson and her accomplices left Philadelphia with a plan to kidnap Snyder or one of his children from his home in Selinsgrove. They stopped in Harrisburg and then rode on to Armstrong's Ferry, ten miles to the north, to rest for the night. The authorities caught up with them there the following morning.

Hurly in turn informed his friend, and fellow Catholic, John Binns, that an attempt might be made on the governor, or possibly on one of Binns's own children. The Catholic connection was Carson's undoing. John Binns knew of Carson's plan a week before she arrived at Armstrong's Ferry. Such a bold plan put too much at stake for many of those who knew of it: the sentence for conspiracy to kidnap a head of state was life at hard labor.[28]

The law officers sent to arrest Carson and her fellow conspirators were surprisingly polite. When Carson challenged the legality of their warrant, they brought a local magistrate to the inn to verify that it was "right and proper." Resigned to the inevitable, Carson still insisted on "partaking of an excellent breakfast" and making the officers pay all of her expenses at the inn. Only then did they set out for Harrisburg.[29]

The evidence of Carson's intended crime was overwhelming: she was apprehended on her way to the governor's residence, armed with pistols. She could claim that her actions were performed in the heat of the moment, but this defense alone would not save her from a conviction of conspiracy to kidnap. She needed a powerful and persuasive weapon in her legal arsenal. Fortunately for her she had one: the alleged "shrine of interest" that guided Snyder's motives when he refused to pardon Smith, now worked to Carson's advantage. As she and her fellow conspirators were transported back to the Harrisburg jail, a gentleman flagged down their carriage and asked to speak with Carson. He offered her some advice, suggesting that she not "submit to any private examination, but demand a public investigation of the affair." He told her to "send for messrs. Elder and Fisher as your counsel, and communicate your business to none else." Carson followed his instructions to the letter. When she appeared before the grand jury for her indictment, she discovered that this kind gentleman was none other than the judge in charge of the hearing, Joseph Carson (no relation to John Carson). Her attorneys, chosen at the judge's suggestion, were opposed to Governor Snyder's administration; they rejoiced at the opportunity to place the governor in an embarrassing position.[30]

In Harrisburg, Ann Carson, Willis, and Bowen were first taken to Justice Fahnestoch's house for questioning. Armed with her unknown champion's advice, Carson refused to be questioned privately and demanded that she be conveyed to the Harrisburg prison. While she waited, curiosity seekers surrounded Fahnestoch's house. Carson recalled that several women were "peeping through the cracks and crevices of the door to catch a glimpse of us."[31] One of these curious "peepers" was Snyder's wife. Carson found such behavior unbecoming in the spouse of the governor: "the potent lady, governess of the state of Pennsylvania, ought to be better educated, have more spirit, dignity, and respect for the office her husband filled than thus to descend to the conduct of servant girls, whose deficiency of education was their excuse, but in a governor's lady it was unpardonable."[32] Mrs. Snyder, it could be argued, had a justifiable curiosity in the woman who was alleged to have been on the brink of seizing either her husband or her child.

In the Harrisburg jail, Carson and her companions spent their time together in a twelve-foot-by-twelve-foot room. Left on their own for hours and days before the grand jury hearing, they had ample opportunity to get their story straight. Only at night did Carson have the luxury of solitude in a separate room. She was not supplied with a bed, so after spending one miserable night wrapped in a blanket with Willis's portmanteau for a pillow (and bed bugs for company) Carson hired herself one from the Golden Fleece. It was so uncomfortable she returned it.[33]

Carson's presence in Harrisburg attracted a good deal of attention. The local paper publicized her daring attempt on the governor and her subsequent arrest. As Carson noted, she had become "an object of general attention and commiseration." Though Carson was confined to the jail, the keeper, Kelker, gave her the freedom to walk around the building and grounds, trusting to Carson's honor not to attempt an escape. Kelker also allowed Carson to entertain visitors during her stay, including his daughter, Mary, and her teenage friends, with whom Carson often passed "an idle hour away in social chat."[34] She was also visited by her attorneys, Elder and Fisher, who interviewed Carson to prepare her defense. Their task was not easy. Miss Beissel, daughter of the Golden Fleece's innkeeper, testified that Carson had pistols in her possession and that her traveling companions were convicted felons. Clearly she was up to no good.[35]

Despite these handicaps, Carson's advocates did their best for her. The prosecution lent a hand as well. The state attorney pro tem called Elijah Bowen to the witness stand to discredit Carson's claim of innocence. He challenged Bowen, "If her acquaintances are respectable, how came she to associate with you, who was late a convict in the Philadelphia penitentiary?" Bowen replied with a challenge of his own: "and how is it that we see the governor of Pennsylvania the intimate friend of John Binns, who has been in seven prisons, while I was never in but one?"[36] And though Elder and Fisher advised Carson not to demand that the governor appear at the hearing, on this point she held firm: "Well knowing I had no lenity to expect, I resolved to mortify him as far as my power extended." Carson demanded the right to face her accuser. Judge Carson, over the objection of the state's prosecutor, ruled that Snyder must appear.[37]

On the third day of the hearing, Governor Snyder walked into the courtroom. Ann Carson's account of this encounter was colored by her dislike of Snyder. Not surprisingly, Carson's description of the governor was not flattering. She informed her readers that Snyder's "advantages, I had understood, were not mental." Nor did he possess "pleasing manners and prepossessing exterior."[38] She was equally scornful of the unnamed prosecuting attorney, "an Irish gentleman of some eminence at the bar," who Carson claimed was drunk in the courtroom and falsely accused her of vicious crimes. "Perhaps Mr.—— had his eye on a good fat office at the time he was abusing a woman he had never seen or known except by report."[39]

Carson contrasted Governor Snyder's severity with the kindness of Judge Carson. While Snyder's expression was "demonic," and full of "pride and malice, panting for revenge," her champion "beamed with benevolence, intelligence, and humanity."[40] As part of his testimony, Snyder read from John Binns's letter warning him of Carson's plan. Despite hard evidence of a conspiracy, Carson pinned her hopes on the jurors' sympathies with her condemned husband. When Snyder entered the courtroom, Carson rose from her chair and cried out, "Oh! There is no hope for Richard Smith; that face has not one trace of humanity in it."[41] She also hoped that jurors would not take seriously the notion that a woman could kidnap the head of state. When Snyder was compelled to swear on oath that his life was in danger from a woman, his admission produced "a general, but smothered laugh in the court."[42] The *Washington City Weekly Gazette* echoed this derision: "And to suppose that governor Snyder could have been *terrified*, surrounded as he was by a population devoted to him, into the granting of a pardon, is but a sorry compliment to his firmness."[43] Nonetheless, the grand jury did find there was sufficient evidence of criminal wrongdoing to require Carson, Willis, and Bowen to stand trial. The governor convinced Judge Carson that Ann Carson posed a continuing risk to him, and asked for a high bail fee to ensure her captivity. Her bail was set at $5,000, a sum far too high for Carson, or even her family (had they been inclined to do so), to pay. Despite her lawyers' best efforts, and Carson's own performance, she was once again in jail.[44]

The conspiracy trial was scheduled to be held in Philadelphia at the mayor's court in October. As Carson waited in the Harrisburg jail to be transported back to Walnut Street prison, she heard two disturbing pieces

Figure 4. Simon Snyder, Pennsylvania's first German-American governor. Ann Carson described Snyder's face as one of "hard features, thickly pox-marked, with a dark, austere, unbending brow, and a countenance that seemed as if it had never relaxed into a smile, nor melted to soft pity's throe." Courtesy of the Library Company of Philadelphia.

of news: her mother had been arrested as an accomplice for carrying letters concerning the conspiracy from Carson to Mrs. Campbell. But far worse than this, Carson's efforts to save Smith were in vain. On August 10, while Carson was still in the Harrisburg jail, Richard Smith was executed.[45]

The Supreme Court denied Smith's application for a writ of error. Chief Justice William Tilghman explained that the prompt decision was motivated by mercy: "a state of suspense might produce agitations of mind, unfavorable to his present condition." In the Court's opinion, the errors in procedure outlined by Smith's attorneys had not interfered with a fair trial.[46] The press wasted no time. By the third week in July, a written confession was published in dozens of newspapers from Maine to Tennessee. It was a confession written with the assumption that Smith would soon "depart to the world of spirits." The narrative provided readers with Smith's life story, from infancy in Ireland, to a profligate youth in New Orleans, valiant military service at Sacketts Harbor, and finally to his unlucky association with Ann Carson. Smith's "Confession" repeated many of the details of his life that came out at the trial. It was a history of wrongdoing, an announcement of repentance and a cautionary tale for others. It revealed nothing that had not come out in the trial testimony and published transcript. It was also a condemnation of Ann Carson.[47]

As Carson waited in the Harrisburg jail for her grand jury hearing, Smith's narrative had already indicted her. Ann Carson was not Smith's savior. She was an "evil woman . . . who is versed in all the wiles and machinations of that diabolical spirit which possessed the heart of the first of her race, and caused the downfall of mankind." His attachment to Carson was no romantic story of mutual attraction. Smith claimed that he had been "seduced . . . into the bands of matrimony," by the "subtle wiles of a designing and inconstant woman who forgot the ties that connected her to her husband." Paraphrasing the seventh book of Proverbs, he warned other "'giddy and thoughtless'" young men of the "wiles of the 'strange woman,' for her ways are as 'the gates of hell, going down to the chamber of death!'"[48] Smith's story was dramatic. It involved love, violence, and betrayal of biblical proportions. It was popular fiction come to life. By the morning of Saturday, August 10, Richard Smith was the most talked about and read about man in the United States.[49]

Carson had reason to despair over Smith's impending doom. His confession may have wounded her, but she learned at the grand jury hearing that her letters to him, in which she revealed to him the various plans for his liberation (and in which she assured Smith of her constancy), never reached him.[50] Nor had she been permitted to see him. The newspapers reported that Carson had asked to see Smith and he had refused to see her. He may well have gone to his death ignorant of Carson's efforts on his behalf.[51]

Widespread reports of Smith's circumstances, compounded by Carson's bold attempt to liberate him, drew crowds to his execution. "Tens of thousands of spectators, . . . of all ages, sexes, and conditions," lined the mile and a half route from the jail to the execution site.[52] Readers were treated to a minute-by-minute account of Smith's execution from his departure from the Walnut Street prison until his body was cut down from the scaffold. Visual and aural details were supplied in abundance:

The impression made upon the crowd when the gates were thrown open and the cart appeared, was of a character of melancholy not easily to be described. Curiosity itself seemed hushed, not a sound was heard, a solemn silence pervaded the whole assembly. The running hither and thither of boys, the pushing of men, and crowding together of women, was all over, and mothers pressed their little ones to their bosoms with more than a mother's anxiousness.

The cart was driven by the executioner, a black man. Just behind him, and with his back toward the horse, . . . was placed the unhappy Smith. By him sat the Reverend Mr. Hurley, the officiating minister of the gospel, who had attended him since his conviction. In the rear of the cart sat a gentleman who humanely volunteered to hold an umbrella over the heads of the clergyman and the prisoner, to shelter them from the rays of a blazing sun.[53]

Readers learned what Smith wore—a dark blue frock coat and dark underclothes—and even the postures of Smith and his priest, Reverend Hurley, the same man who revealed the kidnapping plot to John Binns, who sat "with his head and body inclining to the prisoner who was in a similar position in relation to the priest, and thus devoutly intent on the solemn religious exercises they were reading." Readers learned exactly how long the procession took to reach the gallows—thirty minutes—and how long after reaching the site Smith spent in prayer before mounting the platform—fifteen minutes.

The newspaper accounts helped readers imagine the execution. This was not simple reportage of fact. This was an evocation—with sight, sound, gesture, and even heat (evidenced by the umbrella needed to shade the prisoner). But the journalist there that day did more than merely set the scene before his readers. He portrayed the emotions of the event as well: "The eyes of the thousands of spectators were directed with more than heretofore anxiety to the scene of sorrow. . . . When Smith . . . stood up a murmur of pity was heard from every mouth. How could it be otherwise!

A stripling about 5 feet 10 inches high, of an interesting aspect, deeply impressed with his awful situation; a youth, but in the morning of his days, stood before them in the full vigor of health, and yet but a moment and he would be violently thrust from the stage of human life and consigned to the grave." Even Reverend Hurley was overcome with emotion: "The trembling agitation of the almost exhausted Priest was evident; . . . he poured forth his last blessing. With streaming eyes [he] implored a last forgiveness and straining the unhappy young man to his bosom he resigned him to the Mercy of his Creator and sank in a state of insensibility into the arms of friends who bore him away."

The crowd reacted with appropriate pity and dismay: "When the fatal arrangements were made and he was launched into eternity, there was a general involuntary shriek of horror; sobs and groans were heard on every side and fervent prayers were offered up [through] a mist of tears by thousands whose hearts ached at the sight." Although the account concluded by acknowledging the utility of the event as "a solemn warning to the youth of both sexes to shun the paths of Vice, and steadily pursue those of Virtue," readers were left with a greater impression of the "awfulness" and the "melancholy" as another account described it, than of an act of public justice.[54]

Coverage of Smith's execution was extensive, evocative, and, what may have alarmed authorities, voyeuristic and emotionally indulgent without being instructive. To describe what occurred journalists used sentimental language that portrayed personal reactions to state-sanctioned violence. Gone was an emphasis on how the event reinstated order and authority in the community. Eyewitnesses and readers alike had a new (and negative) response to watching a man die. One reader's reaction to Smith's death is telling in this regard. Deborah Logan, who had read about (and perhaps witnessed) public executions since before the Revolution, recorded in her diary: "This day poor Smith was executed. . . . I do not think I ever so realized to myself the situation of a condemned criminal, as I did in this instance, . . . It has covered my mind with gloom."[55]

If Smith's execution was the second act in a domestic tragedy, Ann Carson's conspiracy trial was the third and final one. Newspapers followed her every move from Harrisburg back to Philadelphia. When Philadelphia Constable John Hart arrived in Harrisburg to retrieve Carson, Willis, and Bowen, Carson locked herself in a room with the prison keeper's daughter, Mary Kelker, until her lawyer assured her that Hart's warrant was legal.[56] And when Hart broke up their return journey at Lancaster for the night,

Carson found mail (of sorts) waiting in her cell. The gentleman who had last occupied the room, on being informed that he was to vacate for Ann Carson, wrote her a "few original lines" and left his bible open to the seventh book of Proverbs. Richard Smith's confession used these same verses to place the blame for his misfortunes on Carson, "a woman with the attire of an harlot, and subtil of heart," who had slain "many strong men."

Here was a calling card with a vengeance. The publication of Smith's confession allowed at least one reader to articulate his own condemnation of Carson. Yet even this she turned to her advantage. With plenty of time on her hands until morning, she wrote a response to the absent author. Carson blamed the failure of her plan on Mrs. Campbell's treachery and greed. Carson also blamed her family for their "hate and prejudice" toward Smith. Her reply to the absent gentleman found its way into the local paper and was then reprinted in several states. The newspapers acknowledged that Carson was news; readers took an interest "in everything that concerns this woman."[57]

Carson was very good copy. While she spent her evening in Lancaster penning a justification for her activities, her co-conspirators were usefully occupied sawing through their leg irons with a saw Carson had smuggled to them. The following morning, Constable Hart wisely checked the condition of his prisoners' bindings, only to discover the chains were almost sawn through. Once Hart resecured his charges, the trip to Philadelphia was uneventful, though for Carson there was a moment of high emotion when the carriage passed through Hamilton Village, past the cemetery along the Schuylkill where Smith was buried.[58]

Carson attracted enormous publicity. From the moment she stepped into the courtroom in Philadelphia in May to answer a charge of accessory to murder until her trial for conspiracy in November, newspaper readers up and down the eastern seaboard were kept informed of her activities and her whereabouts. The Philadelphia *True American* acknowledged its readers' desire for information about Carson: "Anxious to gratify public curiosity we have taken some pains to gather such incidents as would be interesting, in relation to Mrs. Baker, Mrs. Carson and Smith."[59] Newspapers in Philadelphia, New York, and Baltimore all announced Carson's return to Philadelphia from Harrisburg under guard with Constable Hart to stand trial on conspiracy charges.[60]

Much of the reporting claimed to be simply informative, but even seemingly unbiased reportage was potentially damaging to Carson. One report was a letter purportedly written by a gentleman in Harrisburg shortly after Ann Carson's arrest. The letter revealed that Carson's true plan had been to assassinate, not kidnap, Governor Snyder if he refused Smith a pardon. If she and her men failed to capture Snyder, they would kill the governor's son. Should there be any doubt that Carson could carry out such a vicious scheme, the letter writer added: "I have seen Mrs. C. She is an elegant woman, and from character, capable of executing any thing desperate—well accomplished."[61] One newspaper hoped that Carson was unique: "But what should be said of the woman who has been the prominent cause of the violent death of her lawful husband, and of the ignominious death of her unfortunate paramour?—Respecting the delicacy and honor of the Female Sex, we shall only say, that we most sincerely hope, there is not such another woman in the United States."[62] The *Baltimore Patriot* called her a "profligate woman." *Niles' Weekly Register* said she was "abandoned and wicked." But the term most often used to describe Ann Carson, in 1816 and after, was "notorious."[63]

She earned this description in part because her crime was unprecedented. Female criminals were not rare in early nineteenth century America, but Carson's type of crime was. Women infrequently committed violent crimes. Most women were arrested for vagrancy, assault, fornication, or theft—crimes closely associated with impoverishment and limited economic opportunity. In the early nineteenth century, women represented one-third of all prison commitments for minor personal crimes, larceny, and assault and battery.[64] In contrast, Carson possessed firearms and conspired to commit a violent felony. No other woman or man in the state had perpetrated the type of crime Carson attempted. Although women convicted of assault and battery did hit, kick, pull hair, and punch their victims, they did not, as Carson had, brandish dueling weapons. Carson's crime was exceptional, and the circumstances that led to its commission were equally so.[65]

Carson was also "notorious" because of changes under way in the press. New print technologies, expanded reportage, and developing popular culture venues meant that people like Ann Carson could attain a level of exposure not possible in the eighteenth century. News items were more widely distributed (because there were more papers), more people were reading newspapers (and there were more daily papers available in cities), and newspapers were just starting to include more human-interest stories, especially crimes. Newspapers were beginning to carry more than just shipping news, agricultural prices, politics, and European wars. In 1816, America was on the cusp of the emergence of a new vernacular print culture, one that would quickly become characterized as "cheap, sensational, ephemeral, miscellaneous, illustrated, and serialized."[66] Widespread reportage of Ann Carson's activities was the harbinger of this new era.

The one individual who followed Carson's progress every step of the way and made it his business to report, and comment on, her activities for the rest of her life, was newspaper editor John Binns. As editor of the Philadelphia *Democratic Press*, he was well situated to track her movements. As good friend and political associate of Governor Snyder, Binns took a special interest in Carson's case. As the father of a child whom Carson had targeted for potential kidnapping, Binns had a personal concern about Carson's fate. Soon after Carson's arrest near Harrisburg, John Binns, as a private prosecutor, had Jane Baker arrested for her part in the conspiracy.[67] Through his own testimony and evidence of letters in his possession—the letters from Carson to Smith that Jane Baker had carried to the prison.—Binns convinced the attorney general of Baker's culpability.[68] But Binns's political and personal association with Snyder may have hindered his quest for justice. Binns informed his *Democratic Press* readers that despite his efforts to have Baker locked up, she had been released on bail. He vented his frustrations: "It was distinctly promised by the attorney general and his deputy, that if any attempt was made to liberate the accused by a Habeus Corpus that a notice should be given to the writer of this as the prosecutor and person not only in possession of the written, but best acquainted with the oral testimony, and one the happiness of whose family had been basely threatened, and who was thus deeply involved in promoting the ends of public justice." Binns was also chagrined that Chief Justice Tilghman agreed to reduce Baker's bail to a sum that she (actually a professional bail bondsman, Daniel Broadhead) could afford. But Binns saved the majority of his criticism for the attorney general, Jared Ingersoll, for his failure to carry through on his promises to Binns. Binns was publicly associated with Snyder and the Democrats. His newspaper was a party organ. He enjoyed the lucrative favor of the state's printing business and he was also a director of the Pennsylvania Bank. Unfortunately for Binns, Ingersoll's and Tilghman's political sentiments lay with the opposition. Tilghman had been briefly considered as the Federalist candidate to run against Simon Snyder in 1808 (he withdrew in favor of James Ross).[69] Ingersoll ran for Senator on the Federalist ticket in 1814 (he was defeated by Democrat Jonathan Roberts).[70] Whatever these two men might have thought about the law and justice, they were certainly not inclined to do any favors for John Binns.

The attention given to Smith's trial and execution may also have put Carson's endeavor to liberate him in a positive light. Newspapers in Philadelphia, New York, and Washington decried his verdict as unjust, and they criticized Judge Rush's biased handling of the case. None of this helped Smith, but it may have helped Carson. The harshest criticism of the trial verdict came from the *Washington City Weekly Gazette*. The author wrote that Rush's summation was biased and his address to the jury not only "*bitterly* adverse to Smith," but also "harsh, peremptory, and unwarranted by the testimony."[71] Although the writer did not exonerate Smith from the crime of murder, he did lay some of the blame on John Carson, claiming that Carson was an "accessory to his own death.... Love, jealousy, pride, hatred, and revenge, were busy at his heart." The *True American* (Philadelphia) shared with readers the fallacies in Rush's argument. The *Columbian* (New York) concurred with the Philadelphia paper, going further still in asserting that to execute Smith "would, we *conscientiously* think, be a disgrace to a civilized, christian, community."[72]

Nor was the press silent on the topic of Smith's petition for a pardon from the governor. The *Columbian* was highly critical of Snyder's refusal. A Harrisburg paper called Snyder hypocritical: "*Justice* is said to be even handed; yet Governor Snyder has been in the practice of granting pardons very liberally—and some six months ago he granted one, where the conviction was for the same crime as Smith's."[73] Carson also received a share of sympathy from the press: "As to the lady, we perfectly agree with the editor of a respectable Boston print, that still to detain her on a charge of bigamy 'looks like persecution.' Surely her cup of affliction is full enough; and she has sufficient cause to regret the day she married either Carson or Smith."[74]

Unable to provide bail, set at $5,000, Ann Carson spent the months between her hearing and the trial in the Walnut Street jail. Her conspiracy trial began November 7, 1816, at the mayor's court, with Judge Jacob Reed presiding. Carson, Willis, and Carson's mother, Jane Baker, were present to answer the charges against them. Elijah Bowen had paid his bail and fled. Though Carson's Harrisburg attorneys failed to prevent her indictment for conspiracy, her Philadelphia defense team, consisting of Joseph R. Ingersoll, the same lawyer who defended her at the accessory to murder trial, Zeligman Philips, Thomas Armstrong, Benjamin Chew, and Joseph Lloyd, planned a strategy similar to the one used before the Harrisburg grand jury. They had their work cut out for them: there were numerous witnesses to Carson's various plans for Smith's liberation. She and her codefendants, two recently released felons, were apprehended in the vicinity of Selinsgrove with arms in their possession and using assumed names. This did not look like innocent behavior. However, several circumstances worked in Carson's favor: the character of courtroom trials in the early nineteenth century, Carson's demeanor in the courtroom, and the trial's location in Philadelphia.[75]

There were sound legal reasons to hold the conspiracy trial in Philadelphia rather than in Harrisburg. Carson's arrest had occurred near the capital, but the conspiracy had originated in Philadelphia, where the majority of the prosecution's witnesses—Walnut Street jail keepers, Reverend Hurley, John Binns, Mrs. Campbell, and many others—resided. Logistics and expense dictated the change of venue.[76] This accident of circumstance shifted the political influences on the outcome of Carson's trial. The conspiracy happened during a volatile time in state politics. Pennsylvania's political atmosphere was highly charged and partisan.[77] Although the next gubernatorial and presidential elections were more than two years away, election rhetoric was already much in evidence in the newspapers. Snyder was not running for governor, having served his three-term limit. But he was talked about (at least by Binns) as a presidential, or vice presidential candidate. Carson's fame (or infamy) became linked with the political atmosphere in Pennsylvania. As the New York papers reported, with some sarcasm: "The democrats . . . conclude that Pennsylvania is entitled to a little more consideration—that having made herself conspicuous, for her Whiskey Insurrections, Perpetual Motions, Ann Carson conspiracies, and Banking Institutions; she is entitled to the honor of giving the U.S. a President—or, if that cannot be granted, at least a vice president, at the ensuing election."[78]

Simon Snyder had been governor since 1808. His political opponents, after enduring eight years of Democratic rule, Democratic appointments, and Democratic cronyism, were eager to undermine his chokehold on the state. They were also eager to bring down his chief political ally, John Binns. Binns ran Snyder's campaign in 1808. His newspapers, first the *Republican Argus* in Northumberland and then the *Democratic Press* in Philadelphia, were highly partisan and always pro-Snyder. Described as "a one-man kitchen cabinet to Governor Snyder," Binns benefited from his loyalty to the governor.[79] Snyder handed Binns all government printing business and he helped Binns to an appointment on the board of the Bank of Pennsylvania. Many Federalists and Old School Democrats were eager to seize an opportunity to take both men down a peg or two.[80]

Carson's arrest drew interest on two scores: the audacity of her actions and the fact that the governor was the subject of them. Attorneys with anti-Snyder leanings rushed forward to lend her legal assistance. The prosecution at her grand jury hearing in Harrisburg complained that Carson's advocates seemed to "fall from heaven."[81] Certainly many lawyers would have been eager to associate themselves with such a notorious case and client. But they may also have taken satisfaction in helping to spread negative publicity for a governor and an administration they disliked. The Federalist *Harrisburg Chronicle*, for instance, used the occasion of Carson's arrest to criticize Binns: "Binns, of late, seems to devote the principal part of his time to the administration of justice. When Mrs. Smith or Carson, was first committed to our prison, the Press was 'quite sure that insufficient bail would not be taken.' ... His opinion is entitled to much weight, no man in the commonwealth having had more *experience* in criminal jurisprudence than himself."[82] Carson's Harrisburg advocate, Thomas Elder, was an Old School Democrat who backed the losing side when John Ross ran against Snyder in 1808. He was also good friends with Joseph Heister, an anti-Snyderite who was elected governor in 1820.[83]

Whether the change of venue from Harrisburg to Philadelphia was politically motivated is hard to determine, as there were clear reasons for the trial to be held where the majority of witnesses lived. But when the conspiracy trial began in Philadelphia in November, Carson's legal counsel was composed of leading Federalists, including William Rawle and Joseph Reed Ingersoll.[84] The prosecution was led by Deputy Attorney General Thomas Kittera, also a Federalist.[85] These men did not just have political sympathies, but were politically active. Carson had reason for optimism.[86]

Carson's lawyers faced the challenging task of persuading a jury to acquit a woman whom witnesses claimed intended to kidnap the governor. The state brought several witnesses from Harrisburg, including Henry Antes, who had followed Carson to the Golden Fleece in Harrisburg and watched her closely during her stay there, and the Golden Fleece's owner, Frederick Beissel.[87] Carson's jailors in Harrisburg, her jailors in Lancaster, and Smith's jailors in Philadelphia were all there to attest to Carson's suspicious, if not downright criminal, behavior. The prosecution also put Sarah Jane Campbell and her maid, Mary Connellin, on the witness stand, along with their priest, Father Hurley. Each witness could attest to a piece of the plan—from talk of breaking into Walnut Street prison to liberate Smith, to capturing the governor or one of his children, to attempts at escape once in custody. Prosecutor Kittera read a memorandum of the convictions, sentences, and pardons of Elijah Bowen for offenses punishable by hard labor, proving that Carson's chosen companions were no Sunday school teachers.[88] Carson's defense team needed something weighty to counter this body of evidence.

Carson's attorneys subpoenaed the governor as a material witness for the defense. Their strategy was to once again force Snyder to swear his life was in danger from Ann Carson—a claim they hoped the jury would find incredible. But Snyder declined to testify.[89] Nevertheless, his nonappearance may have swayed the jurors' sympathies toward Carson; in the struggle between political factions, the governor's decisions in criminal matters were often viewed more as politics than justice. These perceived biases may have helped Carson to appear as a victim at the mercy of a cruel and cowardly Simon Snyder.

But the defense could not rely solely on local prejudice against Snyder. They also had a courtroom strategy: when the prosecution called its first witness, Smith's cousin Sarah Campbell, Carson's counsel asked that during her examination (and while each subsequent witness was examined) all other witnesses on behalf of the commonwealth be barred from the courtroom. Judge Reed complied with this request. Each witness testified in isolation. The result was that none of the witnesses was able to corroborate the testimony of the others.[90]

The prosecuting attorney, twenty-seven-year-old Thomas Kittera, was up against some of the best legal minds of the era: William Rawle and David Paul Brown.[91] Both men exercised their talents of courtroom showmanship to win sympathy for their client and discredit the prosecution's witnesses. Court trials in the early nineteenth century were part of the "grand, free, popular theater" in nineteenth-century urban America. Spectators eagerly awaited sensational trials (publicized well in advance by the press), especially criminal trials such as Carson's. In a crowded room of the Old State House, "clients, witnesses, lawyers, and spectators crammed together. Much like a theater audience, the spectators booed or applauded, and even the attorneys sometimes played to the crowd with jokes and asides."[92] Rawle and Brown summed up the evidence against Carson in an "able, rational, and humorous manner." More important, they discredited the prosecution's witnesses (including the governor *in absentia*), by placing "the whole transaction in so contemptible a point of view, that the court was a scene of mirth and laughter."[93]

Finally, Carson's own behavior played to the sympathies of the court. When the prosecutor called Carson a liar for denying she planned a conspiracy, she responded in a way sure to evoke sympathy. "Stung to the soul," by Kittera's "rude attack on my veracity," Carson recounted that she involuntarily "started from my seat, and gave vent to my resentment by observing that my sex alone hindered me from chastising his insolence. . . . I, oppressed by feelings now indefinable, lost my fortitude, and gratified his malice by bursting into tears." Just as she had done at the grand jury hearing, Carson exhibited emotional behavior of a particularly female kind.[94] Her pose of helpless, and indignant, womanhood went hand in hand with her attorneys' strategy: who would believe that a crying, fearful woman would try to kidnap the governor?

At four-thirty in the afternoon of the third day of the trial, the jury retired to consider its verdict. Their task was to weigh the evidence against the three defendents. Baker and Willis could not be guilty unless Carson was guilty; they were charged as participants in a conspiracy instigated and carried out by Carson. The evidence against Jane Baker—that she carried letters to the prisoner that contained plans for his escape—was damaging only if she knew what the letters contained. But Baker could say she had no knowledge of the contents. And given her vigorous testimony against Smith at the murder trial, it seemed implausible that she would have been a willing party to his escape. Likewise, judgment for or against Henry Willis depended entirely on whether the jury believed Carson had deliberately traveled to Harrisburg and then toward Selinsgrove to kidnap the governor. Willis' recent pardon by that same governor may have served as a bona fide of his behavior.

An hour and a half later, the jury returned to announce that the defendants Ann Carson, Jane Baker, and Henry Willis (aka John Ryde) were not guilty.[95] The verdict was not only a triumph for Carson, but a defeat for the prosecution, emphasized by the jury's determination that the prosecution pay Carson's court costs. Their decision implied not only that Ann Carson was innocent, but that the case against her was unfair.[96] Carson viewed the judgment as a defeat for her persecutor, Simon Snyder: "Thus the puissant governor and his coadjutor's malice were defeated by a verdict of *not guilty*."[97] Carson, her mother, and Willis were free. As Carson left the courtroom, she was warmly congratulated by the crowd, who were "loud in the exultation at my acquittal."[98]

Why was Carson acquitted? She believed that the prosecution had insufficient evidence against her to obtain a conviction. John Binns claimed that anti-Snyder "party prejudice" was responsible for the trial's outcome.[99] The press, which had so avidly followed Carson's activities, declined to offer analysis. The papers reported the verdict without comment. Carson and Binns may both have been correct in their assessments of the legal and political aspects of her case. Another element that neither of them would have recognized, or at least been able to give a name to, was the gender ideology of the time. Ann Carson was caught with pistols and with criminals she hired. A host of witnesses attested to her various plans to liberate Smith. Yet to convict her would have thrown these nineteenth-century jurors into a gray area they were not prepared to contemplate; they would have had to acknowledge that she was all the things a woman was not supposed to be: active, dominant, intelligent, and physically brave. Certainly her defense strategy was to deny that she was any of those things. What was the truth? The judge, the jury, and the press did not know. But six years after her acquittal, Ann Carson wrote and published a memoir in which she revealed her true self. For eight months, she had been the "notorious" Ann Carson, with her story, not always accurately, reported in the newspapers of the nation. In 1822, she determined to take advantage of the notoriety that still clung to her and to shape her story for her own benefit and purpose.

4

Courting Notoriety

BETWEEN NOVEMBER 1816 and January 1822 Ann Carson did her best to stay out of the public eye as she continued to associate with Henry Willis and other criminals. Inevitably, this connection proved dangerous—twice she was arrested. On the second occasion, she was convicted, sentenced, and served almost a year in the Walnut Street prison. In the summer of 1822, with no employment, no family support (her father was dead, and her mother had left Philadelphia), Carson chose to capitalize on her notoriety. As one of her companions suggested, Carson had "so long played the heroine, for the amusement of the public, gratis, it [was] time they should pay the piper." And so she sought out author Mary Clarke, whom Carson knew by reputation, to ghostwrite a memoir. When Clarke and Carson finally met, Clarke warned Carson of "all the difficulties attending the publication of a native work."[1] Clarke was also concerned for her own reputation—she was known only for her women's magazine, songs, and plays. Clarke recognized the potential for the book to sell well, but she was a respectable woman and wished to remain that way—both for her public character and for her future professional opportunities. Association with Ann Carson was dangerous.

Carson persuaded Mary Clarke to write the book with the promise that Clarke would not "appear in the affair."[2] Thus began a collaboration from which both women hoped to profit. The risks seemed small: Carson persuaded printer Robert Desilver to publish the book on speculation of sales; she did not have to come up with cash to pay for publication. And Carson's reputation could not possibly suffer from a public recounting of her life; as the proven associate of outlaws, the entire nation knew of her kidnapping attempt. And everyone in Philadelphia knew of her recent imprisonment in connection with a robbery. Carson hoped to benefit from a retelling of her affairs—and perhaps seek a little revenge in the process.[3] Mary Clarke would shape Carson's story into a readable, appealing narrative, but her name would not appear anywhere in the book. If it sold well,

Clarke would make money. If it didn't, she lost only the labor she put into writing it.

The *History of the Celebrated Mrs. Ann Carson* was designed to sell. Even the title created allure: who would not wish to read about a famous woman, especially if one already knew that she had led an interesting, tumultuous life?[4] With Smith's execution and the kidnapping conspiracy still in the public's mind, the book told readers the details of Ann's marriage to John Carson, her relationship with Richard Smith, and the events that culminated in her conspiracy trial. The *History* sought to appeal to readers in several ways. The memoir is styled like a sentimental novel, a genre many readers were familiar with. It is also a paean to the middle-class values beginning to spread beyond the social and economic base with which they were identified. Finally, the *History* is a scintillating account of Carson's romantic (and sexual) relationships and her criminal escapades. Reminiscent of the memoirs of courtesans and actresses, Carson's book was meant to shock.

The *History* satisfied the public's curiosity about Carson's activities between her acquittal on conspiracy charges in November 1816 and her release from prison in the spring of 1821. Carson's legal woes did not end when the conspiracy trial concluded. Two weeks later, she was served with an arrest warrant for bigamy. Desperate to avoid imprisonment, she fled to Baltimore with fellow conspirator Henry Willis. There, she resolved "at once to initiate myself among that class of people who set *law*, *justice*, and *forms*, at defiance."[5] Carson went looking for trouble, and trouble is what she got. When a bank robber showed up at her boardinghouse, it was not long before Carson herself was once more in a courtroom. She was again arrested on suspicion of consorting with thieves. Just as the Baltimore County judge was about to dismiss Carson for lack of evidence against her, the prosecuting attorney, a Mr. Montgomery, announced to the court that "the lady that is before you, whom you have arrested as Mrs. D———s, is no other than the celebrated Mrs. Carson of Philadelphia, a lady whose talents when united with outlaws, such as she is at present connected with, renders her a dangerous inhabitant to any state."[6] Montgomery had never met Ann Carson, but a Philadelphia attorney, William Meredith, was in the courtroom that day and identified her. The judge gave Carson forty-eight hours to leave the city.[7]

Carson and Willis traveled further south to Richmond, Virginia, then to Norfolk, and turned north to New York City. Carson intended to reside there indefinitely. But when Willis again departed for the south, "as the eastern states did not afford them a prolific harvest," Ann's money ran out. Thomas Newlin, her children's court-appointed guardian, offered to post Carson's bail for the bigamy charge so that she could return to Philadelphia and her children.[8] Carson took up temporary residence with her parents (with whom her children had been living since her arrest in February). Carson and her family soon removed to lodgings. She earned money sewing "fancy work." She was also helped by Newlin, who clothed and educated her children, and treated them "as an indulgent father."[9]

But she did not abandon her association with Henry Willis. Sometime in early 1820, after his return to Philadelphia, Willis introduced Carson to Charles Mitchell. Carson was interested in Mitchell because he had been a friend of Richard Smith, his "companion in arms, and his visitor in the hour of death."[10] For Carson, this created a "bond of unity" with Mitchell. Because he needed a place to live, she offered to take him as a lodger. Mitchell moved into Carson's home, and, she claims, earned his living by his pen—"in drawing bonds, deeds, and other legal writings, in which he had almost constant employment." Though he was trained as a clerk, Mitchell's true calling was a counterfeiter, which is how Henry Willis came to know him. When a prolonged illness during his residence with Carson prevented him from working, Mitchell fell in with a robbery scheme designed by another acquaintance of his, Dr. Charles Loring.

Loring's target was Thomas Mann, who was known to have nine thousand Spanish dollars hidden away in his home on South Third Street. Loring devised a scheme to lure Mann out of town to break into his house and steal the money. The plan succeeded, thanks to Charles Mitchell's forged letter to Mann directing him to go to Delaware on business. When Mitchell and the others arrived at Mann's house, Mann's wife answered the door. They forced their way in, tied her up, threatened her with pistols, and ransacked the house until they found the hidden money.[11]

Mitchell, Loring, and their associates were quickly arrested. Carson, though she claimed she had no knowledge of the scheme, was arrested as an accessory for accepting money from Mitchell that was part of the loot. The evidence produced against her at the trial was a note that Carson hid in a half pound of butter she sent to Mitchell after his arrest, and which was subsequently found by the keeper at Walnut Street prison. Carson swore that the words, "we are betrayed" in her unguinous message referred to the intimate relationship between Carson and Mitchell, not to the robbery.[12] Despite her lawyer Zeligman Philips's arguments that the court was at fault for trying accessories to a crime before it tried the principals, Carson was pronounced guilty as charged and sentenced to two years in prison. Phillips immediately motioned for another trial. Eleven months later, after a review by the Pennsylvania Supreme Court, the charges against Carson were dropped and she was freed from prison.

With no income, no family, and a bad reputation, Carson was living in a boardinghouse used as a gambling den when she asked Mary Clarke to write her memoir. Clarke's experiences between the demise of the *Tea Tray* in 1816 and her meeting with Carson in the summer of 1822 are a mystery. She was briefly an editor of another short-lived literary magazine, the *Parterre*. And she claimed to have conducted a school somewhere near the Schuylkill River for a few years. By the time she met Carson, Clarke was living at the opposite end of town, near the Delaware at 1 Bryan's Court, a street inhabited by a "sober, industrious class of mechanics." She earned money from her four boarders, wrote songs and pamphlets, and collected a small annuity (possibly from her deceased husband's military pension).[13] One of Clarke's pamphlet peddlers, who boarded in the same house with Carson, brought Mary Clarke to Carson's attention. Clarke was probably no more financially solvent in 1822 than she had been in 1814. A chance to earn money from a sensational memoir was too good to pass up. Consequently, Clarke agreed to write the book and take 50 percent of the profit. She also agreed to board Carson in her house, on the condition that Carson "renounce all improper conduct and society, likewise that you pledge your hand and word, that you will never deceive me." On this basis, Carson dictated the history of her life.[14]

Neither woman explained how they divided the task of constructing the memoir. But Mary Clarke later wrote that she sat for hours at a time writing the book. Carson probably recounted her experiences to Clarke, who then shaped them into a coherent tale. Clarke may have put Carson to work writing out a fair copy for Robert Desilver—Clarke recalled the trouble she had correcting the proofs because Carson was such a bad speller.[15]

It is not accidental that the *History* resembles a sentimental novel. Clarke was a writer, and probably a reader, of this type of fiction. Her magazine, the *Tea Tray*, is rife with tales of star-crossed lovers, innocent young women victimized by evil-doers, and heroic young men who come to their rescue. Such stories were familiar to Mary Clarke. More important, they were familiar, and popular, among readers. Clarke designed the form as well as the content of her narrative to appeal to her audience. As a literary text, the *History* would have been both familiar and enticing to an early nineteenth-century reader. An exposé of a scandalous series of events, the *History* was a precursor to the fiction (in the form of dime novels) and nonfiction (in penny papers such as the New York *Sun* and *Herald*) that attracted readers.[16]

The *History* is a deliberately crafted document intended to entertain, shock, instruct, and gratify. In this regard, it belongs to the tradition of the "true-crime" story: narratives related by criminals themselves. Gallows-side confessions and accounts were readily available at the numerous booksellers and circulating libraries in Philadelphia and other eastern seaboard cities.[17] An immediate precursor to Carson's autobiography was the *Memoirs of Stephen Burroughs*. Burroughs argued to his readers that his character put him at odds with social conventions and legal authority, insisting that his behavior was justified by circumstances. Carson explained her activities in the same way. Carson also followed Burroughs's lead by turning the tables on the legal system and its representatives: Burroughs apparently "regularly challenged the motives of his persecutors and the fairness of the legal proceedings undertaken against him." Carson did likewise. Thus she and Mary Clarke had a rich body of crime narratives to draw on as they constructed the *History*.[18]

The *History* contains fainting spells, lovers' vows, duels, and drama. It weaves together themes of duty, love, and betrayal—typical elements in popular eighteenth- and nineteenth-century sentimental fiction. In structure, style, and content, it closely follows the prescriptions of this literary genre, giving an entertaining twist to the tradition of crime narrative. Carson took up the themes of filial duty and loveless marriage, true love found at the expense of social condemnation, conflict, and, ultimately, betrayal at the hands of a loved one. Carson's account of the circumstances that led to her loveless marriage, for example, is a story of the dutiful daughter sacrificed for the sake of parental will. A device used again and again in early American fiction.[19]

Familiarity with such themes explains part of the appeal of Carson's story to readers who reveled in sentimental fiction such as William Hill Brown's *The Power of Sympathy* (1789), Susanna Rowson's *Charlotte Temple* (1794), and Hannah Foster's *The Coquette* (1797). These were three of the most popular novels in the early republic, and all were based on real-life scandals. Carson's autobiography was one step closer to reality than such stories, but the *History* shared many characteristics with these fictional depictions of actual events.[20]

The *History* also shared a structural conceit with early American fiction such as *The Coquette*, an epistolary novel. The *History* begins with a

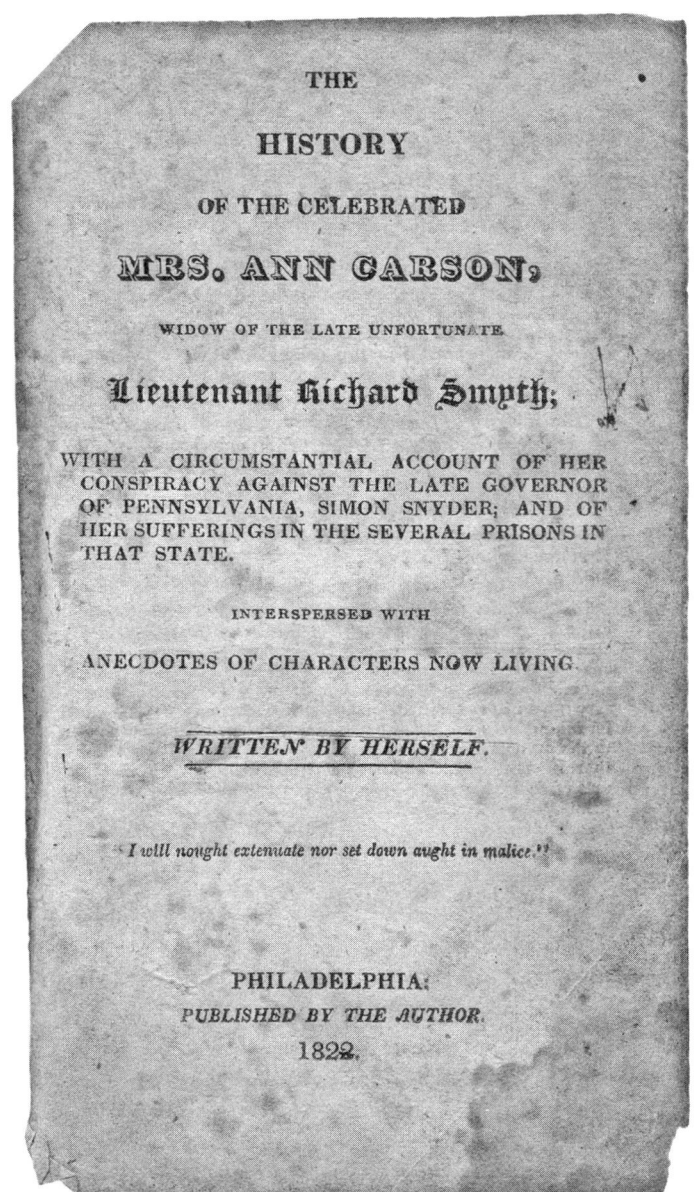

Figure 5. Ann Carson chose her book's title to advertise its contents and to clearly identify herself as the widow of Richard Smith, not the widow of John Carson. She may have added the aphorism "I will nought extenuate nor set down aught in malice" as satire, given the highly critical, if not downright malicious, comments Carson made about many of the "characters now living" depicted in the memoir.

series of letters between Ann Carson and Mary Wallingford of Richmond, Virginia. Their correspondence reveals that Carson met this woman during her travels in the south (while she was with Henry Willis). It is Wallingford who asks Carson to write down her experiences. Carson obliged. Thus Carson's readers read the book from the perspective of this sympathetic friend—a good strategy to put readers in the right frame of mind and to create a sense of intimacy as one woman tells another her life history. This frame for Carson's memoir may have been Mary Clarke's idea—it was very much like the atmosphere Clarke meant to create for her magazine, the *Intellectual Regale*—the subtitle of which, the *Tea Tray*, evokes a cozy chat at tea time. The final letter, from Carson to Wallingford, assures Wallingford that Carson's "most secret thoughts and actions shall be revealed." Thus the *History*'s reader is positioned as a sympathetic, emotive friend. At the same time, Carson's promise to Wallingford entices the reader with anticipated revelations.[21]

For readers eager for drama, there is passion, sex, and murder in Carson's account. Here is an extraordinary tale of a woman who co-opted her husband's authority, supported herself and her children, took a younger (and financially dependent) lover, and chose to fight her way out of a tragic set of circumstances by perpetrating an outrageous crime. Hers is a unique case, dependent on a set of unfortunate events. But Carson's story also shows how one woman dealt with the social and legal constraints of her time. There is a didactic element to the *History*: Carson's memoir vigorously argues for female empowerment and greater autonomy.

Many of Carson's attitudes and ideals were shaped by her education in the 1790s. Carson attended one of the new coeducational academies in Philadelphia. There Carson may well have encountered girls like Priscilla Mason, who stated publicly, in her "Salutatory Oration" for the Young Ladies' Academy in 1794, her views on the possibilities open to women, including the right to vote and hold public office. Carson may also have been exposed to the public debate on gender roles in magazines of the era, including Charles Brockden Brown's *Alcuin*, or Judith Sargent Murray's *Gleaner* essays.[22]

Carson credited her father, who had served in the American Revolution, with giving her a patriotic identity. And he encouraged her to think of independence in personal as well as political terms.[23] Carson acknowledged that as a consequence of her father's influence, from early youth she acquired, as she put it, "ideas almost masculine."[24] Among these ideas were the ideal of companionate marriage and the equality of husbands and wives; Carson was raised to expect "the tender affection that ought to be the basis of all matrimonial engagements." Circumstances, unfortunately, dictated otherwise.[25]

Carson assumed that a certain measure of freedom and independence were hers by right. But she was forced into a marriage in which she had little of either. Carson said that her union with John was an act of "parental authority, contrary to the laws of God and the dictates of Nature, whose voice I then obeyed."[26] Captain Carson demanded a marital relationship in which his wife recognized his authority. This was at odds with Ann Carson's character, expectations, and upbringing. She refused to accept John's "Turkish bashaw" behavior.[27] Their life together was one long pitched battle for supremacy: "If Captain Carson ever presumed to command me, I recoiled with abhorrence from this presumption of power; and, when after our difference, his harshness melted away, and he would sue for forgiveness, I would repay him back with scorn and contempt. Thus I learned how to control and despise him."[28] She began to look forward to his sea voyages because it was the only time she led a peaceful existence. Strong-willed, independent, and stubborn, Ann Carson articulated self-assertion against her spouse's command in terms of republicanism: "I was an American; a land of liberty had given me birth; my father had been the Captain's commanding officer; I felt myself his equal, and pride [prevented] my submitting to his caprices."[29] Her struggles with John strengthened, rather than diminished, her sense of self: "I was no longer the mild, tender, gentle girl I had hitherto been, yet something I must be, nature did not create me for a *non entity*, so I became a heroine, and bravely bid defiance to Captain Carson's authority."[30]

In Carson's account of the gradual deterioration of her marriage, husband and wife gradually reversed roles. From a young, dependent wife, Ann Carson developed into a strong-willed, assertive independent proprietor. John Carson, who thought he had married a girl who would be his devoted, faithful, and submissive companion, raged against Ann's assertion of her personality. Over time, he abdicated his position as head of the household and primary wage earner. Ultimately, he abandoned his responsibilities altogether. Ann Carson's experience left her with a low opinion of both men and marriage. "I had frequently seen the most ardent, impassioned lovers, become cold, arbitrary, unfeeling, austere husbands; and I therefore fancied marriage the grave of love, and that Hymen's flames consumed Cupid's arrows in the heart."[31] Yet she married Richard Smith. Smith, a native of Sligo, "so celebrated for producing men of strong minds and ungovernable passions," was "indefatigable in any scheme he set his heart on; to conquer or die was his motto."[32] It was Smith's desire to make Ann Carson his wife after an acquaintance of only two days.

Carson's description of the circumstances of their marriage ceremony reads like an abduction scene from an eighteenth-century novel. Carson agreed to a carriage ride into the country one Sunday afternoon. When they stopped at a tavern on the Bristol road, Smith proposed to her. She declined. Smith persisted, using "all the wiles of love, to win me to his will."[33] They stopped again at the Jolly Post in Frankford. In a private room, Smith continued to press his suit. Carson again refused him. A few minutes later, the landlord entered the room accompanied by a clergyman. Carson fled the room and Smith pursued her: "He approached and entreated me not to be alarmed; there was a tenderness in his air, voice, and manners that pleased, blended with a flash of fire from his eyes that excited wonder, and terrified me."[34] Still Carson refused him. Smith "swore he would never leave the house alive, unless I consented to become his wife."[35] When Carson persisted in her refusal, Smith agreed to leave the inn but insisted that they first offer an apology to the clergyman for inconveniencing him unnecessarily. Carson agreed and as they entered the room, the clergyman "instantly commenced the marriage ceremony." Carson's reaction was dazed amazement: "I stood astonished; wonder suspended all my faculties; my powers of articulation forsook me, and the whole passed in awful silence. Not one word escaped my lips, and I now declare solemnly, I did not then pronounce the irrevocable yes, so essential in the marriage ceremony, nor utter an assent to any thing that was said. Indeed, the first thing that aroused me from my lethargic stupor, was the clergyman pronouncing us man and wife, and Lieut. Smyth taking the accustomed salute from my lips. Great God! What were my sensations—"[36] Smith played the role of the impassioned young man who would not be denied. Carson was the resisting heroine overpowered by his schemes.

Yet once married, she acquiesced to her fate. They returned to Philadelphia, and the following day Smith entered Carson's house "as its master."[37] Why did Carson marry Richard Smith? She may have known, or heard, enough about Smith to anticipate a different kind of relationship with him than she had had with John Carson. Ann wanted "a man of sense, honour, and feeling."[38] And despite her use of the term "master," to describe Smith's role in her household, Ann Carson may have been the more dominant partner. She was nine years older than Smith, she had a great deal of experience with personal relationships (too much, from her perspective), and she was the one with a steady income. Carson may have been quite confident that her life with Richard Smith would be more to her liking than her life with John Carson. Despite their fiery beginning, she said that Smith "proved to a tender, affectionate husband, and from being a gallant, gay, dissipated man of pleasure, he was, in a few weeks, metamorphosed into a calm domestic family man, a kind father to my children, and a rational companion to myself."[39] Ann Carson never wrote an unkind or a critical word about Richard Smith. Although he cast her as an evil seductress in his confession, Carson never mentioned this betrayal nor indicated that she even knew about it. Nevertheless, this instance of connubial bliss did not tempt her to repeat it.

Carson wrote the *History* as an explanation, but not an apology, for her actions. It is not a trivial matter that she included "celebrated" as a self-description in the book's title. She meant to draw attention to herself in a very positive way. It was important that her readers understood her; sympathized with her; and, to the extent she was able to persuade them, identify with her. One way that she did this was by positioning herself in terms of class. She wrote with pride of herself as a working woman and a "useful and active member of society," but she worked out of necessity, not choice.[40] Carson clung to the class identity with which she started out in life—the middle class. The *History* offers readers a window on the values and self-identity of this segment of society. Carson helps us see who the members of the middle class are by drawing a boundary around their likes and dislikes, fears and aspirations—some of which were shared with members of other social and economic groups.

To be a member of the middle class in early nineteenth-century America meant one needed to possess material attributes: money, dress, and education, as well as certain values and beliefs.[41] Ann Carson's memoir takes inventory of many of these middle-class traits. This class shared certain values with those beneath and above, and they appropriated certain behavior and prejudices from those above them on the economic and social scale. The middle class also consciously sought to exclude those below from association or identification with themselves.[42] It was this exclusion and criticism of social and economic inferiors that Carson used to identify individuals and groups who were not of her class. The comments she makes about behavior, dress, education, and speech—all markers that distinguished class—show us what was important to Carson and her readers.

Members of the middle class developed their sensibility against a background of dramatic economic, social, cultural, and political circumstances in the late eighteenth and early nineteenth centuries. The proletarianization of workers pushed (or kept) some individuals economically down. Yet this same transformation provided others with new relationships to the marketplace and allowed them to attain a measure of affluence that had not been available to them before. Economic forces facilitated the rise of some artisans to merchants, bankers, or professionals. In many families, such as the Baker's and the Carson's, this happened in one generation. Ann Baker Carson's grandfather was a house carpenter in Britain. Ann's father, after coming to America, served as an officer under Stephen Decatur's command during the Revolution. By the time of Ann's birth in 1785, her father captained ships for a Philadelphia merchant and was able to keep his family "in a style suitable to his rank and fortune."[43] John Carson's grandfather was a barber who was able to educate his sons as professionals. Carson's father became a wealthy Philadelphia doctor who in turn provided his son with the means to become, as Ann's father was, a well-to-do ship's captain in the West India trade.[44]

Ann Carson believed in the power of her own abilities to overcome adverse circumstances (such as a ne'er-do-well spouse) and to achieve economic success and financial security. At least this is the way she portrayed herself. In fact, Carson's business acumen was not quite so sharp. In 1811, she asked wealthy Philadelphia merchant Stephen Girard for a $1,000 loan to purchase more chinaware (she had overextended her credit with the local china wholesalers). Sometime thereafter, perhaps because Girard did not give her the loan, Carson spent time in the Prune Street debtor's prison—a fact she did not mention in the *History*.[45] But the truth of her business affairs, and especially her dependence on generous cash infusions from other people, clashed with this story of strength, initiative, and talent. Carson sought admiration, not contempt, from her readers.

Perhaps the more tenuous her grasp on middle-class status became, the more intent she was to distinguish herself from mechanics and shopkeepers "whose ideas soared not beyond the art of making money."[46] She claimed to place a different value on work than did these crass dwellers in the marketplace. The people she criticized valued the making of money for its own sake—as an end rather than a means to an end. Carson, however, positioned herself as a genteel provider who worked out of necessity; she claimed that she "valued [money] for its utility alone, and was anxious only for sufficient to answer my purposes; this my store produced."[47] This was largely a distinction without a difference of course. Carson sought to retain for herself (and in the eyes of her readers) her status as a genteel, middle-class woman. Her slide down the economic ladder robbed her of many of the outward markers of her class. Her words and her demeanor were the only means left with which she could prove her status.

Carson defined her class identity in part by her distinction between manual and nonmanual occupations. She disparagingly referred to an ignorant farmer as "Mr. Ploughshare" and deliberately contrasted the uncouth behavior of a plasterer, whom she called a "man of mortar" and "Mr. Lath and Plaster," to the "civility" of a merchant "gentleman."[48] Carson turned these working men into mere tools and materials, making them objects rather than persons, and thus reinforcing their inferiority to men of the merchants class. According to Carson, the judge who presided over her trial in February 1821 was unqualified for his station because of his profession. He was "a man of weak and superficial understanding." He lacked sufficient education to fill such an important civic role because he had spent his life "toiling for bread" as a hatter.[49] Carson was even less satisfied with the jurors, "men from the lowest grades of society, apparently ignorant and uninformed, consequently the slaves of prejudice."[50]

Carson did not spare women in her class distinctions. She condemned those who failed to meet her standards of "politeness and feminine delicacy," such as two "witless" women she encountered on a boat ride from New York to Philadelphia: "One of these curious ladies was the wife of a grocer in Kensington, of the genuine Camptown breed and manners; ignorant as the tawdry finery with which she was profusely loaded; yet purse-proud, and wrapped in self-consequence."[51] The woman's manners and clothes indicated she was of a lower class. Her husband's occupation, though superficially similar to Carson's, was not by itself a marker of their class. Acquisition of wealth was not a sufficient condition for middle-class membership—much depended on what one did with it. Carson, though a storekeeper, had education and manners that distinguished her from the grocer's wife.

Indeed, Carson's notion of class, not surprisingly, had little to do with economics. She defended her middle-class identity despite her fall from prosperity. Although one needed to be raised in a family in which affluence could provide the means to acquire education and proper training, even without an income to support a genteel lifestyle individuals such as Carson could indicate their class origins. According to Carson, many of her partners in crime came from "families of the first distinction, who, having squandered their patrimony, resort to illegal means to replenish their empty pockets, to procure those indulgences they have been accustomed to."[52] These men and women dressed, spoke, and behaved like middle-class Americans. They did not forego the clothes, style, or living conditions they were used to. This situation highlighted one of the increasing dangers of urban life: the business, social class, and legitimacy of a stranger could not be known from his or her outward appearance. Carson and others used this anonymity to their advantage. With the proper clothes, manner, and sufficient amount of money, criminals could "pass" in respectable society; they preyed on others by exploiting social conventions and expectations.[53] As C. Dallett Hemphill has noted, manners were "gate-keeping devices to serve the cause of social exclusivity" for the middle and upper classes. There is no better example of this in Carson's narrative than her social call on Dolly Madison. Carson looked, talked, and behaved like a middle-class woman, and therefore gained access to the president's wife.[54]

The importance of clothing to maintaining a middle-class identity was also highlighted by Carson's reaction to wearing prison clothes, an act that removed the outward vestiges of her social standing. The prison authorities allowed her to wear some of her own things and put her in charge of selecting and repairing the female prisoners' wardrobe. Among the many criticisms Carson had of her fellow inmates was their inability to repair their clothes. She attributed this to their being "generally the lowest grades of society, scarce one removed from Hottentots." Carson said, "I undertook to civilize and bring into some kind of order." To her surprise, she recalled that "many of them hated me for the care I manifested for them, toiling all day to keep them decent and comfortable."[55]

Another reason for Carson's low opinion of her fellow inmates was the fact that a large number of them were black.[56] Carson's racism was shared by most nineteenth-century white Americans. And, though Carson employed a black woman and talked fondly of the "faithful servant" whom Richard Smith had "emancipated from the horrors of slavery," her contact with black prisoners in the Walnut Street jail evoked virulent comments and behavior.[57] She was particularly disgusted by the dining arrangements. Women were seated "promiscuously, without any distinction of age or color." She watched as her fellow inmates caught their meat "in their fingers, and gnaw[ed] it like dogs, no knives or forks being then allowed them."[58] Carson refused to sit at a table with black women, and she asked to have them removed. Though she did not get her wish, Carson was able to persuade her jailers to force the women to sit at the lower end of the table. She was repulsed by the religious hypocrisy of the black prisoners whom Carson perceived as merely attempting to ingratiate themselves with visitors by "affect[ing] to feel the powers of religion to so violent a degree, that persons in their immediate vicinity were endangered by the surprising feats of agility they performed." Carson also complained that these women gave off "a noisome effluvia."[59]

Carson's unapologetic depiction of these women as coarse, dissimulating, and smelly may disgust the modern reader, but most early nineteenth-century white readers would have agreed with Carson's opinions. For example, Carson related the following episode to exonerate her from rumors that she was cruel: "In my walk from the prison to the court house, my sister Sarah Hutton in company, an impertinent black woman insulted me as I passed. Sarah having a parasol in her hand, struck her a smart blow in the face with it, and report has ever said that I beat a poor black woman unmercifully for only looking at me." Hitting a defenseless woman without provocation was considered wrong, but smartly cracking a social and racial inferior was not.[60]

In addition to racial prejudice, the *History* also evokes religious and nativistic antipathies. Anyone not white, Anglo-Saxon, and Protestant, was the target for Carson's spleen. The Catholics she encountered were written off as untrustworthy because they were "like the greater part of the ignorant Irish of that persuasion, *priest-ridden*."[61] She disparagingly commented on the greed, corruption, and incompetence of the politicians and members of the legal profession of immigrant origin. Carson described the prosecuting attorney at her kidnapping trial as an Irishman of some eminence at the bar, whom she claimed was drunk in the courtroom and who had his eye on a good fat office. But Carson reserved most of her condemnation for Governor Snyder, of whom she noted, "Some of Simon Snyder's friends have said that he would have suffered death rather than commit an act derogatory to his dignity as governor; but those persons should have remembered that he was of mean spirit, and low [and immigrant] origin." Nor did she spare Snyder's wife. This "would-be fine lad[y]," whose conduct Carson complained was no better than that of servant girls, "ought to have been better educated, have more spirit, dignity, and respect for the office of her husband."[62] Carson was explicit about the motivations for the *History*'s publication: to exonerate herself from the malicious rumors about her character, and to turn a profit.[63] Inflammatory comments like those about Snyder and his wife may well have been included for their shock (and money-making) value, but they may also have helped readers distinguish Carson's status from those beneath her.

Carson worked hard in the *History* to justify her class position despite the fact that she violated its norms. She told readers she had refinement, delicacy, education, sensibility, morality (of sorts), and maternal feelings—all characteristics cultivated and valued by the middle class. Her robust racial and ethnic prejudices and her disparaging remarks about artisans and the pretensions of their wives would all have struck a chord with her readers. The *History* is also framed by assumptions about the private and public duties and obligations of men and women: Carson measured her expectations of marriage and work against the prevailing ideas of her time. Though a series of circumstances denied her economic stability and a secure, affective family life, she nonetheless championed the values embraced by many of her readers. If anything, Carson proved how much she believed in these ideals when she exposed the deficiencies in her own family and the failure of first her father and then her husband to be family providers.

Carson's articulation of a middle-class point of view may not have been enough to win her sympathy with readers. In some ways, Carson was an equal opportunity offender. The *History* would certainly have titillated, but also affronted, many people. John Binns, not surprisingly, was among those who despised Carson's book. In his scathing review of it in the *Democratic Press* he warned: "It is a reproach to our police that such a book is publicly advertised and sold in our city. Its details of crime, however glossed over, are calculated injuriously to effect [*sic*] the morals of young people."[64] Carson's portrayal of herself as a victim was intended to justify her descent into the criminal world, but her abandonment of middle-class virtues—such as marriage and a legal means of earning a living—would have been condemned by the very people with whom Carson sought to identify.

Carson's effort to secure her berth in the middle class by espousing a proper attitude toward blacks, grocers, and immigrant governors was all well and good. But to sell copies of the *History*, she had to create a compelling desire to read it. Her account of putting the lower class in their place may have been satisfying, but it was not a topic that would generate sales. The inside scoop on her marriage, the kidnapping, and her later criminal associations were good copy. But the real teaser was Carson's love life—especially her amorous attachments before, during, and after her marriage to John Carson. This was the stuff readers were eager to know.

Ann Carson, like most young women of her class and circumstances, met eligible men who were within her social circle. As the daughter of a navy captain, she associated with many of her father's fellow officers, including John Carson. Before she met Captain Carson, Ann's first amorous experience was with Mr. Willock, purser of the U.S. sloop of war *Pickering*. She met Willock shortly before her father introduced her to Captain Carson. Ann's acquaintance with Willock was short-lived. His ship was lost at sea a few months after they met.[65] John Carson was also a visitor to the Baker's home at this time and became Ann's primary wooer once Willock was gone.

Even before Mr. Willock began his overtures, however, Ann had already formed a strong attachment to another young man, her Southwark neighbor Nathaniel Hutton. Like many other residents of the area, the family had naval ties. Nathaniel Hutton, Sr., was a successful shipwright. He and his brother Benjamin worked closely with Joshua Humphreys, Jr., who constructed the Philadelphia Navy Yard.[66] Nathaniel Hutton, Jr., was the playmate and companion of Ann's adolescent years, and she remained strongly attached to him for many years after her marriage to John Carson. When her parents told her they had arranged for her to marry Carson, Ann railed against her parents' determination to marry her to an older man with financial prospects whom she did not love, rather than to a man of her own age with whom she shared affection, if not amorous devotion. But Hutton was too young to marry, and he had yet to make his way in the world (he was apprenticed to the mercantile house of Willing and Francis).[67]

What might have been merely a sad episode in another woman's life became high drama in Carson's narrative. John Carson was away at sea more than he was home for most of the years of their marriage. And rumor of his death, sometime in 1803 or 1804, though unconfirmed, was enough to attract suitors to Carson. A Captain Harris, who boarded with the Baker family, wrote a proposal of marriage to Ann. She declined, but she kept his letter nonetheless. When John Carson returned without notice in 1804, Captain Harris was no longer around, but Nathaniel Hutton was. John Carson surprised his wife in the company of Hutton. Ann described her reaction to his arrival as "something like horror at seeing one I had supposed numbered with the dead, rise as it were from the bosom of the ocean, come to exercise an authority over me, from which my heart recoiled."[68] With anger and jealousy uppermost in John Carson's heart, he rummaged his wife's drawers and discovered Captain Harris's marriage proposal and Hutton's love letters.

Despite this strained situation and John Carson's obvious jealousy, Ann continued to receive Nathaniel Hutton. Ann told her readers that she was unwillingly pursued. Yet Hutton seems to have easily caught her again and again. Even when she traveled to New Castle to await her husband's return from China in 1806, Hutton joined her there, thus encouraging, as Carson recollected, gossipmongers to spread scandal about them. When John Carson arrived, he immediately moved his wife to Jenkintown, out of Hutton's reach. But Hutton went there too, though he confined his visits to when John was away. When the captain learned of Hutton's visits, he rushed back to Jenkintown and invaded his wife's bedroom at one in the morning, sword drawn, in search of Hutton. Nathaniel was not there. But Carson sought him out the following morning and challenged him to a duel. Nothing came of this. Captain Carson soon moved his wife back to their Philadelphia house, having determined that hiding her in the country was useless. John Carson, who by this time suspected that the attraction was not all one-sided, agreed to give Ann a divorce so that she could marry Hutton. But Ann did not want a divorce. She did not love Nathaniel Hutton or anybody else. She claimed to be "a stranger to this soothing sensation."[69]

Yet as Hutton continued to lay siege to her with "letters, prayers, tears, and entreaties," Ann weakened. Hutton's mother joined his cause. Carson said she was "ensnared in the net that love had spread for me, and vainly struggled to emancipate myself from the toils that thus surrounded me." She agreed to elope with Hutton, taking her youngest child with her.[70] She planned to travel with Hutton to New York City and wait there until Captain Carson granted her a divorce. Ann recalled her departure in the middle of the night:

How shall I describe the horrible sensations that assailed me on quitting my own home, and the honourable protection of a husband, for that of a rash, impetuous young man; every object in the house recalled scenes of misery, although filled with tokens of my husband's affection, brought from the distant shores of India; I gazed on them with an indescribable sensation; no language can portray or convey an adequate idea of the agonies of the moment. I took my boy by the hand, and softly closed the door of my house; its motion, and the gentle sound it made as it softly turned on its hinges, was horror to my soul; my heart palpitated with unusual force,—a trembling ran through my veins—my head grew giddy—I scarcely breathed—I hesitated. A neighbouring clock struck four—it was the hour agreed on for my flight; it seemed the knell of death to all my future hopes in this life; but the remembrance of my domestic misery flashed on my mind, I hastily caught the hand of my son, and rushed forward.

As Carson prepared to enter the waiting coach, she changed her mind. "The precepts of honour impressed upon my heart in infancy by my parents, recurred to memory, and strengthened my wavering resolution; every feminine weakness vanished from my heart, and I was again myself."[71] Meanwhile, Captain Carson discovered that she was missing. In despair, he stabbed himself. Ann ran back to their home and assured him of her change of heart. She then wrote to Hutton, dismissing him forever. Whether Hutton sensed that this time Ann meant what she said or he had simply grown tired of a never-ending pursuit, he left Philadelphia and two weeks later married a woman in New York.

But Ann Carson's relations with her husband did not improve. As the *History* attests and testimony from the murder trial confirms, Captain Carson's ability to hold down a job was increasingly impeded by his alcoholism. Ann had neither peace nor happiness with her spouse, so she sought elsewhere for companionship. Around the time Ann Carson opened her china shop in 1811, her attitude toward romantic dalliance changed. Financial independence seems to have endowed her with emotional independence as well. Her disastrous relationships with Captain Carson and Nathaniel Hutton "had steeled my heart from *la belle passion*."[72] But she was not averse to male attention. Several gentlemen, including married ones, called on her. She counted a Quaker and a Spaniard among her conquests. Carson assured her readers that she did not seek them out. Although she was accused "of using every art to entice men of property to [her] house," she claimed this was untrue. Her admirers must simply have found their way to her. After all, she was young, beautiful (by her own admission), and interested in mild flirtation. Carson assured her readers, "Had I been disposed to sell my favours, numberless indeed would have been my purchasers."[73]

Dalliance led to something more serious. A man she referred to only as "Mr. M——n" followed her home one day as she passed Barry's hotel on Chestnut Street. He soon became her "declared Ciscebo."[74] Here, finally, was Carson's first love. Their connection lasted two years, during the time that Captain Carson was in Charleston and then abroad on his final voyage. They met almost every evening—she confessed to her readers that she had "sacrificed every thing dear to woman."[75] She did not hide from readers her sexual relationship with Mr. M. But once again Captain Carson discovered her activities by reading a love letter. (He was probably now permanently distrustful of his wife.) Captain Carson challenged yet another of his wife's lovers to a duel. No duel occurred, but

Mr. M showed Ann the pistols he carried with him just in case; Richard Smith was not the first man to walk about the city with a gun to protect him from Ann's violent spouse. Soon Ann and her husband left for New York to try and find him a ship. Captain Carson secured a job and sailed off, not to be heard from again until January 1816.

In the meantime, Carson's relationship with Mr. M began to cool. She entertained other men and, as she wrote, turned coquette: "I vowed to play off my powers of attraction, ensnare, trifle with them [men], laugh at, and discharge them. Vengeance was my only desire.... I became, in some measure, careless of the world's opinion, and by that incurred its resentment and contumely."[76] The commencement of hostilities in 1812 brought the military to Philadelphia. Carson boasted of several officers that she numbered among her beaux, including "a certain general, commander of our forces in the northern department of the army, and a gallant major, who had lately arrived from the green shores of Erin—named Dunn. Her former lover, Mr. M (now Major M), challenged Dunn to a duel over Carson's affections. By this time, Carson's connection with Major M was publicly known. This caused her some trouble with "many contemptible men of pleasure," who assumed that Carson would become their mistress if the price was right. Among these was a Quaker flour merchant who made her, "the most liberal offers of an establishment, and even a settlement, on condition of my receiving his visits."[77] Rumor must have spread quickly in the city, especially because Carson was on public display as she sold her wares in the china shop on Second Street. This was precisely how Richard Smith made her acquaintance—after peeking at her through the doorway for several days running, he finally approached her and introduced himself.

Among Carson's admirers was a "Captain H," a friend of Major Anthony Gale, commander of the navy yard. Once again, Carson says she fell in love. She had already heard the rumor that Captain Carson was dead, so she agreed to marry Captain H.[78] When the captain was ordered to join his ship in Boston, Carson followed him there, posing as his wife at a "private boarding at Charlestown, where we could reside together without suspicion."[79] This was Carson's second admission of extramarital sex. Captain H sailed off to the Mediterranean and Carson returned to Philadelphia, where she seems to have quickly recovered from her attachment to the captain. She invited several gentlemen, "whose conversation served to amuse an idle hour and banish ennui," to her home.[80] For entertainment, they wagered Carson that she could not attract a happily married man. She proved them wrong, of course, and described for readers the details of her maneuvers. Her account provided another titillating episode. It was also an occasion for Carson to lament "inconstancy in man."[81] Yet despite her strong feelings against committing her heart once more, not long after this diversion Carson met and married Richard Smith.

If youth, beauty, and availability made Carson attractive, notoriety made her even more so. Her association with outlaws may have, as she claimed, "depreciated me in the estimation of the public," but it enhanced her allure.[82] Carson received several offers from gentlemen asking her "to change my situation."[83] One of these was a doctor from Kentucky who began a correspondence with Carson while she was in the Harrisburg jail. After her conspiracy trial, the doctor (whom Carson referred to as "Dr. Sangrado") traveled to Baltimore to meet her. Despite reservations (she says she dreaded marriage as "the greatest of all human evils"), she agreed to marry him.[84] But on the day of their wedding, she changed her mind. Soon after she sent the Kentucky swain packing, a "Dr. G" of Philadelphia proposed to her. Once again she called marriage the "grave of love, happiness, and peace."[85] But this time she meant it. Carson gave him a firm rejection.

Her relationship with Charles Mitchell in 1820 brought her love affairs up to date for the *History*'s readers. She ended the memoir with her release from jail in the early spring of 1822. A few months afterward, she went to live with Mary Clarke. Because Clarke insisted that she remain behind the scenes, the *History* did not relate their meeting or collaboration. As far as the world knew, Ann Carson wrote her memoir alone.

Instead of living quietly and hoping that her notoriety would eventually fade away, Carson chose to capitalize on it. She was bound by certain facts that were common knowledge, such as John Carson's death, Richard Smith's execution, and her own trials. But she had a unique opportunity to interpret and embellish her actions. Most of all, Carson could turn herself from a criminal into a heroine. She told her readers that she "never intended doing wrong, but somehow or other my evil genius continually led me into quagmires, and then left me to extricate myself as well as I could."[86] Her book was not an apology for wrongdoing. It was her refutation of the supposed lies, gossip, and rumors spread about her. She did have extramarital affairs, but these, she explained, were the expression of love, not lust. According to Carson's code of conduct, her relationships were not a betrayal of her marriage to John Carson because she no longer considered him her spouse. She had not freely chosen Captain Carson out of love. Rather, she accepted him out of duty. Even so, Carson's sexual escapades and her coquettish behavior set her far outside the bounds of middle-class propriety. Female sexuality was not a public topic—unless the topic was a public woman.[87] Carson's behavior was at odds with nineteenth-century conventions for respectable women. But she chose to make a virtue out of a necessity: she embraced her notoriety. She also admitted that she tried to kidnap Governor Snyder. But her action, she asserted, was a last desperate attempt to save the man she loved. The governor, not Ann Carson, was in the wrong.

Carson's readers may not have believed her version of events, but they must certainly have found them entertaining—and probably shocking. This response was all the more reason for Mary Clarke to remain invisible. But Clarke learned an important lesson from the *History*: sex, scandal, and crime sell a lot of books. Clarke claimed that Robert Desilver sold fifty copies a day for several days after the book appeared. The president and vice president of the United States, the governor of Pennsylvania (Findlay, not Snyder), and "a great number of members of Congress, of both houses," all requested it. Clarke put this knowledge to use in her continued pursuit to earn a living with her pen.[88]

5

An Unsuitable Job for a Woman

ANN CARSON SOUGHT to make money from her own notoriety. Mary Clarke sought to make money from the notoriety of others. Nothing in Clarke's writing before 1822 indicated that she wanted to do anything other than play it safe with the published work to which she signed her name. She was a widow with children who depended on her labor to make ends meet. Clarke had only been semisuccessful at professional authorship. Her play, *The Return from Camp*, was performed for a few nights in 1814. Her magazine, the *Intellectual Regale, or Ladies Tea Tray*, folded after a little more than a year. Another periodical, The *Parterre*, had an even shorter life span. She did sell songs and pamphlets here and there, but a small annuity and an income from boarders were a necessary part of her financial stability. She continued to seek out ways to earn money as a writer. When Ann Carson contacted her, Clarke saw the potential value of Carson's life story—the drama, pathos, and illicit relationships were like one of Clarke's stories come to life. When she agreed to write Carson's book, Mary Clarke stepped into the uncharted, but potentially lucrative, territory of gossip and sensationalism.

The idea of profiting from scandal had already occurred to Mary Clarke when Carson approached her in the summer of 1822. Just a few months before their meeting, Clarke anonymously published a transcript of a trial that had caught Philadelphians' attention. In April, Catholic priest William Hogan was accused by his servant, Mary Connell, of attempted rape.[1] The mayor ultimately dismissed Connell's rape accusation and Hogan was tried on a lesser charge of assault and battery. As mayor's court records and alderman's accounts testify, Philadelphians routinely battered each other in the early nineteenth century. But this case stood out—William Hogan was already a household name for his role in a divisive controversy over the powers of laymen in Philadelphia's Catholic community. And though the rape charge was dismissed, it was public knowledge that a priest had tried to sexually assault a woman who was not only his servant but also one of his parishioners. Mary Clarke was familiar with Hogan's battle with the bishop of Philadelphia. It was Clarke's pamphlet defending Hogan that brought her writing to Carson's attention.[2] Clarke's experience with the Hogan trial transcript (according to Robert Desilver, it sold better than his version of the trial) and with Carson's *History* may have confirmed for her that there was an avid, and growing, audience for sensationalism. Her writings in the 1830s took advantage of this demand.[3]

Clarke seized an opportunity that had only recently become available. The second quarter of the nineteenth century was remarkable for an explosion of print. There were more readers and more things to read than ever before. More important, the types of things people read were new. Vernacular print culture burgeoned. This material was, according to one scholar, "cheap, sensational, ephemeral, miscellaneous, illustrated, and serialized."[4] Carson's *History* was all of these. It was sensational in its revelations of private affairs as well as in its unapologetic depiction of criminal activities. In 1822, the *History* stood out as singular. By the early 1830s, its subject matter was common fare in the news, books, and occasionally on the stage. All of Clarke's published writings in the 1830s fit into this "carnival on the page," where curiosities, sensations, and scandals jostled for readers' attention. The *History* taught her that these topics would sell.

Clarke published a melodrama, *The Benevolent Lawyers*, in 1823. In it a beautiful married woman is victimized by a lecherous villain while her sea captain husband is presumed to be lost at sea. (A circumstance she may have borrowed from Carson's life story). The heroine is a virtuous and devoted wife: certainly not an idea she took away from her contact with Carson. There is a ten-year gap between *The Benevolent Lawyers* and Clarke's next extant play. Clarke's whereabouts between 1823 and 1833 are a mystery. She disappeared from the Philadelphia city directories, there are no surviving publications for this period, and she volunteered little information about her activities. She also changed her name: in 1823, she began to use Clarke instead of Carr.[5] She moved back and forth between Philadelphia and New York City, writing theater reviews in both cities, and she continued her association with several actors and actresses.[6]

In 1833, Clarke published a play, *Sarah Maria Cornell, or, The Fall River Murder*.[7] Hers was just one of many publications that year about the murder of a Massachusetts mill girl and the subsequent trial of Methodist minister Ephraim K. Avery for her killing. The circumstances of Cornell's death were dramatic: working in the New England mills, like many other men and women of the day, she was swept up in the religious fervor of the Second Great Awakening. She joined the Methodist church, attended camp meetings, and was allegedly seduced and impregnated by the Reverend Ephraim K. Avery, a married man. Avery was tried for murdering Cornell to prevent exposure as both her seducer and the father of her unborn child. The Cornell case caused an uproar in New England that year, partly because of the circumstances of the case and partly because Avery was acquitted of the murder. The trial transcript, letters, related documents, and a narrative of the circumstances were rapidly published to capitalize on public interest as well as to argue for and against Avery's guilt. In early September, in the middle of this flurry of publications, the Richmond Hill Theater in New York City staged *Sarah Maria Cornell*. Mary Clarke made Avery the villain of the piece; in the play, he is unquestionably the seducer and murderer of Cornell. The play was condemned by critics as tasteless and libelous. The *New-York Mirror* said, "So gross a violation of propriety and public decency has seldom been committed in this city; and it may doubtless be classed as an offence for which the author, his aiders and abettors, may be presented and indicted."[8] But audiences flocked to it nightly—for the same reason that the *Mirror*'s critic panned the "deep and bloody tragedy." Advertisements for it around the city consisted of "enormous wood-cuts . . . which embellish the pumps, fences and corners of streets."[9]

Clarke remained blessedly anonymous in this condemning review of her work. In fact, the reviewer assumed the author was male, not female. But when she published the play later that year, she signed her name to it. Clarke's play, though a critical disaster, was a popular success. It demonstrates her determination to write what the public wanted to read about: sex and murder. Such popular entertainment was not without its critics. Mary Clarke chose to openly associate herself with this kind of subject matter. She had company. The Fall River committee, a group of citizens determined to investigate the case and pursue legal action after the criminal trial concluded, hired novelist Catherine Williams to write a narrative of Cornell's story.[10] Williams faced far less criticism than Clarke did: Williams's book was journalism that sought to uncover the truth. Clarke's play was sensationalism that pandered to baser human interests. Yet Williams and Clarke agreed on several points—both criticized the licentiousness of camp meetings and both condemned Reverend Avery. Williams described him as "a man of wicked, and revengeful, and persecuting temper; and his frequent closetings in the famous study with females, and the sad and grieved appearance of his wife, speak volumes."[11]

Clarke blamed Cornell's predicament on her too-fervent attachment to the itinerant evangelical ministers and their camp meetings, at which young women were often pinched, and sometimes seduced, while older women were persuaded to part with their jewelry.[12] Clarke's view was reinforced by Frances Trollope's published firsthand account of a camp meeting in Indiana:

But how am I to describe the sounds that proceeded from this strange mass of human beings? I know no words which can convey an idea of it. Hysterical sobbings, convulsive groans, shrieks and screams the most appalling, burst forth on all sides. I felt sick with horror. As if their hoarse and overstrained voices failed to make noise enough, they soon began to clap their hands violently. The scene . . . Many of these wretched creatures were beautiful young females. The preachers moved about among them, at once exciting and soothing their agonies. I heard the muttered 'Sister! Dear sister!' I saw the insidious lips approach the cheeks of the unhappy girls; I heard the murmured confessions of the poor victims, and I watched their tormentors, breathing into ears consolations that tinged the pale cheek with red."[13]

Clarke's play and Williams's exposé were polemics against evangelicals and their charismatic hold over innocents such as Cornell. Yet this moral high ground was also a convenient venue for reveling in the unsavory consequences of sin and sexuality. Clarke depicted Reverend Avery and his fellow itinerants as money-loving, fornicating evildoers who would not hesitate to murder if it suited their needs. Cornell's seduction is portrayed as a rape. Although it occurs offstage, there is enough onstage prelude to the act to leave very little to the imagination. And Cornell is murdered onstage. Although Avery had been acquitted of Cornell's murder in a court of law, he faced a tougher sentence in the court of public opinion. Clarke's reenactment of Cornell's rape and murder gave her audience what it had been deprived of in real life: proof of Avery's guilt. It was this aspect of Clarke's play that the *Mirror*'s critic so thoroughly condemned. The play ends as the real trial did, finding Avery not guilty because of lack of evidence. But one character vows that "Heaven will, in its own time, avenge the murder; till then may the execration of ten times ten thousand virtuous hearts pursue the assassin of poor Sarah Maria Cornell."[14] Clarke chose to walk a fine line between respectability and sensationalism. She continued this balancing act in her next two publications.

Nothing is as fascinating as the backstage of anything. Then, as now, audiences were curious to learn about the private lives of public players. Clarke's biography of Edwin Forrest gave readers a behind-the-scenes look at a popular actor's early life (now a common practice but just becoming so in the early nineteenth century). Clarke latched onto popular interest in theatrical personalities, especially colorful or controversial ones. She assured readers of the authenticity of her narratives by inserting herself into them; the "proof" of her facts was verified by her associations. To provide this authenticity, Clarke positioned herself as a participant in the theatrical world—something still suspect for respectable women to do.

Clarke was no stranger to the theater. At the same time that she was struggling with the *Tea Tray* in 1815, her play *Return from Camp*, a patriotic piece set during the War of 1812, was performed in Philadelphia.[15] Two more plays, though never staged, were printed in the *Tea Tray* in 1816: *Lake Champlain, or The American Tars on the Borders of Canada*, "a speaking pantomime in two acts," and *Venture It, A Comedy in Five Acts*.[16] It is no accident that Clarke was writing plays during this time. By her own account, Clarke was already involved in the theater: she claimed to have managed one in Philadelphia sometime in the early 1810s.[17]

As a consequence of her activities, Clarke was friends with several Philadelphia thespians, including Joseph Hutton. Though Ann Carson castigated her n'er-do-well brother-in-law for his shiftless ways, Hutton was a supporter of Mary Clarke and she of him. Clarke described Hutton as one of the best readers in Philadelphia, a poet and a player. Hutton signed as a witness on Clarke's insolvency petition in December 1815. He also subscribed to the *Tea Tray* and to the *Parterre*.[18] Hutton's career as an actor was brief (it was one among many professions he tried, including business and education) and his name was not well known outside Philadelphia theater circles. But Edwin Forrest was the best-known American actor of his day. At the time Clarke's biography was published, Forrest had already achieved star status. He was born in Philadelphia in 1806. He began his professional career at the tender age of fourteen when he debuted in John Home's tragedy *Douglas* at the Walnut Street Theater. Six years later, he played Othello at the Park Theater in New York City. His notable roles throughout his career (which ended around 1852) included the Shakespeare protagonists Hamlet, Othello, and Macbeth. As Forrest's fame and income grew, he encouraged American writers by offering cash prizes for new plays. John Augustus Stone's *Metamora*, one of these solicited works, became one of Forrest's trademark plays.[19]

Clarke enticed her readers in two ways: the title announces that she knew Forrest "from his boyhood," and her preface states that she plans to correct "various vile fictions" put about by another recently published

Forrest biography.[20] Much of Clarke's book was based on her knowledge of his activities in his early years in Philadelphia theaters in the 1810s and on conversations she had with William Forrest about his brother's later adventures. Clarke was a frequent visitor to the green rooms of New York's theaters—most notably the Chatham Street Theater, where William Forrest was a part owner.[21] She was not personally acquainted with the actor, yet she took credit for introducing the young Edwin Forrest to the theater by letting him in for free to performances at the theater she managed. Lest she claim too much—and be repudiated by Forrest for false claims, Clarke was careful to say that, though she knew him from boyhood, she was "not then in a situation to hold personal intercourse, or even speak to him"[22] Though she had only a distant association with Edwin Forrest—one that he may have been completely unaware of—Clarke claimed that she helped him rise to fame by giving him a "puff" (as favorable theatrical notices were then called) "on his first coming into New York."[23]

The History of Edwin Forrest is as autobiographical as it is biographical. As she had done in the *Tea Tray*, Clarke brought her personal woes to her readers' attention. Clarke compared her situation with Forrest's: "He had risen from his obscure origin, while I had descended from a high standing in society, to an humble dependence on my own industry—not talents—they were lulled to rest by over exertion which were poorly rewarded, and my mind sought relief from its mental toil in the labor of my hands."[24] Her continual reminder that she had a connection (however tenuous) with the great actor reinforced the authenticity of her account; readers were assured that what they read came from a source close to Forrest. This personal testimony cut both ways: it reassured readers that she spoke from personal experience, but those who knew anything about the New York theater world would also know that Clarke's admission that she frequented the Chatham Street Theater indicated that she went slumming. In the 1820s and 1830s, New York's premier high-brow theater was the Park. The Chatham opened in 1824 to give the Park competition for its first three seasons. The newer theater quickly descended into low-brow entertainment, including equestrian demonstrations. Frances Trollope, who attended a performance there sometime in its less salubrious years, claimed that the theater had been "so utterly condemned by *bon ton*, that it requires some courage to decide upon going there.... The interest must have been great, for till the curtain fell, I saw not one quarter of the queer things around me; then I observed in the front row of a dress-box a lady performing the most maternal office possible, several gentlemen without their coats, and a general air of contempt for the decencies of life, certainly more than usually revolting."[25]

The atmosphere in American theaters was far removed from the respectable order and dignity of a lady's tea table. Audiences were not quiet. They routinely interrupted performances with "groans, animal noises, missiles thrown at the stage or other parts of the audience, and witticisms shouted out at opportune moments."[26] Trollope complained about the constant chatter, tobacco spitting, singing along with music, crying babies, and even breast-feeding that took place during a performance. Theater audiences were physically segregated by class and to a certain degree by sex (women were not seated in the pit). Most decent women sat in boxes or in the gallery, and prostitutes were confined to the third tier.[27] Theaters were also identified by class: according to David Grimstead, "the Park Theater was associated with the upper classes, the Bowery with the middle, and the Chatham with the lower."[28]

Clarke's admitted connection with the Chatham Street Theater may have been a ploy to attract readers—sin is always sexier than virtue. And the timing of her biography was good. Audiences and readers interested in the popular performers' of the day were increasingly gratified by newspaper snippets of gossip and performers' own accounts of their lives in front of, and behind, the curtain. The *New-York Mirror* and the *Spirit of the Times* both carried weekly theater reviews and gossip. William Dunlap, a prolific playwright and former manager of the Park Theater in New York, published his *History of the American Theater* in 1832. (The "Catalogue of American Plays and Their Authors" at the back of Dunlap's *History* included Clarke's *Fair Americans*.) When the British actress Frances Kemble made a splash in American theaters in 1832, audiences wanted to know about her clothes, her activities, and her likes and dislikes. Kemble gratified fans by publishing her *Journal* in 1835. Readers learned what Kemble ate, where she traveled, and whom she associated with. It helped that she was treated royally by the Americans—including dinners with luminaries such as Daniel Webster and former president John Quincy Adams.[29] Though at least one reviewer, Edgar Allan Poe, thought that Kemble's book conflicted with "notions of the retiring delicacy of the female character," Faye Dudden claims that "Fanny created a powerful new image: the female performer whose dignity was as undeniable as her talent."[30] Clarke revealed just enough about her own life to make it credible that she actually knew and associated with these famous actors and actresses. Yet she left much out. She gave no specifics about the theater she managed and no particulars about which papers she wrote theater reviews for. Just once in a while she placed herself in a specific time and location to comment on her subject's activities.

At a time when theater was still a controversial venue for women—especially at theaters such as the Bowery where working-class audiences still pelted performers, vomited in the aisles, and caroused with prostitutes—to openly declare an association with the stage, even behind the scenes, was risky. Prostitutes were not only in the audience, they lived close by. Most theaters were located in areas with a high concentration of brothels. Ninety-three of New York City's brothels (34 percent) were within two and a half blocks of a theater between 1830 and 1839.[31] One contemporary described the close association between the theater and the sisterhood: "In addition to the dressing rooms for performers [behind the Park in Theater Alley], Rebecca Fraser ran a brothel in the early 1820s before moving around the corner at Ann Street in 1825. For nearly a decade, from 1831 to 1839, [Sarah McGindy and] Mrs. Newman ran a house with at least eight girls only a few doors behind the Park Theater [that specifically catered to performers and patrons alike]."[32] Fanny Kemble was admired for both her talents and her respectability. But plenty of actresses in the stock companies of American theaters endured ogling, jeers, or worse on a nightly basis from male audience members who assumed that these women were sexually available.[33] Mary Clarke risked something to gain something. Although she made it clear that she was not an actress but rather a playwright and critic, she admitted to being a confidant of those who were.

Clarke's second biography revealed how intimate she was with some of the popular personalities of the day. *A Concise History of the Life and Amours of Thomas S. Hamblin* was based on Clarke's firsthand acquaintance with Hamblin, his former wife Elizabeth, and at least one of Hamblin's mistresses. The book contained everything a reader could want in a gossipy exposé: scandal, sexual impropriety, and death under suspicious circumstances. Clarke hinted at malice and murderous deeds; her account of Hamblin's activities was like a melodrama come to life. Clarke told her readers that she felt compelled to expose Hamblin's corrupt, and possibly criminal, behavior in order to defend his former wife, Elizabeth Blanchard Hamblin, from rumors her ex-husband spread about her. Clarke had many opportunities to view the private lives of these public personalities through her work as theater critic, her friendship with William Forrest, and her involvement with theater production (Elizabeth Hamblin managed the Richmond Hill theater when *Sarah Maria Cornell* was performed there). Clarke was also the confidant of Hamblin's mistress, Naomi Vincent, a relationship that gave her privileged information to share with her readers, but edged her closer to questionable associations.[34]

Clarke began her book by describing the circumstances surrounding the Hamblins' breakup and Thomas's subsequent relationships. Clarke hoped to vindicate Elizabeth by refuting the lies promoted by playwright Louisa Medina—who just happened to be Hamblin's mistress of the moment. Clarke's "Authoress' Address to the Public" explains that Medina's published sketch of Hamblin's life was intended not only as "a eulgium on her protector, with a puff for herself," but, more insidiously, as a device to "win golden opinions in favour of her protector, in opposition to his highly injured wife, Mrs. Elizabeth Hamblin, once Miss Blanchard, the partner of his early life, the participator of his poverty, and the mother of his legitimate children." Medina did more than laud her protector. She blamed Hamblin's financial misfortunes, and lack of professional success on the mistakes of his former wife. Medina did indeed "puff" herself as "the most talented woman of the day."[35]

With these injustices simmering behind her writing, Clarke's narrative unfolds a series of wrongs Hamblin committed against his wife. First he cheated on her and shipped her off to England so that he could have free reign. Then he openly consorted with prostitutes—before and after Elizabeth Hamblin sued for divorce on grounds of adultery. Clarke remarked, "Was I to attempt presenting my readers with a catalogue of his dulcinias, I fear the Printers capital letters would be exhausted, and my pamphlet swelled out too large to be marketable."[36]

But the biography goes far beyond the grounds for Elizabeth Hamblin's divorce. The book is a public recitation of the rumors and scandals that swirled around Thomas Hamblin for most of his professional life. Clarke used Elizabeth Hamblin's injury as an excuse to describe all Thomas Hamblin's indiscretions without seeming to be merely a gossip-monger. She claimed to have a legitimate excuse: the defense of Elizabeth Hamblin's reputation. Like many intent on moral condemnation, Clarke found it necessary to explore in detail the ways in which the sinner had sinned.

English actor Thomas Hamblin and his wife, Elizabeth Blanchard, moved to the United States in 1825, making their professional debut in New York and Philadelphia. Clarke related the deterioration of the Hamblin marriage from its halcyon beginnings to Thomas Hamblin's sexual, financial, and emotional betrayals. Clarke said that Hamblin beat his wife, "not only with his fists, but taking a whip to lash her with like a beast, when maddened by his telling her, after she had been toiling for hours on the stage, that he was going to pass the night with Mary Gallagher or some other of the sisterhood."[37] Hamblin was unfaithful—not with just any women, but with a series of notorious prostitutes, including Gallagher (named as Hamblin's co-respondent in the divorce case), and Philadelphia madam Mrs. Fermor (whom Mayor Robert Wharton despairingly described as a woman "too bad to live, and too wicked to die").[38]

Clarke used Elizabeth Hamblin's unhappy circumstances to remind her readers of married women's vulnerability. Clarke first raised this troubling situation in Carson's *History*. Men legally, sexually, and emotionally exploited their wives with little or no consequences. Ann Carson was a too-obedient daughter who was forced to turn tyrant herself after years of emotional abuse at the hands of her alcoholic spouse. Clarke told her readers, "In every matrimonial fracas, (and where jealousy exists, they are too frequent) the unfaithful husband ever has the advantage, as his power is superior to that of the wife's; he has the sole command of all they possess—he can come and go at leisure, and expend his property in vice and profligacy." Elizabeth Hamblin was a too-loving and trusting wife. Despite the fact that her earning power kept the Hamblin's financially afloat—she was "the magnet that filled the house every night she performed"—Thomas Hamblin pocketed her earnings. Elizabeth received only "what he chose to give her." Her legal status gave her no alternative but to allow her spouse to take her money and spend it as he wished.[39]

Elizabeth Hamblin was not the only woman at the financial mercy of this tyrant. Clarke pointed out that Hamblin repeatedly used women's legal inferiority for his own financial benefit. As manager of the Bowery Theater, he fabricated stars, beginning with Josephine Clifton (1831) and Naomi Vincent (1832) (niece of the same Mary Gallagher with whom Hamblin carried on).[40] Clifton and Vincent signed three-year contracts at the Bowery that paid them expenses but no salary. These actresses benefited from Hamblin's promotion of them (and the public relations campaign that was part of the promotion—Hamblin paid to have favorable notices inserted in James Gordon Bennett's *New York Herald*), making them instant "stars" instead of rising through the rank and file for years.[41] Hamblin made enormous sums from the houses packed with audiences who came to see these attractive young women. Clarke emphasized the dependency created by this arrangement—one much more to Hamblin's advantage than to Clifton's or Vincent's. Josephine Clifton served out her time with Hamblin (and Clarke alleged that she was pregnant by him when she left New York) and went on to tour in Britain and the United States. Naomi Vincent was less fortunate. Like Clifton, Vincent performed without a salary. Unlike Clifton, she became Hamblin's public mistress: he referred to her as Mrs. Hamblin after his divorce from Elizabeth in 1834, even though the New York court forbade him to marry again.[42]

Mary Clarke acknowledged her friendship with Vincent. Clarke visited her at the house on Broome Street where she lived with Hamblin. There Vincent confided to Clarke that Hamblin exploited her: he not only took all her earnings, but he controlled her personal life to the extent that she was forbidden from associating with her former acquaintances. Clarke met with Vincent secretly until Hamblin discovered this and ordered Vincent to refuse to see Clarke.[43] As confidant to Naomi Vincent, Clarke could give her readers inside information on Hamblin's misdeeds and a young woman's fall from grace. But Clarke was careful to write that her association with Vincent began—and ended—before Vincent became Hamblin's mistress: "I was well and personally acquainted with that talented victim of a base, artful, designing seducer, before her fall from her high estate, to become what she latterly was—Mr. Hamblin's mistress and the mother of two illegitimate children; one born previous to Mrs. Hamblin's obtaining her legal divorce in the state of N. York."[44]

Clarke believed that Clifton and Vincent were innocent young women before Hamblin got hold of them. But what they gained in stardom, they lost in virtue: "Some of Mr. Hamblin's advocates assert, that his bringing out Miss Clifton and Miss Vincent on the stage, was highly meritorious, as it perhaps prevented them from becoming members of the Cyprian corps, and placed them in a situation to gain an honest living by their talents. All this is very fine rhodomontade, and would have been very proper had he so acted; but as both ladies lost their characters by their connexion with him, I wonder where the difference lays between a public prostitute, or being the private mistress of a married man; and both their appearances prior to leaving the stage, gave strong indications of their being not so immaculate as they pretended."[45] Clarke asserted that Hamblin took many of his other actresses right from the brothels: "Everything he touched turned to gold, extracting it from the vilest filth of the earth in the human form; the scum of brothels became candidates for public favour under his patronage."[46] Clarke was not alone in claiming

Hamblin's affinity with prostitutes. The *New York Sun* interviewed a Chapel Street prostitute who said, "We girls always patronize the Bowery—moreover the manager here is a very clever man."[47] One of Hamblin's fans was the prostitute Helen Jewett. Jewett visited the theater weekly, though sometimes more frequently.[48] It was a short walk from her brothel on Thomas Street, where she was murdered, to the Park Theater. Perhaps Jewett was more than just a fan: Patricia Cline Cohen speculates that Hamblin may have been one of Jewett's clients. Jewett teasingly wrote to Richard Robinson, the man accused of killing her: "I had a little private chat with the manager of a certain theatre since you have been gone; which, however, I intend to explain and obtain entire absolution for."[49] Hamblin gained admission to the closed grand jury hearing on her murder case. Possibly he was worried about what details of his relationship with the murdered prostitute might be made public.[50]

But Clarke suggested that Hamblin was involved in still darker deeds than frequenting prostitutes. In 1838, he introduced another protégé to the stage, Louisa Missouri Miller. Miller was Josephine Clifton's half-sister and, like Clifton, the daughter of Philadelphia brothel-keeper Mrs. Fermor. In the spring of 1838, Miller made her debut in Louisa Medina's adaptation of Bulwer-Lytton's novel *Earnest Maltravers*. Miller fell ill shortly afterward and died suddenly, at Hamblin's house. Clarke suggested that Miller was in line to become the next Mrs. Hamblin, and that Medina, who had played "too deep a game" to secure Hamblin's affections, murdered her rival. Clarke ended the Hamblin biography with a reprint of the coroner's report on Miller's death and a newspaper account of Miller's last days. But Clarke says the account was written by Medina "and of its truth I leave them to judge as also to decide on the singularity of her sudden death."[51] Clarke certainly flirted with libel with these suggestions. She may have been emboldened by the numerous attacks on Hamblin that followed Miller's death. The editor of the *Spirit of the Times* remarked that Hamblin "has yet to learn that female reputation is forever blighted by the mildew of his society—that there is contamination, a most leprous and loathsome contamination, in all association with him." An anonymous broadside also blamed Hamblin for Miller's death (though it did not claim she was murdered): the "Attack on Thomas S. Hamblin, following the death of actress Louisa Missouri in 1838," includes an illustration of Hamblin as "The Great Seducer."[52]

Clarke made good use of the sensations of the moment. She also exploited the social tensions and prejudices of her era. The nativism so evident in the *History* is also present in the Hamblin biography. At a volatile time in the history of immigration, the theater was one of several venues for clashes between native-born Americans and European immigrants. The Anderson riot at the Park Street Theater in 1831 was ignited by British singer-actor Joshua Anderson when he supposedly uttered slurs against Americans from the stage. This volatility between players and audiences prompted Hamblin to rename his playhouse the "American Theater, Bowery."[53] Hamblin marketed his actresses by proclaiming them to be "native talent," in contrast to the steady stream of British performers, such as Edmund Kean and Fanny Kemble, who played at the rival Park Theater and elsewhere. Clarke argued that Hamblin was a hypocrite. He was British, not American. He simply pandered to his audiences. And the name change did not protect Hamblin from attack. During the Farren riot in July 1834, Hamblin was pelted by the audience—despite having wrapped himself in an American flag.[54] Behind the scenes, Clarke witnessed Hamblin condemn American actors: "This was in the green-room of the Walnut Street Theater, in answer to Mr. Maywood's observation, that the American actors are too generally very bad readers. Mr. H than fancied I was an English lady, and when by my answer, resenting the ungrateful wish, he learned I was an American and gloried in the name, he turned really pale."[55] Nor did Hamblin, according to Clarke, wish to stage "any damned Yankee trash." Clarke blamed Hamblin and other immigrants for exploiting Americans and despising the hand that fed them:

Now these are the men who come into the United States penniless, cajole the citizens in public, and laugh at them in private, while they fill their pockets by their labours and carry the money to be spent in England. Nay, so thoroughly do Mr. Hamblin and Mr. with Mrs. Flynn, despise their audience at the Bowery Theater, that one day when I had censured Mrs. Flynn for playing Erina in Brian Bhrome, dressed in white, when she should have appeared in a rich green Satin—'Pho, what do they know about the propriety of dress; just talk to them of their country and liberty, that is enough for such ignorant fools,' said she. Yet it is to enrich these persons many a boy robs his master, or cheats his parents of the slender pittance he has earned during the week, which he expends to obtain an entrance to the Bowery Theater, and then invents a lie to conceal his fault. This is too frequently the first step in vice, and proceeds to depredations on the public, which ultimately terminates in their becoming inhabitants of the State Prison in manhood. Such is the real character of Thomas Hamblin and his establishment, both public and private; nay, he has even made the silly people enrich his mistresses, while he participated in their prosperity.[56]

Clarke's animosity toward British players generally and toward Thomas Hamblin specifically was personal as well as political. When Hamblin said in her hearing that he didn't want any "damned Yankee trash," he included Mary Clarke's plays. Clarke told her readers that Hamblin refused to allow his theater manager, Mr. Flynn, to stage *The Fair Americans*. This was after Hamblin assured Clarke that "he would be glad to see her prosper." Clarke believed that Hamblin wished to promote Louisa Medina's work by suppressing all other original plays. Clarke's endeavor to succeed as a professional writer was an uphill battle. Her attempts with the *TeaTray*, the *Parterre*, and production of her plays demonstrate how difficult it was to earn a living this way. Clarke was not the only female playwright in America in the early nineteenth century.[57] Comparison with Louisa Medina, of whom Clarke had no high opinion, is useful. Medina (1813–1838) was governess to Hamblin's daughter Elizabeth (Betsy) by Elizabeth Blanchard Hamblin. Clarke says Medina stole Hamblin's affections away from Naomi Vincent, who was pregnant with his child. Clarke referred to Medina as "the dumpy Medina," who had a "vulgar face, and clumsy person."[58] Why was Clarke so catty about this woman? Because Medina, a relative newcomer to professional writing, had something Clarke did not—a sponsor. Thomas Hamblin served as a conduit for Medina's success as a playwright. It was Hamblin who got her plays produced. His star power and influence guaranteed Medina an audience. Once her first play, *Wacousta*, succeeded, momentum built for her subsequent plays to be performed.[59] Medina may have been genuinely talented. Or maybe she knew, more than Clarke did, what appealed to audiences. Unquestionably, Medina had important opportunities that were denied to Mary Clarke.

Clarke's desire to expose the outrages that drove Mrs. Hamblin to divorce her husband prompted her to investigate Hamblin's life. But Clarke's own sense of abuse and injustice at his hands might have been the fuel that fired her vicious attack. She claimed that Hamblin was "the infringer of almost every law, both human and divine, but one."[60] After enumerating his "adultery, seduction, tyrannizing, double-dealing in business, intoxication, rioting and gambling," Clarke concluded that if such practices "do not draw a man's picture as near the devil's as it can go, and sink him up to the eyes in infamy among the respectable citizens of the United States, then has my dear, my native land forfeited every claim to morality, and [I] shall no longer glory in being an American."[61]

Hamblin literally wrapped himself in an American flag to save his skin. Mary Clarke did so metaphorically; her prose was meant to rouse indignation in her readers—against Hamblin's immorality to be sure, but also against his foreignness. Clarke was as guilty in her own way of exploiting sensibilities as Hamblin was. And she was just as good at exploiting other people (as Hamblin learned to his chagrin), including Ann Carson.

6

Betrayal and Revenge

SOON AFTER MARY CLARKE published the Hamblin exposé, she began a revised and expanded version of Ann Carson's *History*. Having mastered the increasingly popular genre of scandal-mongering, Clarke chose to tell the rest of Carson's story. Sixteen years elapsed between Carson's book and Mary Clarke's *The Memoirs of the Celebrated and Beautiful Mrs. Ann Carson*.[1] In 1838, Ann Carson was no longer a nine days' wonder. And Clarke no longer wrote tame plays and romantic stories. Her professional activities were now part of the tabloid culture which, with mushroom-like growth, had begun to dominate the public prints. The *Memoirs* contains all the text of the *History* and then relates the events in Ann Carson's life after her release from prison in 1822. Clarke told her readers how she and Carson met, why Clarke agreed to ghostwrite the *History*, and what Carson's subsequent activities were. But these events unfold from Clarke's perspective rather than Carson's. Clarke's style in the *Memoirs* is concise. She gives her readers a rapidly unfolding plot devoid of the purple prose that encumbered the *History*. And where Carson's narrative dwells on her feelings, Clarke's account focuses on Carson's activities: the *Memoirs* has dynamic action rather than dramatic sensibility. Nor is the *Memoirs* a vindication of Carson's behavior. Clarke was the author of scandalous histories. Her revelations of Ann Carson's life emphasize vices and misdeeds. Whereas the *History* argues that Carson was a wronged woman, the *Memoirs* shows that Carson was simply bad.

Clarke began the *Memoirs* with Carson's release from prison in January 1822. Carson was destitute and nearly friendless. Yet she was not forgotten: in Philadelphia, Carson was still notorious. Mary Clarke described how Carson and a fellow prisoner, Mrs. Stoops, took a carriage from the Walnut Street prison to the Hutton family's house. Carson hoped to find a friendly welcome and a temporary lodging with these old friends. But the Huttons refused to have anything to do with her. As did the brothel owner. Ultimately ensconced at Captain Parrish's gambling house, Carson spent her days playing cards with his clients and winning enough money to purchase clothes. With no long-term financial prospects in view, Carson thought seriously about publishing her life story. Mrs Stoops encouraged this idea, reminding Carson, "You have so long played the heroine, for the amusement of the public, gratis, it is time they should pay the piper."[2] According to Clarke, her essay concerning the Hogan schism caught Carson's attention. By chance, one of Mary Clarke's pamphlet sellers, William Butler, lodged at the Parrish house. Carson asked Butler to sound out Clarke about ghostwriting the autobiography.[3]

Thus Clarke was introduced into Carson's story. When Clarke and Carson finally met at Captain Parrish's house, Clarke warned Carson of "all the difficulties attending the publication of a native work."[4] It would not be easy to find someone willing to publish such a scandalous account. Nevertheless, Carson persuaded Mary Clarke to write the book with the promise that Clarke would not "appear in the affair."[5] Clarke worried about her reputation; in 1822, she was known only for the *Tea Tray*, songs, and plays. She had published her more controversial writings, the transcript of the Hogan trial and her Hogan pamphlet, anonymously. Clarke was a respectable woman and wished to remain that way—both for her personal reputation and for future professional opportunities. Thus when one of the Commissioners of Southwark informed Clarke that the Parrish boardinghouse was a gambling den, she refused to return there. But she did agree to take Carson into her home while they wrote the *History*.[6]

When Mary Clarke invited Ann Carson to reside with her in Bryan's Court, Clarke already had a full house: four paying boarders (whom she never named); her youngest son (also unnamed); and Sam, a young black servant.[7] Soon after Carson's arrival in July 1822, Carson's youngest son, Joseph (age fourteen) came to live with them.[8] Keeping everyone fed and the house clean consumed much of Clarke's time. When not occupied with household chores, Clarke began the memoir. Carson dictated, while Clarke wrote, revised, and shaped the narrative.[9] Despite Clarke's doubts of finding someone to publish the book, Carson persuaded Robert Desilver to the job. This was not his usual line of work, and it was a financially risky undertaking. But Desilver agreed to publish the autobiography because he said he owed a debt of gratitude to Carson's father, Captain Thomas Baker. Desilver had served under the captain as a teenager. Baker, according to Desilver, treated him "more like a father, than a commander."[10]

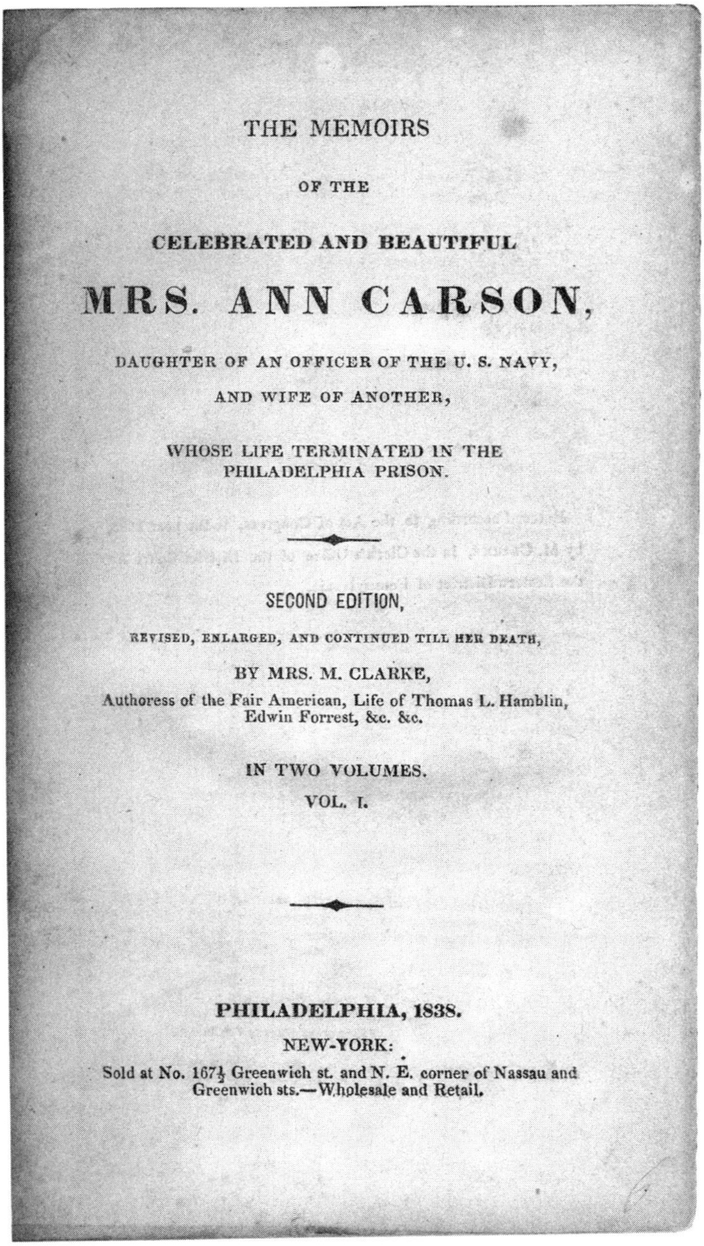

THE MEMOIRS

OF THE

CELEBRATED AND BEAUTIFUL

MRS. ANN CARSON,

DAUGHTER OF AN OFFICER OF THE U. S. NAVY,

AND WIFE OF ANOTHER,

WHOSE LIFE TERMINATED IN THE
PHILADELPHIA PRISON.

SECOND EDITION,

REVISED, ENLARGED, AND CONTINUED TILL HER DEATH,

BY MRS. M. CLARKE,

Authoress of the Fair American, Life of Thomas L. Hamblin,
Edwin Forrest, &c. &c.

IN TWO VOLUMES.

VOL. I.

PHILADELPHIA, 1838.

NEW-YORK:

Sold at No. 167½ Greenwich st. and N. E. corner of Nassau and
Greenwich sts.—Wholesale and Retail.

Figure 6. Title page to Mary Clarke's continuation of Ann Carson's life. She publicly acknowledged authorship of some of her theatrical publications, including the exposé of Thomas S. Hamblin's misdeeds.

Even before Clarke finished writing the book, the printer, "Mr. W," took the opening chapters away. When Clarke received the proofs sometime later, she spent so much time correcting them that Desilver despaired it would ever be finished, or stay within his budget. Clarke blamed the mistakes on Carson: she claimed that Carson's spelling was so bad that the typesetters freely interpreted the text. But typographic errors were the least of Clarke's worries. Desilver advertised the coming publication as soon as the printer had a copy to work with in the late autumn.[11] Word spread quickly that the infamous Ann Carson was about to reveal all. This made many people nervous, including the publisher. Desilver feared possible libel suits—against Carson, Clarke, himself, and the printer. It was probably the phrase "anecdotes of various persons now living," that really worried everyone. Desilver hired lawyer George Shaw to read the manuscript and to point out anything potentially libelous.[12] When Shaw informed Desilver that much of the book would draw fire, Desilver reconsidered his offer. Meanwhile, Clarke also sought legal opinions. "Mr. B," whom Clarke described as a trusted friend of Carson, and Clarke's own friend, "Mr. G," both read the memoir.[13] Their verdict was not so dire as Shaw's. Clarke tried to persuade Desilver (via his wife) to go ahead with publication. Mrs. Desilver told Clarke that her spouse "had not had a quiet nights rest, this two weeks." Desilver himself expressed his frustration to Clarke: "Damn you all, said he, if I had the money back I have expended on it, I would not care if the Devil had the whole of you."[14] Clarke calmed the printer and persuaded the couple to read through the manuscript together. Robert Desilver, in consultation with his wife (who may have persuaded her spouse that the financial rewards outweighed any risk), agreed to publish the memoir. A few passages were rewritten (to tone down Carson's vituperative accusations) and several names were changed to initials.

Yet as Clarke resolved one crisis, another arose to torment her. One evening in January a "gentleman of the black cloth, or banditii" paid a visit to Bryan's Court. The respectable citizens of Philadelphia were not the only ones concerned about their reputations. The unnamed gentleman was an emissary from Carson's former associate Henry Willis. (Willis was incarcerated somewhere in Virginia at the time.) He offered the two women seven hundred and fifty dollars if they agreed to suppress the book. Clarke ordered the unknown man out of her house: "What, said I, laughing, to initiate my son and me, in the whole art and mystery of roguery, to write your lives first, and perhaps your confessions afterward, when you are hanged?"[15] But Ann Carson wavered in her commitment to earn an honest living. When the man placed five hundred dollars in cash on the table along with two gold watches and a quantity of jewelry, Carson determined to go with him. Clarke reminded her that if she abandoned the book and went back to her life of crime, she would harm and betray Desilver, and all the other individuals who placed their confidence in Carson's reformation. Even this admonition failed to change Carson's mind. Only after Clarke ordered the man to leave her house and locked the door behind him was she able to stop Carson. Clarke contrasted Carson's weakness with her own fortitude: "Oh! The money was so tempting said she. And those gold watches just the thing for us; had you, said I, left the house with that man, you should never have entered the door again, your boy would have been given up to the orphan's court, and the book published in spite of you."[16] Clarke's depiction of this scene showed Carson in a bad light: Carson was weak-willed, avaricious, and selfish. She was unconcerned about the harm her actions would cause others, including her benefactress Mary Clarke. Clarke emphasized her own virtue (not to mention self-sacrifice) while revealing Carson's vices.

The book went on sale soon after this encounter. It was an instant hit. Desilver was well-compensated for his risk, Clarke was congratulated by passersby as she did her errands, and Ann Carson was once again in the public eye. Clarke claimed that Desilver sold fifty copies a day for several days. These brisk sales were likely aided by a review John Binns wrote for his *Democratic Press*. Binns condemned Carson's book, saying that it was "a reproach to our police that such a book is publicly advertised and sold in our city." But Binns believed that Carson's worst offense was that she made "the discovery of the conspiracy and her apprehension and commitment to prison, a cause for abusing the writer of this article and grossly libeling the Memory of the late Governor Snyder." Binns's chagrin and frustration is palpable: "It is unnecessary perhaps, to add, that according to this *veracious* history, Mrs. Carson is a woman of exemplary morals and manners, and that whenever she made a slip or did those things she ought not to have done, it was always the fault of others and not her own. Her innocent credulity she admits, often made her the dupe of the artful and criminal. I am, says she, a woman 'more sinned against, than sinning.' Binns warned his readers that the *History*'s "details of crime, however glossed over, are calculated injuriously to effect [*sic*] the morals of young people." Such an advertisement of the guilty pleasures awaiting readers of the *History* was too great a temptation for many. According to Clarke, the president and vice president of the United States, the governor of Pennsylvania, and "great numbers of members of Congress, of both houses," all requested copies.[17]

This initial flurry of success was short-lived. By the agreement they had with Robert Desilver, he was to sell his five hundred copies before Clarke and Carson could begin to profit from theirs. In the meantime, Clarke had rent to pay and mouths to feed (including Carson's adolescent son Joseph). She had only a small income from the sale of her songs and recently published comedy, *The Benevolent Lawyers*. Carson was no help at all. Clarke complained that Carson spent all her money on clothes. And Carson took Joseph's income from his job with the printer to buy clothes for him. Nor could Clarke devote her energies to further writing while she was preoccupied with the constant flow of men who called on Carson with the pretense that they needed clothing mended. In the *History*, Carson claimed to be "dependent on her needle for support." These admirers took her at her word, "saying they wanted shirts made, stockings mended, waistcoats and pantaloons made or repaired; and after taxing our time for an hour or two in frivolous conversation, they took their departure."[18]

In an effort to retrench, Clarke moved from Bryan's Court to a house owned by Desilver far out on Chestnut Street near the Schuylkill River (a move that pained Carson because she could see Smith's tomb from her window).[19] But even this economy was not enough to ensure financial stability. The *History* sold well enough that a second edition would soon be needed. But Desilver refused to print it—probably feeling that he had more than paid his debt to the memory of his old commander. To obtain the much-needed cash to publish the book a second time, Clarke suggested that she and Carson tap the New York market, where a dozen copies had sold in two hours. Clarke and Carson decided that only one of them would go to New York. The two women flipped a coin: Carson would go. At the beginning of March, carrying two hundred and fifty copies of the *History* (one hundred belonged to Clarke and the rest to Carson) and copies of Clarke's songs and plays and having Clarke's best ruffles, collars, and nightgowns, Carson made her way north. She had a letter of introduction to a bookseller on Wall Street with whom Clarke was acquainted. When she arrived in Manhattan, Carson took up lodging with an acquaintance, Mrs. Ferras, who kept a boardinghouse "for gentlemen of the black cloth." Carson had first met her landlady in the Walnut Street jail, where Ferras served time for passing counterfeit money. It may have been Carson's intention all along to rejoin her friends, perhaps from the moment that Henry Willis's emissary set foot in Clarke's house. Clarke claims to have believed that Carson set out for New York fully intending to fulfill her promise to sell the books. Carson later told Clarke that she boarded with Ferras only as a last resort: she did not have enough money for a hotel. Even under pressure from Ferras and the counterfeiters, Carson assured Clarke that she deliberated for a week before she joined their enterprise.[20]

Certainly Carson's good intentions, temptations, and capitulation made a better story for Clarke to tell than premeditated scheming: "For one week she wavered, gratitude to me, regard for her children, were placed in one scale, and the ease, elegance, and comfort she enjoyed there, when contrasted with my humble residence and economical expenditure in the other, early habits prevailed over prudence, penitence and promises, and she once more joined the association."[21] Carson sold the books to Wiley, the Wall Street bookseller. With the cash, she purchased one hundred counterfeit dollars of "New England money," and one thousand counterfeit dollars of Stephen Girard's bank's notes, forging the Girard cashier's signature herself.[22]

Meanwhile, Clarke had not heard from Carson, or about Carson, for two weeks. When she returned to Philadelphia, Carson happily informed Clarke that their money worries were over. They could now have a life of ease and plenty by passing off counterfeit money. Carson already had a plan in place whereby they could easily and effortlessly profit from passing notes. She had arranged that Rosanna Overn, another of her prison acquaintances, would be their servant and help pass the counterfeit money. Carson had also recruited Clarke's pedlar, William Butler, whom Carson had met at Parrish's boardinghouse.

Clarke greeted this news with a wail of despair: Carson had robbed her of her "little all."[23] She adamantly refused to participate in Carson's schemes. Mary Clarke knew exactly what Ann Carson was capable of: "Do you think I have so small a share of pride and spirit, as to put myself in your power, by committing an overt act, if I were to pass one single note, I should be completely in your power, and knowing as I do your overbearing temper, I should become a servant instead of being mistress of my own house."[24] Clarke reminded Carson that it was not wealthy bankers like Stephen Girard who were hurt by counterfeit money. The real victims were the small shopkeepers (such as Carson had been) who took the bad currency. Even when counterfeit bills were detected, storekeepers were not compensated for the money they had lost.

But Carson was undeterred by empathy or moral reasoning. Having failed to persuade Mary Clarke with money, she tried to tempt her with the prospect of literary success. Carson offered to give Clarke six hundred dollars in counterfeit bills, enough money to enable Clarke "to get out your History of America this summer, and set you completely at ease in pecuniary matters."[25] This angered Mary Clarke even more. She scolded, "That might have been the case, replied I, had you not squandered our money in that spurious trash, and been so foolish as to come and tell me of it, have I not frequently said to you, if you ever go to your old tricks again, do not let me know it; and mark me lady fair, if you persevere, you will not be three months out of prison; and if Bobby Wharton [the mayor of Philadelphia] gets you, and the inspectors, they will have no mercy on you."[26] Clarke's anger was more than an expression of righteous indignation, it was fear for her own prospects. Carson's treachery placed Mary Clarke in a difficult position. She had pledged for Carson's good behavior to the Philadelphia authorities. Now, on Clarke's watch, Carson had once again plunged into reckless, unlawful activity.

Clarke did two things at this point: she attempted to persuade Carson to give up her plans, and she took steps to protect herself. She gave Carson one week to change her mind. Otherwise, Clarke planned to turn her out of the house and be done with her forever. She reminded Carson, "As you well know I am security to the civil authority for your good conduct, and must do my duty for the sake of my children, and my own character."[27] Clarke warned her black servant that Carson was "a dangerous woman," who might sell him. While Clarke waited for Carson's decision, she showed the notes to Alderman Badger and told him of Carson's plans. Badger examined the notes and said that they looked genuine. She then went to Robert Desilver's shop, where several gentlemen congregated. None of them could say with certainty if the notes were genuine. This inability to tell good money from bad worked to counterfeiters' advantage: with such a profusion of different paper monies in circulation, spurious notes passed the uncritical eye of merchants with relative ease. When Clarke asked lawyer George Shaw to give his opinion, Shaw remarked that counterfeit or not, the Girard notes would be readily accepted, as the bank had "not yet been touched."[28] Armed with several opinions but no conclusive answer, Clarke took the notes to an exchange broker, whose business depended on recognizing counterfeits. He told her without hesitation that the notes were indeed bad.[29]

Betrayal and Revenge

Figure 7. Stephen Girard purchased the building used by the Bank of the United States and opened his bank there in 1812, only a few blocks from Carson's china store. Despite the building's imposing presence, Carson's counterfeiting activities proved the vulnerability of early nineteenth-century banking institutions. William Birch and son, 1799. Courtesy of the Library Company of Philadelphia.

Clarke continued to adjure Carson to abandon her criminal plans; the two of them could live perfectly well on honest earnings. Though Desilver declined to publish a second edition of the *History*, another printer, Probasco, agreed to print the work and bind it on a risk: "He will deliver them to us, one hundred at a time, and we can pay him as the books sell." The publisher Isaac Riley told Clarke he could easily sell hundreds of copies in the Southern states.[30] And the two women could supplement their book profits by sewing uniforms. Clarke explained her plans to Carson: "Sam [Clarke's young servant] can carry the work backward and forward, that we may not be exposed; we can easily earn a dollar per day, that will support our family and the proceeds of my songs will do more than pay our rent; I will sew all the long seams and do the rough work; come now dear Ann, do not let us part, we have lived nine months happily together." But Carson would have none of it: "She burst into a horse-laugh, and asked me rather scornfully, if I supposed she was going to make soldier cloths?—Employment only fit for the meanest and lowest females of the city." Clarke reminded her that she happily made soldier shirts, "When your character was as clear as the noon-day sun, in comparison to what it is now."[31] No amount of argument could deter Carson from returning to a life of crime. At the end of the week, the two women agreed to part. Clarke still feared that Carson had her eye on Sam; Clarke warned her not to attempt to take him away. Carson told Clarke that her motive for writing her memoir was vengeance on those who had caused her grief. This announcement prompted Clarke to declare that had she known this, she would never have agreed to write the book. So they parted on less than friendly terms. Clarke was disappointed in her efforts to keep Carson honest. And Carson may have regretted that Clarke refused to serve as a cover for her illegal activities.

Carson left the house the following day while Clarke was in another part of the city. When Clarke returned in the evening, Carson was gone and so was most of Clarke's furniture. She immediately went to Mayor Wharton, informed him that Carson had returned to crime, and asked him how to get her furniture back. Wharton was less sympathetic than Clarke would have liked. He told her to be content it wasn't worse: Clarke lost her furniture, but she still had her reputation—without which she had no prospects of any kind. Several of Clarke's acquaintances, including a lawyer she referred to only as Mr. H, counseled her to sue Carson. Informing the authorities was not enough; for the sake of her children as well as herself, a public reputation required a public act. Clarke had severed relations with Carson, but only a few people knew this. Mr. H reminded Clarke, "of that transaction, the public at large know nothing, and it is them with whom you at present reside; it therefore behoves [sic] you as a respectable and unprotected female, the mother and mistress of a family, to defend yourself as far as possible from petty scandal."[32]

Clarke took her lawyer's advice. She made her separation from Carson public. She sued Carson for board charges Carson had neglected to pay her. When the two women confronted each other in the courtroom, it was full of observers "almost to suffocation." Thus there were many witnesses to the fact that Clarke and Carson were no longer associates. In an insulting twist, Ann Carson accused Mary Clarke of taking the fifteen dollars in counterfeit money that Clarke had burned. Carson denied that the bills were counterfeit. Clarke recalled, "She produced her bill, and I was extremely surprised to see myself charged with $15, counterfeit money that I had burnt, and the making of a great coat which she had volunteered to do, and worn much more than ever I had done."[33] Carson's lawyer quit in disgust and left the courtroom. But Alderman Raybold informed Clarke that if she no longer had the money and could not prove it was counterfeit, he (reluctantly) had to rule in Carson's favor. Clarke lost her temper and declared to the court that it was no wonder counterfeiters got away with their schemes when the law sanctioned their behavior. Clarke argued that she had witnesses to the bad bills—she had shown them to several people, including Alderman Badger and Mr. Allen, the exchange broker. Raybold finally dismissed Carson's claim against Clarke. In the end, Clarke won her judgment against Carson, though there was slim hope she would ever get her money. But the court appearance had served its intended purpose: the public knew that Mary Clarke and Ann Carson had parted company. And there was no doubt with whom the public sided. As Carson left the courtroom, she was followed by a crowd, "some saying she ought to have been hanged instead of Smyth." When she stepped outside, boys attempted to pelt her with stones, prompting Alderman Raybold to order an officer to escort her home for her own safety. Mary Clarke was the heroine of the day. Several gentlemen congratulated her and offered her financial assistance. All this was too much. She told her readers, "Wearied with the conflict I burst into tears."[34]

Poor, but respectable, Mary Clarke returned home. Ann Carson journeyed to New York City, taking Clarke's furniture with her. There she resided in comfort in a rented house on Chapel Street. Surrounded by her fellow counterfeiters, Clarke says Carson "commenced a career of vice, and low vulgar dissipation."[35] She frequented the race course and other, according to Clarke, "shameful places" such as oyster cellars and pie shops. Oyster shops were usually located in cellars with a street-level entrance down to them. Many were in the working-class parts of Manhattan. The typical shop sign for an oyster cellar was a red balloon—reflecting more than a coincidental relationship between such places and prostitution.[36] Clarke's deliberate mention of these locales indicated Carson's descent into low life. Oyster cellars and pie shops were not places to which respectable women went.

From March until the beginning of June, Carson shoved counterfeit bills onto unsuspecting New York shopkeepers. Her success had as much to do with her appearance and demeanor as it did with the quality of the notes she shoved. Carson appeared to be everything a respectable woman should be—well-dressed and well-spoken. And, as Stephen Mihm notes, she also gave a "convincing performance of class identity." Carson seemed much too ladylike to be a criminal.[37] Indeed, her appearance at the race course would have calmed any misgivings. Elegantly attired, she drove there in a hired barouche, made bets with the counterfeit bills, and after several visits cleared almost five hundred dollars in legitimate currency.[38]

With so much success in New York, Carson determined to "come a pull" in Philadelphia as well. At the beginning of June, she returned to Captain Parrish's house along with Butler and two women: Sarah Mayland and Sarah Willis (no relation to Henry Willis). They were all received with enthusiasm. Carson became a counterfeit distributor, selling bills to customers obtained by Butler, and she employed women, who could not afford to purchase the counterfeits themselves, as shovers.[39]

Carson would have been safe and wealthy if she had stayed out of the public eye. But her overconfidence in her abilities as a con woman led to her downfall. Early one morning, Carson used a counterfeit five-dollar Girard note to purchase a pair of stockings from a dry-goods merchant at the corner of Prune and Fifth streets. The shopkeeper, James Brady, did not recognize her, but as he followed Carson out the door, he remarked to a fellow shopkeeper, John Saville across the street, that she was a "fine conversable lady." To which Saville replied that she was Ann Carson, just come from New York to pass counterfeit money. Panicked by this calmly delivered piece of news, Brady sent his assistant after her. When he caught up with Carson, she feigned ignorance, gave him a real bill, and went on her way. But she failed to take back the counterfeit note. Within the hour, the counterfeit note was in the hands of Mayor Wharton. Within the day, he issued a warrant for her arrest.

Clarke sarcastically described to her readers how Carson, once more "the lioness of the day," sought refuge "in a cockloft next the roof, covered over with carpet-rags, on a hot day in June, in the house where she boarded, while 'Phoebus shed his glories on her head.'" With obvious satisfaction, Clarke added, "thus it is that vice treats her votaries; first leads them into a quagmire and then leaving them to wade out as they can."[40]

Butler and Willis were soon arrested, but Carson managed to leave town and catch the mail coach to Trenton. It was Mary Clarke who suggested to High Constable John McLean that Carson was almost certainly headed for New York. This tip was enough for McLean to ride off for Trenton, arriving there in time to catch Carson alighting from the mail coach. Carson's fellow passengers were incredulous "that such a handsome, elegant, intelligent lady companion, was a criminal flying from justice, and no less a person than the celebrated Mrs. Ann Carson."[41]

Carson tried several ploys to avoid arrest. She insisted that she was the wife of Charles Mitchell (she wasn't). With the legal name of "Ann Mitchell," a warrant with "Ann Carson" on it was invalid. But McLean had taken the precaution of getting a warrant issued with the names Carson, Smith, *and* Mitchell.[42] He also ignored her claim that his Pennsylvania warrant was null and void in the state of New Jersey. She was taken into the mail stage inn and searched by the landlady and another woman. They undid her corsets but found nothing concealed in her clothing. Carson had fifty dollars in her pocketbook, all of it legal tender. After suffering this indignity, Carson tried her best to reestablish her poise. She proclaimed herself the daughter of a patriot and "widow of two American officers," who did not deserve to be treated as a common criminal.[43] This appeal to patriotism earned her the jailkeeper's sympathy; he refused to put Captain Baker's daughter in prison until she was proven guilty. Instead, he sequestered her in a room on the second floor of the Trenton courthouse.

Carson's searchers did not find the five hundred dollars in Girard notes she had sewn inside her dress. And the jail keeper failed to take into account Carson's sympathetic admirers, one of whom smuggled a rope to her room. Two days after her capture, Carson escaped from the courthouse. But the rope was not quite long enough. As she fell the distance from the too-short rope to the ground below the second-floor window, Carson injured her knee and her ankle. Nevertheless she managed to hobble out of town in full daylight, her handkerchief shielding most of her face from view. She made it as far as a rye field two miles away, where she fell asleep until midnight.

Clarke related these dramatic events as she heard them directly from Carson. According to Clarke, alone and injured in the middle of the rye field in the middle of the night, Ann Carson had a vision of "her Father, Capt. Carson, Richard Smyth, and myself hovered round her." She heard Mary Clarke's voice "as distinctly as she ever heard it in her life, telling her to rise, and not lay there and die like a dog on the ground."[44] With this spectral encouragement to aid her, Carson summoned enough strength to make her way back into Trenton, leaning on a piece of fence rail. When she reached the jailhouse, she threw away her crutch and knocked at the door. This ended Carson's break for freedom. She remained in the Trenton jail until she was well enough to travel back to Philadelphia for her hearing at the Mayor's Court a week later.[45]

Carson's bold escape attempt generated considerable publicity. The *Baltimore Patriot* announced, "The notorious *Ann Carson*, of Philadelphia, who was a few days since lodged in a jail at Trenton, has made her escape. She was charged with passing counterfeit money."[46] A few days later, the same paper gave further information about Carson's activities: "A desperate gang of counterfeiters has been arrested in Philadelphia; the celebrated Mrs. Carson is one of them. She may be called the Abelino of that place. Possessing talents, skill and personal attraction, every art is used to promote her nefarious views."[47] Carson's arrest was reported as far south as South Carolina. The Charleston *City Gazette and Commercial Daily Advertiser* article, "An Active Woman," related the details of her escape attempt.[48] Some papers reported that Carson already had plans to profit from her crime: "[She] says that this *adventure* will aid in furnishing matter for a second volume."[49]

Not surprisingly, John Binns made it his business to report Carson's activities. He alerted his *Democratic Press* readers that a gang of counterfeiters had been apprehended, and he described the counterfeit notes in detail. Two days later, in an article beginning "As we expected," he announced to the public that Ann Carson was in custody in connection with the crime.[50] On June 19, he apologized to his readers for any omissions or discrepancies in the paper—he had spent the day at the hearing for Carson and her associates. Binns recorded verbatim the grand jury hearing and printed long excerpts in the *Democratic Press* the following day.[51]

Mayor Wharton examined Carson and her confederates to determine who had been guilty of what and to sort out the masterminds from the minions. Sarah Willis and Sarah Mayland traveled with Carson from New York but did not possess any of the counterfeit notes until Carson sold them some when they stopped in Bordentown, New Jersey. When Carson arrived in Philadelphia, she sold William Butler one hundred dollars of Girard money for twenty dollars. He told the mayor that he planned to play it off at the Baltimore races. Carson also gave Dr. Charles Loring money with which to purchase a pair of shoes for her. Sarah Willis still possessed all of her notes at the time of her arrest. Two other women, Elizabeth Shepherd and Sarah Parrish (Carson's landlady), could not afford to buy notes from Carson. Instead they agreed to "push" it, or pass it, for her. Elizabeth Shepherd helped Carson "mull" the money (make it seem used) by rubbing it over her hair. Sarah Parrish was to accompany

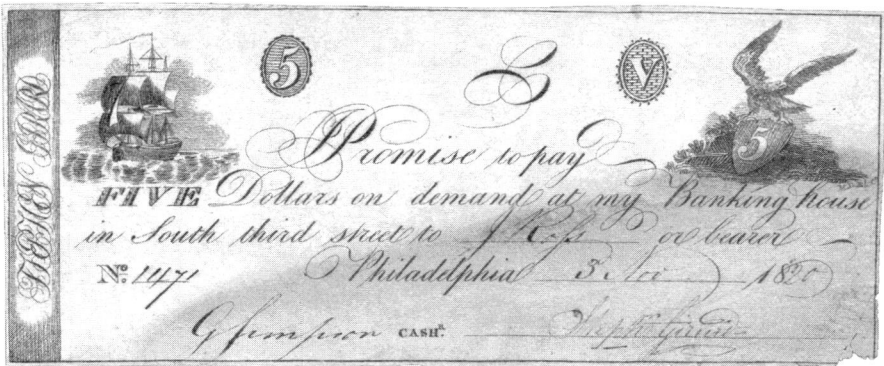

Figure 8. Shopkeeper James Brady accepted a five-dollar note similar to this 1820 counterfeit Girard bank note from Ann Carson in 1823. Courtesy of National Numismatic Collection, Smithsonian Institution.

Carson to the countryside and handle the "bootle" (the bundle of counterfeits) while Carson passed the notes. (This arrangement lessened the risk of discovery: the pusher handled only one counterfeit note at a time, leaving a companion outside with the bundle of notes.) But when word got out that the authorities were on their trail, Shepherd and Mayland buried the notes in Parrish's yard. As these stories unfolded, it became clear that Carson was at the center of this activity. Without her distribution of Girard banknotes from New York, none of the suspects would have had counterfeit money in their hands. Ann Carson headed this conspiracy to defraud.

Carson herself had been caught in the act of passing a counterfeit. James Brady narrated his early morning encounter with her and the purchase of black stockings with the five-dollar note. John Saville retold how he enlightened his fellow merchant about Carson's identity and intentions. Carson questioned each witness. She demanded that Saville describe the dress she wore and what bonnet she had on—presumably to challenge his assertion that it was she, and not someone else, that he saw come out of Brady's store. Saville seemed not a wit disordered by Carson's questions. His disparaging rejoinder to her was, "I was remarking that you were much worse dressed than you used to be."[52]

The most damaging testimony came from Sarah Willis, who, for a plea bargain, turned witness against her confederates. Willis confirmed that Carson arrived in town with deliberate intent to sell and to pass counterfeit money. She also informed the mayor that Carson was not finished with counterfeiting. She planned to return to New York, where a large shipment of notes was expected from Canada, to purchase a further three or four thousand dollars in notes on Girard's bank and the Camden (New Jersey) Bank. Moreover, Carson admitted to Willis that she had passed the five-dollar Girard note. When Mayor Wharton referred sarcastically to the turncoat Willis as one of Carson's "bosom companions," Carson, with spirit, replied, "It could hardly be believed I was so foolish as that. I have no bosom companion."

Throughout the examination, Carson repeatedly badgered witnesses, questioned their honesty (especially that of Sarah Willis), and made comments to the mayor. When Wharton asked Willis, "Did you take the bootle with you then?" Carson said, "I see your honor is up to the slang." In another exchange, Wharton questioned Carson about the money she gave Loring to have shoes made for her. Carson denied the transaction, stating, "I don't know anything of Shoemakers." To which Wharton replied, "They are a very respectable class of men, I was a hatter and covered the head;—the Shoemakers cover the feet, and I do not wish to hear anything disrespectful of them." Carson rejoined, "You covered the more honorable part."

Their exchanges were not all so polite; as Wharton questioned Elizabeth Shepherd, Carson interrupted him:

Mrs. Carson. Will you allow me, Sir, to speak for this woman.
The Mayor. No! indeed, I will not. You are not her Counsel.

Sarah Willis then testified:

I received a note in prison in which Sarah Maland [*sic*] told me Ann would have [Mr.] Willis taken up at New York, if I did not speak the truth here.

Again Carson interrupted:

A.C. Will you hear me Sir.
Mayor. No! I will not. I will hear this woman as she began first.

Carson talked anyway, prompting the frustrated mayor to interject, "I cannot have my time taken up by New York stories, and business not before me. I have little time enough to do the public business without it occupied in listening to stories which I know to be untrue." Wharton's temper grew shorter as Carson's interruptions continued. When she objected to Sarah

Willis's statement that she saw Carson "go into a house, not a respectable house," Carson asserted, "It is not true. It is no such thing." Her outburst provoked Wharton to command, "Mrs. Carson, hold your tongue or I will make you." When Carson continued to talk, Wharton threatened, "If you do not be quiet I will have you gag'd." This threat finally silenced her.

Carson's appearance before the mayor and grand jury in 1823 was quite different than her prior court appearances. She was now neither deferential nor cooperative. She was assertive, commanding, and defensive. And the verdict went against her. Carson was indicted on two counts: for passing the five-dollar note to Brady and for conspiracy to distribute counterfeit money. Her companions were all similarly charged. Carson's bail was set at three thousand dollars—a sum far too large for her to raise. She was taken to prison to await her trial.[53]

The evidence certainly warranted Carson's indictment. But her behavior before the mayor may have helped persuade the jurors of her guilt. Perhaps even more damaging to Carson was the presence of printer Robert Desilver on the grand jury. He had risked money to aid the daughter of his former navy commander. Carson failed to live up to his expectations for her reform. She had also betrayed Desilver's friend, Mary Clarke. Furthermore, his fellow jurors were mostly artisans and mechanics, people whom Carson so viciously criticized in the *History*.[54]

Carson and her associates were tried in the Mayor's Court at City Hall (now Independence Hall) on Wednesday July 2, 1823. It was a hot summer morning and the room, according to Mary Clarke, was close and smelly. Clarke, summoned to appear as a witness for the prosecution, waited in the packed courtroom for the defendants to arrive. When the carriage from the jail pulled up to City Hall, spectators already assembled in the courtroom rushed to the front door, eager to see, as Clarke put it, the "poor limping heroine."[55] Sarah Willis, as the state's most important witness, was seated next to Alderman Duane. The rest of the accused were escorted to the enclosed area in the center of the room—literally behind a bar, as if caged in a pen. Mary Clarke, her emotions already in turmoil at the prospect of testifying against her former friend, asked William Duane the favor of seating Ann Carson elsewhere "out of respect to her father." Clarke intended to sit with Carson, and, as she put it to Duane, "you surely would not wish to see me among criminals and convicts."[56]

Carson's knee injury was so severe she had to be carried from the carriage into the courtroom by two constables. Carson was taken to a bench against the wall. Before she could sit down, Mary Clarke joined

Chapter Six

Figure 9. The mayor's court, complete with prisoner's bar. All four of Carson's trials took place here. Courtesy of the National Park Service, Independence National Historical Park.

her. Clarke burst into tears and almost fainted into Carson's arms. Carson, who could barely stand, held up her near-hysterical friend until the constables took Clarke by the arms and seated both women. Clarke recalled, "She passed her arm round my neck, she drew our veils over our faces, and held her essence bottle to my nose."[57] Clarke told Carson that she had been "sick at heart" over their parting. Clarke could not write. She had no appetite. She spent her days wandering the streets and visiting alderman's offices to get news of Carson. Ann Carson, however, was "fat and healthy," which Clarke credited to the "rich substantial diet such as kings might envy," served in New Jersey.[58] As they talked, the spectators crowded them, eavesdropping on the women's conversation. They pressed so close that they pushed on Carson's injured knee "until she groaned with agony—in vain the officers called out, 'Gentlemen you annoy the ladies, and have hurt Mrs. Carson's knee.'"[59] The officers moved Carson and Clarke to a seat by the window at the back of the room, overlooking the garden. Not all the spectators were so inconsiderate. One gentleman, who stood near Clarke and Carson the entire morning, gave them fruit and lemonade and offered his sympathy.[60]

The court's first order of business was Carson's two petitions for postponement. Her lawyer, Zeligman Philips, had succeeded in delaying the trial for one week (from June 25 until July 2) on the grounds that Carson was unwell.[61] Once in the courtroom, she again requested postponement—arguing that necessary defense witnesses were unavailable and that her injuries prevented her from giving proper time and attention to her defense. Her second reason for postponement had to do with her notoriety. In her sworn statement, she claimed that under the present conditions in the city, she could not receive a fair trial.[62] Her assertion was not without foundation: newspapers printed reports about Carson from the day she fled the city in early June until she appeared at the grand jury hearing. The Philadelphia *Aurora*, The Trenton *True American*, and papers as far away as Salem, Massachusetts, and Charleston, South Carolina, reported her activities.[63] Carson blamed her unfavorable publicity on one person: John Binns. His *Democratic Press* items, which appeared almost daily, were reprinted and paraphrased in area newspapers. Binns was not an unbiased reporter. Carson told the court that one item in particular, titled "As we expected," had "enflamed" the public mind, and that "sufficient time has not elapsed for the fervor to have abated, so as to afford [her] a fair and impartial trial." Nor did it help that Binns was an alderman of the city and, thus, a judge of the court. Although Binns did not participate in Carson's trial in his official capacity, to have an alderman discredit her character could only be bad. Undoubtedly, John Binns did not pretend to be impartial—in his opinion, the woman who had planned to kidnap his friend, the governor of the state, with a backup plan to grab one of Binns's own children, was not a person to be given the benefit of the doubt. Moreover, as Binns told his readers, though Carson had been acquitted on the conspiracy charge in 1816, she had since been in prison in connection with a robbery and had admitted in her recently published memoir that she deliberately tried to kidnap Governor Snyder.[64]

After duly noting Carson's requests, Mayor Wharton dismissed them and proceeded with the trial. But Carson's lawyer, Zeligman Philips, was absent from the courtroom. Mary Clarke found him as he was leaving the building on his way to Washington, D.C. When Clarke asked him why he had abandoned Carson, Phillips replied, "'My dear Mrs. C. said he, I can do nothing for her, there is you, the only friend she has to testify she knew the note to be counterfeit, and the man she passed it on, to swear she is the person—now what can I do for her?' . . . He then handed me a note for Mr. Duane—'Prevent her from speaking, do not let them appoint her a lawyer, and by carrying the case into the Supreme Court, I may get her off, and a few weeks in prison will tame her; if she will do such things she deserves punishment.'"[65]

Clarke returned to the courtroom and informed Wharton that Phillips had left town. Wharton ordered a not guilty plea to be entered on Carson's behalf and the trial continued. The testimony began with Stephen Girard's cashier, Roberts, who examined the note Carson passed to James Brady, along with the other notes confiscated from her associates. He confirmed that they were counterfeits, and bad counterfeits at that, "as the name of Mr. Girard was improperly spelled, and the paper had no water mark." He then offered his opinion that he would not "take it upon his conscience to swear a forgery against [Carson]," because the notes were so badly done. Furthermore, he volunteered, "those persons who had received the notes deserved to sustain the loss."[66] This opinion must have [dismayed] James Brady and the other merchants present in the courtroom: the official representative of Girard's Bank blamed the shopkeepers for their gullibility rather than the counterfeiters for their deception.

Clarke made a nervous witness. She was reluctant to condemn her former friend, but she alone could verify that it was Carson's handwriting on the bills. Wharton asked her if to the best of her knowledge, the signature on the notes was Ann Carson's handwriting. In a trembling voice, Clarke answered yes, returned to her seat next to Carson, and again burst into tears. When she had recovered, Wharton told Clarke to sit near him: "I know you will publish this trial, so hear all that is said; and see that she gets a fair one."[67]

Carson was no more cooperative at the trial than she had been at the grand jury hearing. She again argued with Sarah Willis during Willis's testimony. The frustrated mayor asked Mary Clarke to try to make Carson be quiet. Clarke replied, "Can you sir, stop the falls of Niagara?" Wharton: "No madam, said he; neither can I stop her tongue." In desperation, Clarke tried to cover Carson's mouth, hissing at her, "'Will you keep silence, are you crazy, or has the D——l got into you?' . . . I put my handkerchief on her mouth, but she was outrageous, and pushed me away." Even one of the spectators admonished Carson to calm down, or "all Mr. P. can do will be in vain."[68] Clarke gave up the struggle and returned to her seat near the mayor. As Carson continued to rant at Sarah Willis, spectators laughed openly. Wharton finally ordered Carson removed to the front of the room, threatening to put her behind the bar with the others if she continued her outrageous behavior. This subdued her.

Once more in control of herself, Carson cross-examined Willis in a calm manner. As the state's witness, Willis provided damaging evidence against her. All Carson could do in return was to discredit Willis. When a juror asked Willis where she first made Carson's acquaintance, Willis answered at Mary Clarke's house. Now it was Clarke's turn to express outrage. She leapt to her feet and called Willis an "audacious lying huzzy." Now Carson silenced Clarke, and forced Willis to admit the truth—that she had met Carson while they were both in the Prune Street prison— Carson for her role in the Mann robbery and Willis for adultery. Testimony ended in the late afternoon and Wharton adjourned the court for dinner. The prisoners were escorted back to Arch Street prison, but Carson, as the star of the trial, was escorted by Constable McLean to a nearby inn, where the proprietress, Mrs. Holt, had specially prepared a meal for the famous Mrs. Carson. After dinner, the accused reassembled and the jurors were given their instructions and dismissed to consider a verdict. Twenty minutes later, they returned: Ann Carson was guilty on all counts. So were Butler, Loring, Mayland, and Overn. Charges were dismissed against Elizabeth Shepherd and Sarah Parrish. Sarah Willis, for her cooperation and incriminating testimony, walked away free. Carson seemed unsurprised by the jury's verdict, given the "popular prejudice predominating against her." She further commented that she "cared not if the court gave her 20 years."[69]

Wharton ordered them all to return to prison until sentencing the following week. Carson once again pled that her injuries made her unfit to attend the court, and her sentencing took place two days after the others. All the principals in the case—Carson, Butler, and Loring—were given the heaviest sentence possible—seven years of hard labor. Sarah Mayland was given six years. Rosanna Overn, deemed feeble-minded and alcoholic, was given a lighter sentence of five years—still a long spell to serve under spartan conditions in the penitentiary.[70]

The papers buzzed with the news. Binns's *Democratic Press* carried an extensive transcript of Carson's sentencing. Binns included Carson's sworn affidavits and notes by the court recorder. He even printed the letter from the prison doctor attesting that, despite her claims, Carson was fully fit to attend her sentencing. He reminded his readers that Carson was already a hardened criminal who admitted, in her memoir, that despite a convincing performance of innocence in the courtroom, she had deliberately planned to kidnap Snyder. (And that he, Binns, was responsible for thwarting her scheme). He offered the opinion that Carson's seven-year sentence reflected the fact that "the court considered Ann Carson as too dangerous a woman to be lightly sentenced or soon liberated."[71]

Binns seemed to relish this orgy of information. He printed in full Judge Reed's speech to Carson after passing sentence on her. Reed's speech is remarkable for its length as well as its severity. He stated that Carson was the instigator and director of the conspiracy to defraud; she had brought counterfeit notes from New York and encouraged the others to participate in her scheme. Thus Carson shouldered the blame for their crimes as well as her own. She truly was dangerous to know.[72]

Because Carson was "no ordinary offender," and because of the "notoriety and profligacy" of her conduct, Reed thought it proper to make a public statement as to why Carson deserved the maximum sentence the law could impose:

If the court could flatter themselves that a less severe punishment than they are about to inflict, would, as respects yourself, be attended with any good effect, they would cheerfully impose it. But when they reflect upon your open and profligate course of life for many years—your association with the vilest characters of both sexes—your various projects and schemes of fraud and villainy—that you have been charged with adultery, and a conspiracy to rescue the murderer of your husband from the hands of justice by means and associates the most infamous and desperate—that you were convicted as accessory to a Burglary to a large amount—and finally of the offence for which the slow but certain hand of justice has at length overtaken you. Although you have [been] acquitted of some of these offenses, but little doubt remains at this time that you have had some participation in many if not all of them. Of others you have been convicted but escaped by the forms of law. In short you have evinced such a determined propensity to crime of almost every kind and degree; exhibited such a persevering course of infamy, in which impunity has hitherto encouraged your progress, that but little hope remains of reformation except from the operation of that punishment from which you have hitherto so wonderfully escaped.[73]

Reed added that he had never before encountered an individual of either sex involved in such a variety of crimes. He marveled at the degree to which Carson seemed to positively embrace crime and vice. Her upbringing, education, and respectable family connections should have been sufficient to make her an upstanding citizen rather than a notorious criminal. He could only account for Carson's behavior by speculating that she must have a "natural attachment to vice." Carson was intelligent, resourceful, and willfully criminal. Her intentional rejection of society's expectations for a woman of her background condemned her to the harshest penalty the court could inflict. Reed expressed his hope that seven years of hard labor would "correct those evil propensities, which so constantly beset you, by which your life has been infamously distinguished."[74]

As Reed began his lecture from the bench, he ordered that Carson stand to hear her sentence. When she refused to do so because of her injuries, two court officers offered to assist her. Carson rejected their aid and precariously stood on her own to receive Reed's admonition. When he finished, he asked if she had anything to say. She answered that "she did not come there to hear a sermon preached, and required instantly to be conducted to prison."[75] The court obliged. Carson was taken to serve out her time in the Walnut Street jail. Despite the lengthy sentence imposed on her, Mayor Wharton still held out hope for her redemption. He told Mary Clarke that he would release Carson after three years—providing she behaved herself—on the condition that she live with Mary Clarke.[76] Clarke was not present on the day of Carson's sentencing. At the conclusion of her trial, Carson had promised Clarke that she would pay her back the one hundred and fifty dollars Carson received from Wiley the New York bookseller (and had spent on the counterfeit notes), and she would arrange for Clarke to have power of attorney in order to retrieve her furniture and clothes. But Alderman Duane failed to tell Clarke the date of Carson's sentencing. Clarke lost everything: her furniture remained in New York, and Sarah Willis kept her clothes.

Mary Clarke did not see Ann Carson again until the day before Christmas, when the Mayor, as a special favor, allowed Clarke into the prison (prisoners were not ordinarily permitted to have visitors). Clarke told her readers that Carson still looked "fat and healthy" and was in good spirits. Carson was in a penitent mood that day. She admitted to Clarke that "she merited her present punishment, and took it as a salubrious medicine, that would renew health hereafter." They parted on good terms.[77]

Carson's spirits may have been buoyed by her lawyers' activities: they planned to petition the state legislature on her behalf. She continued to hope that her prison sentence would soon end. In the meantime, she took steps to further matters along. She invited Stephen Girard to add his name to the petition. She reminded him, "It is a fact well known to the Citizens in general, and publicly expressed, that my trial and consequent conviction was contrary to every sense of humanity or justice, rumour has said that I manufactured and signed this bill said to be on your bank That I am the principal, but Sir I assure you its otherwise. I am not capable of such business befitting only a man." Carson continued to use gender roles for her own advantage. How could a mere woman possibly sign counterfeit notes? Carson also believed that Girard's nationality inclined him to mercy: "You Sir are a Frenchman Therefore it would presumption in me to extol that which is well known to you as the national virtues of your Countrymen, sympathy, feeling & commiseration for the female Sex." Why wouldn't Girard take pity on a helpless, unfairly treated woman? Currying favor and sympathy from the man whose bank she defrauded may not have been the best strategy, but Carson was nothing if not brazen.[78]

While she awaited favorable news from her lawyers, Carson returned to the job she had during her incarceration two years before; she was in charge of the women's workroom. Her status allowed her to choose her roommates. She selected women she knew—Rosanna Overn and Kitty O'Brien. But these two resented Carson's superior position and her imperious demands that they follow Carson's orders. One day in early April 1824, Carson returned to their cell to find that Overn and O'Brien had failed to clean it as Carson had requested. An argument ensued in which stewing resentments surfaced. Overn blamed Carson for their present imprisonment: it was Carson's fault that she had given them such badly printed notes. Overn further ventured her opinion that Carson should have been hung instead of Richard Smith. A war of words flew back and forth and finally erupted into physical violence: Overn, though she was half a foot shorter than Carson, grabbed Carson by the hair and pinned her while O'Brien picked up a chair and struck Carson repeatedly.[79] Carson could not free herself from Overn's grasp and ward off O'Brien's blows at the same time. Only after Carson's cries alerted nearby inmates and they began to beat their bars to summon the deputy keeper did O'Brien stop hitting her. The keeper confined the three women to separate cells. The following day, the Board of Inspectors held a hearing to determine who had been at fault. Carson was feverish and so badly injured that she could barely stand. The inspectors placed the blame squarely on Overn and O'Brien. Carson was sent to the infirmary to recover from her wounds. A few days later, she was well enough to walk, with the keeper's assistance, to the mayor's office to testify against the two women. She returned to prison and her condition worsened. On April 27, she died.

The coroner determined that the cause of Carson's death was typhoid fever—a common enough ailment, especially among prisoners. But Mary Clarke told her readers that there was more to the case. Clarke claimed that Carson had been deliberately exposed to typhus germs by the matron of the infirmary, Carson's former associate and fellow counterfeiter, Sarah Mayland. Mayland held a grudge against both Carson and O'Brien—against Carson for the unsuccessful counterfeiting scheme that landed them all in prison and against O'Brien because they were both in love with Charles Loring. Mayland calculated that if Carson died, O'Brien would be charged with murder. Mayland could avenge herself against both women. She placed Carson in a bed where an inmate had just died from typhoid fever and left her there without food or water for twenty-four hours. Remarkably, Carson recovered enough after this treatment to go to the mayor's office. But she then relapsed and finally succumbed to the disease to which Mayland exposed her.[80]

Mary Clarke learned of Carson's death that very day. On more than one occasion during the time they lived together, Carson had requested of Clarke that if Carson died before her to bury her next to Richard Smith. Clarke hastened to the prison to collect Carson's body and fulfill her promise. But she arrived too late; the coroner had already taken Carson's body away for burial in the potter's field on the Ridge Road. Clarke's one thought was to save Ann Carson from the anatomists—doctors who commissioned grave robbers to dig up newly buried corpses for dissection. Clarke, accompanied by her eldest son's friend, Alexander, was determined to prevent this last indignity, and to "sit on her grave all night" if necessary.[81] They walked two miles from Clarke's house on Castle Street out to the potter's field. But the grave digger's house was shut and there was no evidence that a burial had taken place that day. It was already nine o'clock in the evening, and as they made their way back to town, rain and hail started, soaking both of them to the skin. As they neared Cherry Hill prison, they came upon a solitary house. The owners kindly welcomed Clarke and her young companion into their home and gave them dry clothes and beds for the night. The couple confirmed that the coroner's wagon had not passed the road that day. The next morning, Clarke went to Coroner Dennis's house and discovered that Carson's body had been in his tool shed all night. Carson's son, William, along with the Hutton family, had arranged to have his mother buried next to Captain Baker in Dr. Staughton's burying ground. When Clarke reached the home of Nathaniel Hutton, Sr., William Carson assured her that his mother, on her deathbed, had expressed a wish to be buried next to her father. William also informed Clarke that Carson had sent her love to Clarke, "almost with her dying breath."[82]

Clarke had done her duty. As she concluded her narrative, she eulogized Carson in the following manner: "Thus terminated the life of this once beautiful, intelligent, and accomplished woman, the victim to man's passions, and the world's persecutions, in the thirty-eighth year of her age."[83] Clarke was charitable in her summation of Ann Carson's character, but the press was less so. The *Philadelphia Gazette* announced on the evening of her death: "Mrs. Ann Carson, a woman whose history and character are well known to the citizens of Philadelphia, died this morning, in the Walnut Street prison, of typhus fever. She was a woman of strong mind and equally strong passions. In certain circumstances, she would have been a *heroine*; in those in which she was placed, she was what it is unnecessary to mention."[84] The *Baltimore Patriot* was less unkind, but perhaps more insulting: "Great *notoriety*, while living, whether for good and great, or for base and little deeds, entitles individuals, when they die, to have their deaths published 'in all the papers.'—According to custom, and 'conformable to usage,' we announce the death of Mrs. *Ann Carson*, in the Philadelphia Penitentiary, on Tuesday, 27th inst. In the 38th year of her age."[85] Carson's cellmates, Kitty O'Brien and Rosanna Overn, were prosecuted for beating her. But Sarah Mayland's revenge was incomplete: neither O'Brien nor Overn was charged with murder. A month after Carson's death, they were found guilty of assault and battery and sentenced to serve, in solitary confinement, an additional year in prison.[86] Sarah Mayland was transferred to the Arch Street prison to be the matron, and served out her full six-year sentence.[87] Mary Clarke's former employee, William Butler, was already forty-eight years old when he entered prison. He died five years later, two years shy of freedom. Dr. Charles Loring was pardoned a year early—presumably for being a model prisoner.[88]

Mary Clarke claimed that Carson sanctioned a revised, second edition of her life story. Carson planned to publish the book herself, but she told Clarke that, if she died, Clarke was free to publish it.[89] Carson may not have envisioned the book that Mary Clarke wrote fourteen years after her death. It was an account of Carson's life, to be sure. But it was a story in which Mary Clarke, not Ann Carson, was the heroine. Clarke's narrative foregrounded her own experiences. Nor was Ann Carson the sympathetic character of the *History*, who had been more sinned against than sinning. Carson betrayed Mary Clarke's trust, so Clarke took her revenge in the M*emoirs*.

Clarke's version of Carson's character made Carson the victimizer, not the victim. Mary Clarke depicted herself as the charitable woman whom Carson betrayed. Clarke generously took Carson into her home and shared her "widow's mite."[90] After Clarke labored for months to write the *History*, Carson stole Clarke's share of the profits and exchanged them for counterfeit money. When Carson left Clarke's house, she took Clarke's best clothes, she stole Clarke's furniture, and she even contemplated abducting Clarke's servant to sell into slavery. No wonder Mary Clarke no longer felt kindly toward Ann Carson; Clarke's revised opinion was that Carson was "too infamous for any person to associate with, that has any respect for themselves."[91]

Fourteen years after Carson's death, Clarke put her own experiences to good use. The narrative served two purposes: it related the events in Carson's life and it allowed Clarke to explain why she chose to associate with Carson. Clarke told her readers that she did Carson a favor in writing her life story; Clarke had doubts about whether the book would ever get printed, let alone actually sell. What she did not share with readers was her belief that Carson's story was a potential gold mine: it might be worth Clarke's short-term financial sacrifice (and the suspicion of some of her acquaintances when she took so notorious a woman into her home). Clarke did not expect that Carson would betray her trust, but even this unfortunate turn of events ultimately worked to Clarke's advantage. It confirmed her virtues and it made great copy.

Clarke also used the *Memoirs* for self-promotion. As she related her conversations with Robert Desilver about publishing the *History*, Clarke recounted his assurance to her that it would make money. Desilver knew that she had a good record of success with her publications. He reminded Clarke that her version of the Hogan trial sold well while his did not: "'Ha, ha, ha,' said Mr. D., 'Did not you sell one thousand copies of Hogan's trial and clear a thousand dollars by it, while I sunk money on my edition? That black rascal of yours, can sell more pamphlets than any person in this city, and you complain of being poor.'"[92]

As well as using the *Memoirs* for free advertising, Mary Clarke shaped the narrative as she chose. There were documents and people to confirm or deny specific events, but there were no witnesses to the conversations between Clarke and Carson; no one could challenge Clarke's interpretations or assertions of what Carson had said in private. Clarke told a good tale and at the same time avenged herself with an unflattering portrayal of Carson's character and appearance. In the *History*, Carson described herself in glowing terms. She was tall, attractive, vivacious, and appealing to the opposite sex. Clarke's *Memoirs* presents a different Ann Carson. For example, when Clarke finally tracked down Carson to an unsavory, rundown house in Southwark after Carson had taken her furniture, Clarke brought a male escort, the son of a friend, to protect her reputation and to help her secure her stolen property. This young man, upon meeting the famous Ann Carson, whom he was eager to see, commented, "She may have been handsome in her youth, but as that is past, I see nothing in her more than any other woman, to me she appeared rather bold, masculine and vulgar."[93] Carson was no longer attractive—no longer able to inspire passion at first sight in the hearts of young men. Clarke was careful to put these uncomplimentary words into other people's mouths. *She* did not describe Carson this way. Nor did Clarke praise or compliment herself. But she documented occasions when other people did so. Her friend, Mr. Berrit "the painter in Cherry Street," for instance, told Clarke that "Judge Booth observed the other day, it [taking Carson into her home] was one of the most honorable and benevolent actions of your life."[94]

Clarke also gratified her readers' lascivious desires with revelations about Carson's love life. Carson had been candid in the *History* about her relationships with men: she detailed her long-standing attachment to, and near elopement with, Nathaniel Hutton, her connections with Captain H., Mr. M——r, and Charles Mitchell. In the *Memoirs*, Clarke says that during the time Carson lived with her three different men wrote to Carson, "offering her an establishment, and a settled income." Clarke remarked that "one of them was so polite as to invite me to take up my residence with her, but she rejected them all with contempt."[95] Clarke reminded the readers of the *Memoirs* of Carson's illicit relationship with Captain H. and her three-year-long "intrigue" with the married Mr. M——r, whom Clarke said was "a son of one of the first merchants in the city."[96] Clarke also revealed the name of another ex-lover: Thomas Newlin. He had been the court-appointed guardian of Carson's three youngest children and financial benefactor to Ann Carson. His generosity, and his guardianship, ended abruptly when Carson invited Charles Mitchell to live with her in 1820.[97]

Clarke further entertained her readers with a tale of romance and danger: the history of Carson's involvement with Henry Willis, whom Carson hired to help her kidnap Governor Snyder. Willis was devoted to

Carson, but she did not return his affection. She did, however, accept his financial support from 1816, when she left Philadelphia after the kidnapping trial, until his arrest in Virginia sometime before 1820.[98] According to Clarke, Willis proved his devotion to Carson by giving her jewels he had stolen from the former American consul, Tobias Lear, in Washington, D.C. Mary Clarke said that Carson pawned the jewels for cash and was on her way to redeem gemstones (presumably with money from the Mann robbery) on the day she was arrested in 1820.[99] Henry Willis proposed marriage to Carson. When she refused, he threatened to kill her and any man she tried to marry. Clarke informed her readers that this was the true reason Carson did not wed the doctor from Kentucky (not from any hesitation to reenter into the bonds of matrimony as Carson had claimed in the *History*). To lend credence to his threat, Willis told Carson that he had already committed murder in the name of love: he killed a woman he loved on the day that she wed another man. Despite Willis's threats, Carson took up with Charles Mitchell—while Henry Willis served a four-year sentence in another state.[100] Clarke included these dramatic scenes from Carson's love life to throw more light on events already mentioned in the *History*. She told her readers: "The tempter, the tempted, and the temptation, have been presented to them in all their varied forms."[101]

Clarke then presented this sexual fantasy: what if Carson had kidnapped Governor Snyder? What might have transpired while they were alone together in an isolated spot? "I wonder if Mrs. C would have remained immaculate, during their secluded residence together, and how long Simon would have held out, which would have been most effectual, her attractions, or her threats?"[102] This bawdy notion seems strange coming from someone as proper as Mary Clarke—but in the context of Carson's sex life and Clarke's recent biography of Thomas Hamblin, she did not shy away from impropriety.

How did Clarke publicize her intimacy with such a notorious woman and not become notorious herself? The Hamblin biography showed that Clarke had connections with people close to Hamblin, even to one of his mistresses. But the *Memoirs* revealed that Clarke had *lived* with a celebrated criminal. Clarke was careful to show how at every opportunity she not only avoided any association with criminal behavior, she also tried to turn Carson away from crime. Clarke sought to establish her innocence with the authorities and with the general public: she took the counterfeit note to her friends and to a city alderman. She testified against Carson (unwillingly, she claimed) as a public opportunity to declare her innocence, and she ensured that the public knew that she had parted company with Carson by suing Carson for room and board. Clarke tried hard to demonstrate her virtue.

Clarke also used her class position to defend herself. Her social and professional associations were solidly middle class: Clarke emphasized her acquaintance with Mayor Wharton, Robert Desilver, and other artisans such as Berrit the painter. Though she lived among "mechanics" during her residence in Bryan's Court, Clarke claims that she did not associate with them; her social connections lay further up. Nor did she frequent disreputable places: when Clarke discovered that Elizabeth Parrish's house was a gambling den, she refused to return there. When business required her to travel to unsavory locales (to Carson's residence in Southwark, to the potter's field) or at odd times of the night, Clarke was careful to take along an escort. Clarke always behaved, and was treated, as a lady.

But did the content of the *Memoirs* place Clarke outside respectable society? Could a woman write such a book in the 1830s and not be condemned for doing so? The *Memoirs* is not anonymous; Clarke advertised who she was and what her prior publications were (including the Hamblin biography). But Clarke's depiction of the fall of a corrupt woman is more than mere entertainment; the *Memoirs* is a morality tale. Clarke got to have it both ways: she justified her actions and at the same time gratified the desires of her readers for sex, crime, and bad behavior. Clarke manipulated Carson's image for her own purposes; she elicited sympathy and absolution for herself as an innocent, and a respectable, woman victimized by a selfish, immoral one. Yet her association with Carson lent authenticity to a dramatic, true-crime tale. With the right packaging, Clarke took advantage of Carson's notoriety without becoming notorious herself. Carson's trust in Clarke proved to be just as misplaced as Clarke's trust had been in Carson. Mary Clarke, too, was dangerous to know.

Afterword

IN 1838, ANN CARSON had been dead for fourteen years. Mary Clarke was in her late fifties. The conclusion of Clarke's life is as obscure as the beginning. She revealed very little of her personal life in her writings, and no documents—census records, death records, or wills—reveal her last years. In the preface to the *Memoirs* she expressed a desire to be buried "in Christ Church burying ground, along with my mother, and Dr. Franklin—the one I loved, the other I respected more than any other person in the world, excepting General Washington." But no record exists of either a Mary Carr or a Mary Clarke buried there. Her children were grown: her youngest child, the son mentioned in the *Memoirs*, was in his twenties. Her daughters were possibly married with families of their own, and Clarke may have lived with one of her children. Whatever her fate, she disappeared from public records altogether. Clarke informed her readers that she was only able to publish the *Memoirs* through the financial generosity of an unnamed gentleman in New York. She expressed a wish that the proceeds from the book would "smooth my passage to that 'Long-sought home, the GRAVE.'" Financial success, and even economic security, had eluded her for decades. No publisher's records exist to tell us how many copies of the *Memoirs* were printed or sold. There are no reviews of the book, nor any other indication of its success or failure. We cannot know if she was comfortable in her later years.

Ann Carson's public crimes had private consequences for her family. Her mother's incarceration and trial took a financial toll on the Bakers. By Carson's account, Jane Baker sold many of their belongings, moved to a smaller house, and lived "privately." But Ann was not the only member to disastrously affect the family. Within eight months of Jane Baker's acquittal, Thomas Baker was in debtor's prison. In a letter to Stephen Girard, Jane Baker explained that to "save one of my Son in Laws from Prison [Baker] endorsed a Note for 63 Doll." The unnamed son-in-law did a bunk and left Baker with a debt he could not pay. The ne'er-do-well family member could have been her sister Mary's husband, currier Thomas Abbott, but most likely it was Sarah's husband, Joseph Hutton. The 1817 city directory listed Hutton as an accountant, apparently a very bad one. Hutton had tried his hand at many occupations, including actor and schoolteacher, but seems to have failed at all of them. Girard did not reply to Baker's plea for aid and the captain probably languished in the Prune Street apartments (as his daughter had before him) until October. When Thomas Baker died two and a half years later, his widow testified that he was worth no more than seventy-five dollars—a very small sum.

Ann Carson stayed away from Philadelphia (to avoid standing trial for bigamy) for eight months or so after the kidnapping trial. Her children, whom she barely mentioned in her narrative, lived with her parents beginning in early 1816. Even after Carson returned to Philadelphia, her children stayed with the Bakers. By the time Carson was released from prison in 1821, Jane Baker may no longer have been in Philadelphia. Though Carson's second son, Joseph, moved in with Carson and Clarke for a time in 1822, her oldest son, John H. Carson, did not. Nor did her daughter, Jeanette. Piecing together the few references in the *Memoirs*, Jane Baker's letters to the government concerning her widow's pension, and the Baker family's genealogy, it is probable that John H. Carson moved south with one of Ann's brothers, possibly James Baker, a navy captain. By the early 1830s, James Baker was living in New Orleans. By 1837, he, along with his wife, children, and mother, was living in Pensacola, Florida. Jane Baker did not mention her grandchildren in her letters.

By law, Captain John Carson's three children were entitled to his share of his aunt Elizabeth Carson Febiger's estate. When Febiger died in 1818, the children's court-appointed guardians, first Ann's lover Thomas Newlin and later Adam Henchman, repeatedly asked the Orphans' Court to force Febiger's administrators (one of whom was John Carson's brother) to distribute the Carson children's inheritance. In 1824, Henchman was still trying to get the Febiger estate to part with the money. The children may never have received the anticipated funds, particularly if they joined their grandmother in Pensacola, a place Jane Baker described as an "unhealthy southern climate" that had brought disease and death to several of her children. Despite a lifetime of financial hardship, marital trials, and parental heartbreak, Jane Baker lived to her eighty-second year. She died in Florida in October 1850.

Notwithstanding the national attention given to Ann Carson's extraordinary activities, she is barely visible in historical records. Periodically, since the early nineteenth century, chroniclers or journalists seeking a human-interest story have revived Carson's notoriety. Few of them interpreted her story accurately. William C. Armor, a nineteenth-century biographer of Pennsylvania's governors, stated that Carson and her accomplices were all "given a home in the penitentiary" after their guilty verdict. Some writers, including an anonymous Carson family genealogist, glossed over the truth. There is a reference to the marriage of Ann Baker and Captain John Carson, the birth of their children, and the captain's date of death, but no mention of the circumstances. Other writers embellished an already remarkable tale: in 1902, a *Philadelphia Ledger* writer commented: "Indeed, female wantonness, in Philadelphia perhaps has never produced a more audacious specimen of depravity and beauty." In 1933, Frederic A. Godcharles called Carson "the most captivating beauty of the underworld and the most notorious character in the state." Struthers Burt, in his 1946 book *Philadelphia Holy Experiment*, tried to explain how the City of Brotherly Love produced so unique a character: "As for Philadelphia, it regretted her behavior and was puzzled, as it has been again and again in its history, that any Philadelphia girl could behave in such a fashion. . . . Philadelphia has never yet admitted the obvious fact that a woman is a woman first and then a Philadelphian, and not the other way about." The most recent mention of Carson appeared in another Philadelphia newspaper in 1961. The headline of a column devoted to Philadelphia's colorful past referred to her as "The Gay Widow." Ann Carson's history, when it was related accurately, was boiled down to an amusing incident illustrative of the foibles of a beautiful woman.

But the reality for both women was harsh. Family circumstances challenged them to devise their own means of financial support. As downwardly mobile middle-class women, Carson and Clarke sought to retain their status while they entered a world of work outside the home. Without a reliably working spouse, Ann Carson first turned to shopkeeping and sewing military clothing. These were conventional activities for working women. However, as Ann Carson's finances became more precarious, she joined the ranks of con men and counterfeiters. Mary Clarke's husband was alive until 1816, but, according to Clarke, he was so physically broken by his war service that he did not contribute to the family income. Clarke's route to economic stability was more unusual for a woman in the 1810s than was Carson's. Clarke's venture into print with poems, plays, and the *Tea Tray* required that she present herself within a framework of dependence rather than of professional achievement. Mary Clarke's later efforts to write for profit drove her away from traditional boundaries of polite letters and into the uncharted territory of sensationalism. Their paths led both women into dangerous terrain. But neither woman went unwillingly. Carson and Clarke were well aware of the consequences of their actions and the possible benefits and losses.

From a historical perspective, Carson's and Clarke's unusual choices contradict several assumptions about women and gender roles in the early republic. First, their histories demonstrate that prescriptive behavior, heavily relied on by scholars as a key to understanding society, cannot begin to account for the variety of activities women pursued; more alternatives (legal or otherwise) were available for women than our knowledge derived from conduct books, sermons, and other sources have led us to believe. Carson and Clarke were neither elite nor working-class women. Occupations such as servant, huckster, or even prostitute, were not options for them. These women occupied a middle ground that has been largely unexplored for this economically volatile era.

Second, Carson and Clarke were highly conscious of a woman's place in early nineteenth-century society. Part of this book's task has been to examine Carson's and Clarke's rhetorical strategies—how and why those strategies shaped their stories. The *History* and the *Memoirs* were both written with a clear sense of audience. The carefully chosen revelations, self-fashionings, and justifications in these texts were designed to elicit sympathy. Such a response to Carson's *History* may seem improbable, but Carson's criminal associations were exposed only after her death, in Clarke's *Memoirs*. Carson told her *History* readers that she was more sinned against than sinning. And Mary Clarke positioned herself at a careful distance from the illicit activities of the men and women she chronicled. The *History* also has a didactic element: it criticizes married women's legal status and it argues for greater female autonomy. Ann Carson chose to place much of the blame for her bad marriage and financial instability on the social and economic restrictions placed on women. She saw her personal difficulties in gendered terms. Carson claimed that if she had had the freedom to choose a husband for herself and if she had been trained for an occupation, many of her domestic and legal troubles could have been avoided. Carson and Clarke both demonstrate the degree to which they were self-aware of their situation as women.

Carson even rationalized her criminal activities as the result of society's constraints: she argued that her upbringing and circumstances left her no alternative to a life of crime and that her desire for personal independence justified her actions. This rhetorical ploy echoed thoughts, ideas, and writings from an earlier generation of writers, including Judith Sargent Murray and Mary Wollstonecraft. Such forthright advocates for women had fallen out of favor by the 1820s, yet Carson's invocation demonstrates that she and Mary Clarke expected their ideas to resonate with readers: they tapped into a subterranean continuity in the argument for women's rights. At the same time, as the details of Carson's trials in the Philadelphia courts illustrate, gender roles created expectations of behavior that were so ingrained that even individual demonstrations to the contrary could not dislodge beliefs about male and female identities.

Despite these social prescriptions, Carson railed against the injustice of women's lot and admitted that she violated social norms to achieve an independence that was impossible within the confines of respectable social and marital relations. Mary Clarke strove for economic security beyond traditional means of support. Her writing was couched in terms of her exposed situation, fragile financial status, and lack of a male protector, but her actions show that she had a firm idea of how to take care of herself. Clarke had dangerous associations, but they were of her own choosing. Clarke immersed herself in the worlds of criminals and disreputable actors and actresses and she used her acquaintance with the demimonde to shape a career as a sensationalist writer. Yet she was careful to present herself as a participant observer—close enough to give her readers privileged information but distant enough to retain her good name. She pursued financial success through a series of what she hoped would be best-selling exposés. At the same time, she protected her reputation with a careful construction of her character and a justification for her involvement with unsavory individuals. Clarke's writings sought to gratify the schizophrenic longings of a society that valued purity, innocence, and sexual ignorance on the part of women, yet delighted in the exposure of female sexuality and passion. Clarke's editorial ventures highlight women's increasing participation in what was a traditionally male profession. Her writings also show us that she was not afraid to stray beyond accepted topics for women writers; she embraced the voyeuristic sensationalism of the emerging media venues in the 1830s. Clarke took risks to make profits.

Laurel Thatcher Ulrich has written that well-behaved women seldom make history. But even the badly behaved ones often fall away from posterity's view. Attention to the unique experiences and survival strategies of Ann Carson and Mary Clarke affords us an opportunity to reevaluate the interplay of gender and class in the early nineteenth century from the perspective of women who were, if not mad or bad, certainly dangerous to know.

Notes

Chapter 1. Two Working Women

1. Coverture was the legal concept that defined woman's right in early America. The term feme covert referred to married women. They could not own property, sign legal documents, or enter into a contract.

2. *The Memoirs of the Celebrated and Beautiful Mrs. Ann Carson, Daughter of an Officer of the U.S. Navy, and Wife of Another, Whose Life Terminated in the Philadelphia Prison*, second edition, revised, enlarged, and continued till her death, by Mrs. M. Clarke, Authoress of the *Fair American, Life of Thomas L. Hamblin, Edwin Forrest*, &c. &c., in Two Volumes (Philadelphia, 1838): 1: 19. Page numbers for quotations in *The History of the Celebrated Mrs. Ann Carson, Widow of the Late Unfortunate Lieutenant Richard Smith, with a Circumstantial Account of her Conspiracy Against the Late Governor of Pennsylvania, Simon Snyder; and of Her Sufferings in the Several Prisons in that State, Interspersed with Anecdotes of Characters Now Living*. Written by Herself (Philadelphia: Published by the author, 1822) are taken from this second, revised edition.

3. *Memoirs*, 1: 19, 22. After the Revolutionary War, Thomas Baker became partner with his brother-in-law, Robert Loague. Baker and Loague bought a schooner and participated in the West Indies trade for a short time. Thomas Baker later went to work for a merchant with a larger ship for several years.

Both the Baker family's and the Carson family's income and housing ranked them slightly above the average for Philadelphia households. Susan E. Klepp and Susan Branson, "A Working Woman: The Autobiography of Ann Baker Carson," in *Life in Revolutionary Philadelphia: A Documentary History*, ed. Billy G. Smith (University Park: Pennsylvania State University Press, 1995), 156, n. 1.

4. *Memoirs*, 1: 19.

5. Ibid., 1: 21.

6. Jerald A. Combs, *The Jay Treaty: Political Battleground of the Founding Fathers* (Berkeley: University of California Press, 1970), 116.

7. *Memoirs*, 1: 22.

8. Carson described her father's treatment: "The surgeon, anxious to restore my father's health, threw him into a salivation, which reduced him to infantine debility, and then permitted him to drink freely of any intoxicating liquors he chose; this threw the disease on the brain, and his reason was sacrificed on the shrine of ignorance, intemperance, and servility." *Memoirs*, 1: 26.

9. *Memoirs*, 1: 25. Baker's disability left him subject to fits of irrational behavior. Carson says that he tried to strangle Jane Baker while Stephen Decatur and his

wife were visiting. Mrs. Decatur managed to pull Baker away from his nearly asphyxiated spouse. This episode prompted the first of two admissions to the Pennsylvania Hospital for "insanity" and "mania." He was treated and released in June and July 1801. *Memoirs*, 2: 40; Seamen's Admission Records, Pennsylvania Hospital, Philadelphia.

10. Susan Branson, "Women and the Family Economy in the Early Republic: The Case of Elizabeth Meredith," *Journal of the Early Republic* 16 (Spring 1996): 47–71.

11. *Memoirs*, 1: 25.

12. Using the pseudonym Constantia, Murray contributed essays to the *Massachusetts Magazine* in the early 1790s. At the end of the century, she published her colleted essays and plays as *The Gleaner: A Miscellaneous Production* (1798). Many of her writings advocated educational and economic training for women and argued for women's intellectual equality with men. See Sheila L. Skemp, *Judith Sargent Murray: A Brief Biography with Documents* (Boston: Bedford, 1998).

13. Ibid., 1: 32.

14. The Bakers are listed at 14 Dock Street. Stafford, *The Philadelphia Directory for 1801*.

15. *Memoirs*, 1: 33.

16. Ibid., 1: 34.

17. Ibid., 1: 21.

18. Ibid., 1: 30. Betrothals at such a young age were far from the norm in this era. Only 13 percent of young women married before age seventeen, and only 3 percent before age sixteen. Susan E. Klepp, *Philadelphia in Transition: A Demographic History of the City and Its Occupational Groups, 1720–1830* (New York, Garland Press, 1989), 74. The family lived off profits from the sale of some real estate (what was left after Baker paid his debts to Davis. Baker had not yet applied for his half-pay).

19. *Memoirs*, 1: 21.

20. John Carson's ship was probably the *China Packet*. George Street runs from Gaskill to Plumb (or Plum) Street—this is between Second and Third streets. The Carsons lived there from 1801 to 1804.

21. The *Pennsylvania Packet* returned to Philadelphia on August 4, 1806. Seaport lists and Jean Gordon Lee, *Philadelphia and the China Trade, 1784–1844* (Philadelphia: Philadelphia Museum of Art, 1984), 92.

22. Philip Chadwick Foster Smith, *The Empress of China* (Philadelphia: Philadelphia Maritime Museum, 1984). Chapter 12 explains the highly controlled port and trade system set up by the Chinese at Canton.

23. *Memoirs*, 1: 67.

24. Ibid., 1: 68.

25. Ibid., 1: 75.

26. Ibid., 1: 76. Carson rented the house from David Ellis.

27. The city directory listed her as "Sarah Baker, Tutress, at 84 N. 4th Street" in 1807 and 1808. She moved around in subsequent years. The last listing is in 1811 when she was at 23 North Fourth Street.

28. Carson says she had one of these certificates, but no record exists. See *The Trials of Richard Smith . . . as Principal, and Ann Carson, alias Ann Smith, as accessory, for the Murder of Captain John Carson* (Philadelphia: Desilver, 1816), 19-20.

29. Not until Congress passed the NonIntercourse Act in March 1809, which prohibited trade only with France and Britain, did coastal commerce and employment begin to rise back to pre-embargo levels, and then only for a short while, as relations with Britain continued to deteriorate.

30. Diana diZerega Wall, "Family Dinners and Social Teas: Ceramic and Domestic Rituals," in *Everyday Life in the Early Republic*, ed. Catherine E. Hutchins (Winterthur, Del.: Henry Francis du Pont Winterthur Museum, 1994), 270.

31. Ann Carson to Stephen Girard, September 24, 1811. Girard Papers, Series 2, Reel 49, no. 392 (Letters Received 1811), American Philosophical Society; *Memoirs* 1: 130–31. Boston imported far more porcelain than New York or Philadelphia. Nancy Ellen Davis, "The American China Trade, 1784–1844: Products for the Middle Class," Ph.D. dissertation, George Washington University, 1987, 122; Lee, *Philadelphia and the China Trade*; Jonathan Goldstein, *Philadelphia and the China Trade, 1682–1846: Commercial, Cultural, and Attitudinal Effects* (University Park: Pennsylvania State University Press, 1978).

32. *Memoirs*, 1: 85–86. Queensware was originally made by Josiah Wedgwood for George III in 1765 and named in honor of Queen Charlotte. Wedgwood then marketed it to the general public, and soon other manufacturers produced similar ware. Queensware became the descriptive name for this type of tableware, regardless of which company made it. Diana Wall, *The Archeology of Gender* (New York: Plenum, 1994); Paul G. E. Clemens, "The Consumer Culture of the Middle Atlantic, 1760–1820," *William and Mary Quarterly*, 52, no. 4 (October 2005): 609–10.

33. *Memoirs*, 1: 87.

34. Ibid., 1: 79–80.

35. Ibid., 1: 80. Carson resigned in December 1809. The *Wasp* went to sea again after being refitted in September 1812, where it had a notable encounter with the HMS *Frolic*. Thomas H. S. Hamersly, *General Register of the United States Navy and Marine Corps, 1782–1882* (Washington, D.C.: Hamersly, 1882), 130.

36. *Memoirs*, 1: 93.

37. Ibid., 1: 93.

38. Ibid., 1: 100.

39. My thanks to Fred Gaede for this information. Callender Irvine was the commissary general of purchases by 1812. He rented a building in the city for cutting out and inspecting the finished garments. Clothing was taken back to the Arsenal (which was on the edge of town at Grays Ferry Road and Washington Avenue) only when it was ready to be shipped.

As contractors, Carson and her mother chose how much (or how little) they paid the women who sewed for them. The purveyor attempted to eliminate corruption by mercenary contractors who pocketed most of the profits while the poor who actually made the clothes were paid almost nothing. Irvine changed the system by employing a handful of men to cut out and issue these pieces directly to seamstresses rather than to contractors. This change occurred sometime during the war but apparently after Carson and Baker participated in production. Erna Risch,

Quartermaster Support of the Army: A History of the Corps, 1775–1939 (Washington, D.C. Center of Millitary History, U.S. Army, U.S.G.P.O., 1989), 146.

40. Mary Clarke published under the name Mary Carr until 1823. For clarity, I refer to her as Mary Clarke throughout this book.

41. In fact, Clarke had begun publishing the magazine the previous month. She probably issued the "Proposal" in the *United States Gazette* because she lacked a sufficient number of subscribers. In November, she had only two hundred; five hundred was what she hoped for. *United States Gazette*, November 19, 1814.

42. Clarke later revealed that her husband died late in 1816. He seems to have been an invalid for some time prior to this, possibly as a result of wounds sustained fighting in the War of 1812. *Memoirs*, 1: 119.

43. For examples of the handful of colonial women with successful careers in printing, see Okker, *Our Sister Editors* (Athens: University of Georgia Press, 1995) and Marion Tuttle Marzoff, *Up from the Footnote: A History of Women Journalists* (New York: Hastings House, 1977), 1–8.

44. *The Intellectual Regale, or Ladies' Tea Tray*, 1, no. 1 (November 19, 1814).

45. *United States Gazette*, December 1, 1814. A year later, Clarke reiterated her reliance on Philadelphia's women: "The ensuing year shall determine the editress, whether to trust to female patronage for future support, or to suffer the Tea Tray to fall to the ground forever." Preface to *Tea Tray*, 2, no. 1 (May 1815).

Clarke's desire to attract female readers may explain why she left subscription papers at Lydia Phillips's circulating library (199 South Third Street). Circulating libraries (often located within bookshops) were heavily patronized by women. Some, as was the case with Phillips's library, were even owned and run by women. At least two other libraries were run by women in the center of Philadelphia at this time: Christina Neale's library and bookstore on Chestnut adjacent to the New Theater (at Sixth Street) and Ann Shallus's Circulating Library and Fancy Goods Store (90 South Third Street). David Kaser, *A Book for a Sixpence: The Circulating Library in America* (Pittsburgh: Beta Phi Mu, 1980), 69.

46. *United States Gazette*, December 1, 1814.

47. Amy Beth Aronson, *Taking Liberties: Early American Women's Magazines and Their Readers* (Westport, Conn.: Praeger, 2002), 53, 100. Lori D. Ginzberg, *Women and the Work of Benevolence: Morality, Politics, and Class in the Nineteenth-Century United States* (New Haven, Conn.: Yale University Press, 1990). For a full discussion of the subject of sensibility see G. J. Barker-Benfield, *The Culture of Sensibility: Sex and Society in Eighteenth-Century Britain* (Chicago: University of Chicago Press, 1992).

48. Mary Kelley describes the dilemma in this way: "From their literary income they supported or contributed to the support of themselves and their families, yet felt compelled to justify that support on the basis of domestic need. And, most significantly, they struggled in their tales to assess and place a value on women's lives while disparaging and dismissing their own literary efforts." Mary Kelley, *Private Woman, Public Stage: Literary Domesticity in Nineteenth-Century America* (New York: Oxford University Press, 1984), xi; Carolyn L. Karcher, *The First Woman in the Republic: A Cultural Biography of Lydia Maria Child* (Durham, N.C.: Duke University Press, 1994).

49. Susan Branson, *These Fiery Frenchified Dames: Women and Political Culture in Early National Philadelphia* (Philadelphia: University of Pennsylvania Press, 2001), 21–54; Cathy N. Davidson, *Revolution and the Word: The Rise of the Novel in America* (New York: Oxford University Press, 1986); Linda Kerber, *Women of the Republic: Intellect and Ideology in Revolutionary America* (Chapel Hill: University of North Carolina Press, 1980).

50. As Paul Erikson says of a later generation of writers, authorship "looks different from the perspective of people for whom being an author was a *good* career outcome." "New Books, New Men: City-Mysteries Fiction, Authorship, and the Literary Market," *Early American Studies* 1, no. 1 (Spring 2003), 275.

51. This geographical intimacy is confirmed by a comparison of the *Tea Tray*'s subscription list with the Philadelphia city directory for 1814–1815. Even though Clarke moved her residence and the *Tea Tray* office twice during the magazine's existence, these locations were all within the center of the city. In 1815, she moved to 98 Race Street. In 1816, she was living at 133½ South Sixth Street.

52. *United States Gazette*, December 1, 1814. General magazines, such as *The New York Magazine; or Literary Repository*, were remarkably similar to the *Tea Tray*. David Paul Nord's content analysis of *The New York Magazine* found that the "largest proportion of the articles fell into a more nebulous area that I have labeled 'manners and morals.' . . . Many of these pieces were romances—usually sentimental stories of love lost or found, seduction resisted or embraced." Nord also claims that many of the articles and stories were aimed at women. Nord, "A Republican Literature: A Study of Magazine Reading and Readers in Late Eighteenth-Century New York," *American Quarterly* 40, no. 1 (March 1988), 52–53, 55. Publications such as the *Tickler* (Philadelphia, 1807–1813), *Salmagundi* (New York, 1807–1808), and the *Port Folio* (Philadelphia, 1801–1827), as well as *The Lady's Miscellany; or The Weekly Visitor* (New York, 1802–1812), may well have been among the publications Clarke drew on for the structure and content of the *Tea Tray*.

53. Ann Coles, printer, 108 Sassafras; Catherine Clarke, boardinghouse, 112 Swanson; Mary Britt, bonnet maker, 64 North Third; Elizabeth Barnes, milliner, 65 South Sassafras; Christina Neale, bookseller and circulating library, Chestnut adjacent to the New Theater (at Sixth); and Lydia Phillips, bookseller and librarian at 119 South Third Street.

54. *Tea Tray*, 1, no. 3 (December 3, 1814).

55. Ibid., 1, no. 22 (April 15, 1815).

56. Ibid., 2, no. 9 (July 15, 1815).

57. *Lake Champlain* was published in volume 2, no. 2 and no. 3, in 1816; *Venture It* was published two months later in issues 12 through 21. Several hundred copies of two previously printed plays, *The Fair Americans* and *Battle of New Orleans*, were listed in the schedule of property Clarke turned over to Thomas Smith in December 1815, suggesting that there had not been much demand for them.

Nina Baym includes a brief analysis of *The Fair Americans* in *American Women Writers and the Work of History, 1790–1860* (New Brunswick, N.J.: Rutgers University Press, 1995). The play has been reprinted in *Plays by Early American Women, 1775–1850*, ed. Amelia Howe Kritzer (Ann Arbor: University of Michigan Press, 1995).

The Return from Camp was advertised in the *United States Gazette* on January 2, 3, 5, 6, 1815.

58. *Tea Tray*, 2, no. 25 (November 4, 1815); 2, no. 26 (November 11, 1815).

59. Ibid., 2, no. 5 (June 17, 1815).

60. "The Publisher apologizes to his friends and the public for a tardiness not more ungrateful to them than to himself. In future, the Patrons of this Journal may rest assured it shall appear in due season." *Port Folio* New Series, 1, no. 4 (February 1, 1806). Harold Milton Ellis, *Joseph Dennie and His Circle: A Study in American Literature from 1792–1812* Bulletin of the University of Texas, no. 40, July 15 (Austin: University of Texas, 1915).

61. In this regard, Clarke anticipated the later nineteenth-century development of literary realism, when Americans perceived reading as a conversation with an author. A useful discussion of this phenomenon is Margaret Beetham's "Towards a Theory of the Periodical as a Publishing Genre," in *Investigating Victorian Journalism*, ed. Laurel Brake, Aled Joes, and Lionel Madden (New York: St. Martin's, 1990). Barbara Hochman has described such participatory activity in regard to novels as "reading for the author" or "friendly reading." Hochman, *Getting at the Author: Reimagining Books and Reading in the Age of American Realism* (Amherst: University of Massachusetts Press, 2001), 12.

62. Clarke was not completely sanguine about her projected success. In remembering the kindness of her subscribers, she added, "and when perhaps the dark clouds of adversity may lower over her humble abode, their remembrance, like the healing balm, will dissipate the gloom for a time, and make her heart glow with the most delightful of all sensations, gratitude without humiliation." *Tea Tray*, preface, 1, no. 1 (November 19, 1814).

63. *Tea Tray*, 2, no. 5 (June 17, 1815).

64. Ibid., 3, no. 8 (February 24, 1816); 3, no. 7 (February 17, 1816).

65. Ibid., 1, no. 24 (April 29, 1815). Dennis Heartt is listed as printer from November 1814 until April 1815. Thereafter, Clarke is listed as printer through the December 30, 1815, issue. The *Tea Tray* is listed as printed and published by Mrs. Clarke at 8 South Fifth Street for the first time in 1, no. 22 (April 1815). As Leon Jackson has kindly pointed out, Clarke was almost certainly not doing the physical work of printing.

66. Philadelphia City Archives. Record Group 20.30, Common Pleas Insolvency Petitions and Bonds. December Term, 1815. My thanks to Donna Rilling for discovering this petition. Clarke's notice appeared for the first time on December 16, 1815, in *Relf's Philadelphia Gazette*: "Take notice, that I have applied to the Judges of the Court of Common Pleas, for the city and county of Philadelphia, for the benefit of the several acts of insolvency of this commonwealth [Act for the Relief of Insolvent Debtors], and they have appointed the 29th day of December inst. To hear me and my creditors, at the court-house in Philadelphia, at 10 o'clock, A.M. where you may attend." Coincidentally, a local theater was playing the comedy *Debtor and Creditor* the same week Clarke's notice appeared. *Relf's Philadelphia Gazette*, December 7, 1815.

67. *Tea Tray*, 2, no. 9 (July 15, 1815).

68. Ibid., 2, no. 7 (July 1, 1815).

69. Ibid., 2, no. 9 (July 15, 1815).
70. Ibid., 2, no. 4 (June 10, 1815).
71. Ibid., 2, no. 6 (June 24, 1815).
72. Ibid., 2, no. 9 (July 15, 1815).
73. Ibid., 2, no. 25 (November 4, 1815).
74. Ibid., 2, no. 25 (November 4, 1815).

75. Clarke's inexperience may also have been a contributing factor. Her collection of subscription fees on a monthly basis was unusual. And the absence of any advertisements and announcements that would have come from an exchange with the other magazines and periodicals in the city and the region indicates that Clarke was probably unfamiliar with the printing and publishing trade. My thanks to Leon Jackson for this information.

The Philadelphia women's magazines that followed the demise of the *Tea Tray* were no more successful than Clarke's publication. *The Ladies' Literary Museum, or Weekly Repository* went through several incarnations between its inception in July 1817 and its last issue in June 1820. It became the *Lady's and Gentleman's Weekly Museum and Philadelphia Reporter* in July 1818 (perhaps in an effort to appeal more directly to male readers), then it changed its title to the *Lady's & Gentleman's Weekly Literary Museum and Musical Magazine* on January 1, 1819. In the backcountry, William Peirce of Marietta, Pennsylvania, briefly published the *Ladies' Visitor* from 1819 to 1820.

76. Clarke is listed as the "editress" of the *Parterre* in *Robinson's Original Annual Directory for 1817* (Whitehall, Pa., 1817). The office was at 108 Sassafras.

77. Amy Beth Aronson, "Understanding Equals: Audience and Articulation in the Early American Women's Magazine," Ph.D. dissertation, Columbia University, 1996, 84–85; Kenneth M. Price and Susan Belasco Smith, eds., *Periodical Literature in Nineteenth-Century America* (Charlottesville: University Press of Virginia, 1995), 3.

Chapter 2. Marriage, Manhood, and Murder

1. Jane Baker may have had a small grocery store in the shop for a time prior to Carson's china store. James Robinson, *The Philadelphia Directory, City and County Register for 1808* lists Thomas Baker, grocer, 184 South Second Street.

2. The events leading to Carson's death are reconstructed from the *Memoirs* and the transcript of Smith's trial. This account is by no means objective; because much of it relies on Ann Carson's perspective in her autobiography, there is no way to independently verify or refute Carson's version. *The Memoirs of the Celebrated and Beautiful Mrs. Ann Carson* (Philadelphia, 1838), *Memoirs*, 1: 99.

3. *Memoirs*, 1: 136. Carson writes that they stopped at the Sign of the Jolly Post, but the trial testimony states that it was Haines' Tavern. The Reverend. Mr. Doak married them on October 15, 1815.

4. *Memoirs*, 1: 144.

5. Ibid., 1: 146.

6. Ibid., 1: 146, 149. John Carson's extended absence may have been a result of the war. "No ships from Canton arrived in the port of Philadelphia from August 1812 until the *Pacific* docked in May 1816. Several American merchants and supercargo, not anticipating war, were stranded in Canton." Nancy Ellen David, "The American China Trade, 1784–1844: Products for the Middle Class," Ph.D. dissertation, George Washington University, 1987, 14.

7. *Memoirs*, 1: 154.

8. The subpeona served on Ann Carson was printed in the appendix to *The Trials of Richard Smith . . . as Principal, and Ann Carson, alias Ann Smith, as accessory, for the Murder of Captain John Carson* (Philadelphia: Desilver, 1816), v.

9. *Memoirs*, 1: 156, 157, 158.

10. Ibid., 1: 158–59. On January 18, Alderman Badger bound Carson to keep the peace. Ann's brother-in-law Joseph Hutton paid Carson's five-hundred-dollar guarantee.

11. *Memoirs*, 1: 159.

12. Ibid., 1: 163.

13. Ibid., 1: 164.

14. Ibid., 1: 165.

15. Ibid., 1: 166–67. Jane Baker encouraged John Carson's behavior. Prior to this encounter, on the night of January 20 she had suggested that he drag Smith from the house and publicly chastise him in the presence of the merchants at the coffeehouse. *Memoirs*, 1: 160.

16. *Memoirs*, 1: 174. My reconstruction of these events is based on Carson's recollections in *The History of the Celebrated Mrs. Ann Carson* (Philadelphia: published by the author, 1822) and testimony at Smith's trial.

17. *Columbian* (New York) February 8, 1816; *New Jersey Journal*, February 13, 1816. The *True American* article was reprinted in the *Columbian*, January 23, 1816. Carson's death was also noted in Mary Clarke's *Tea Tray*: "Died—On Saturday night, Feb 3 Capt. *John Carson*, of Philadelphia," 2, no. 6 (February 10, 1816).

18. *Poulson's American Daily Advertiser*, February 7, 1816; *Memoirs*, 1: 174.

19. Smith's trial coincided with the rise in the popularity of trial transcripts. "Published trial reports bore the marks of a popular literature: cheaply printed, usually between paper covers, and cheaply sold, often illustrated, and especially in the more sensational crimes, printed in competing editions by several publishers." Karen Halttunen, *Murder Most Foul: The Killer and the American Gothic Imagination* (Cambridge, Mass.: Harvard University Press, 2000), 95–96. Desilver's transcript was published in two parts so that he could get the first part of the trial out as soon as possible. He began to run advertisements for it in the *United States Gazette* (Philadelphia) beginning June 11, 1816. There may have been a competing transcript, by T. S. Manning, advertised in the same paper on June 11 and June 13. No copies of Manning's version have been located.

20. Degrees of murder was defined in a Pennsylvania law of 1794. See Alexander J. Dallas, ed., *Laws of the Commonwealth of Pennsylvania*, vol. 3 (Philadelphia: Hall and Sellers, 1795–1801) H v., 599–600, and Edwin R. Keedy, "History of the

Pennsylvania Statute Creating Degrees of Murder," *University of Pennsylvania Law Review* 97 (1949), 759.

21. *Trials*, 5–6.

22. This quotation from the fourth section of the Act of the Legislature passed September 19, 1785, is on page 60 in the *Trials*.

23. *Trials*, 1: 69.

24. Ibid., 1: 70.

25. Ibid., 1: 70.

26. Ibid., 1: 34.

27. Ibid., 1: 14, 15, 17.

28. Ibid., 1: 17.

29. Ibid., 1: 227. Ingersoll neglected to tell the jury that Jane Baker was not an unbiased observer. She had welcomed Carson warmly on his return and had repeatedly tried to persuade Ann to take him back.

Despite their reputation for dalliance and infidelity, many sailors had strong emotional ties to their wives. See Paul A. Gilje, *Liberty on the Waterfront: American Maritime Culture in the Age of Revolution* (Philadelphia: University of Pennsylvania Press, 2004), chap. 2.

30. *Memoirs*, 1: 41.

31. Ibid., 1: 43. Smith was singled out for his bravery in an article in *The Union* (Washington, Ky.), June 25, 1814.

32. *Memoirs*, 1: 60. Browne referred to a letter published in the *Aurora* (Philadelphia).

33. *Trials*, 44.

34. Ibid., 44.

35. Ibid., 45.

36. Ibid., 45.

37. Ibid., 192. Rawle argued that the case against his client hinged on the legality of Smith's marriage to Ann Carson: "For unless [the prosecution] can establish his adultery with Ann Smith—they cannot make him the murderer of John Carson." *Trials*, 185.

38. *Trials*, 18.

39. Ibid., 18–19.

40. Ibid., 19.

41. Ibid., 21.

42. Ibid., 19.

43. Ibid., 21. The village of Yellow Springs, located about thirty-five miles northwest of Philadelphia, was a resort known for its spa. Carson had reenlisted in August 1808. He was dismissed in December 1809. *List of Officers of the Navy of the United States and of the Marine Corps, from 1775 to 1900*, ed. Edward W. Callahan (New York: Haskell House, 1969), 102.

44. *Trials*, 56.

45. Marital obligations are fully discussed in Hendrik Hartog, *Man and Wife in America: A History* (Cambridge, Mass.: Harvard University Press, 2000). See esp. the Emmerson/Reynolds case, pp. 147–48.

46. *Trials*, 40.

47. Ibid., 135.
48. Ibid., 193.
49. Divorce petition of John Carson. Appendix to *Trials*, 239.
50. *Trials*, 102, 105. The prosecution would argue that because Ann Carson was still John's wife, it was not possible to violate her—there was no such thing as marital rape.
51. *Trials*, 105.
52. Ibid., 219.
53. Ibid., 69.
54. Ibid., 69.
55. Ibid., 70.
56. Ibid., 75.
57. Ibid., 74.
58. Rush's speech is part of the trial transcript. It was also reprinted in several newspapers, including the *Columbian* (New York), July 15, 1816 (reprinted from the *Washington City Weekly Gazette*), *Boston Daily Advertiser*, June 13, 1816.
59. *Relf's Philadelphia Gazette*, May 28, 1816; *United States Gazette* May 28, 1816.
60. *Trials*, 164.
61. *United States Gazette*, June 11, 1816. Smith's case drew crowds from the outset. Because the mayor's office proved "too small to contain the crowd of spectators," Smith's initial examination after his arrest took place in the Oyer and Terminer courtroom at City Hall. *Relf's Philadelphia Gazette*, January 22, 1816.
62. *Trials*, 107.
63. Ibid., 232.
64. It is possible that Barkley's seemingly precise memory may have been more a result of Ann Carson's careful coaching than Barkley's natural ability.
65. *Trials*, 233.
66. Ibid., 236.
67. Ibid., 147.
68. Information about the jurors comes from the 1816 Philadelphia city directory.
69. Horace Binney, *The Leaders of the Old Bar of Philadelphia* (Philadelphia: C. Sherman & Son, 1859), 90.
70. Bell notes, "The flamboyance, tricks, and courtroom antics of those nineteenth-century lawyers was often more a matter of personal flair than any great legal knowledge or skill. Courtroom behavior was needed to create reputations because any lawyer who did not impress the public and gain a reputation found it difficult to survive. The entertainment of the courtroom action continued to be one of few shows in town, and citizens filled the courts and were familiar with the styles and reputations of various lawyers." Robert R. Bell, *The Philadelphia Lawyer: A History, 1735–1945* (Selinsgrove, Pa.: Susquehanna University Press, 1992), 96–97.
71. *Memoirs*, 1: 167.
72. Ibid., 1: 163.

Chapter 3. The "Enraged Tygress"

1. Correspondence of Simon Snyder, Case 76, vol. 1. John Binns to Simon Snyder, July 10, 1816. Philadelphia, Historical Society of Pennsylvania.

2. *The Memoirs of the Celebrated and Beautiful Mrs. Ann Carson, Daughter of an Officer of the U.S. Navy, and Wife of Another, Whose Life Terminated in the Philadelphia Prison.* Second Edition, revised, enlarged, and continued till her death, by Mrs. M. Clarke, Authoress of the *Fair American, Life of Thomas L. Hamblin, Edwin Forrest,* &c. &c., in Two Volumes (Philadelphia, 1838), 1: 183.

3. "The States' Attorney having, by mistake, returned the indictment of bigamy against me to the mayors court instead for the quarter sessions, my bail, by this error, was exonerated from his recognizance." *Memoirs,* 1: 183.

4. *Memoirs,* 1: 184.

5. Ibid., 1: 184.

6. Ibid., 1: 185.

7. Ibid., 1: 187.

8. Ibid., 1: 188. A writ of error is filed to review and correct an error of the law committed in the proceedings, which is not amendable, or cured at common law, or by some of the statutes of amendment. See *Baltimore Patriot,* July 29, 1816.

9. "The governor of Pennsylvania has been censured by some people for not granting a pardon to the guilty man." *Baltimore American and Commercial Daily Advertiser,* August 17, 1816.

10. *Memoirs,* 1: 141–42.

11. *Memoirs,* 1: 191.

12. "Jones [Bowen's real name] stated previously to be arrested that he had been an officer in the same regiment with Richard Smith, and manifested much anxiety for his pardon." *Pennsylvania Republican* (Harrisburg), July 23, 1816. Bowen/Jones also called himself Davis from time to time. He had been arrested for theft in 1808 and horse stealing in 1811. He certainly was not an officer in Smith's or anybody else's regiment. See the *Baltimore Patriot,* July 29, 1816.

13. *Memoirs,* 1: 192.

14. *Memoirs,* 1: 192. "The act of 1790 also ordered the erection of a building in the yard containing separate cells for the solitary confinement of the most 'hardened and atrocious offenders.'" Harry Elmer Barnes, *The Evolution of Penology in Pennsylvania: A Study in American Social History* (Indianapolis, Ind.: Bobbs-Merrill, 1927), 135. Barnes quotes from *The Statutes at Large of Pennsylvania,* vol. 13, p. 515.

15. *Memoirs,* 1: 193.

16. Ibid., 1: 193.

17. Ibid., 1: 195.

18. Ibid., 1: 194–95.

19. *Recollections of the Life of John Binns* (Philadelphia: 1854), 275.

20. *Recollections,* 275. Binns was not the only individual to get the story wrong. Fifty-seven years after Carson's trial for conspiracy, one chronicler provided the following account: "During the administration of Governor Snyder a

notorious woman, Ann Smith, alias Carson, formed a bold scheme for abducting the Governor's youngest son, then a lad at school, and for holding him until the pardon of her paramour, who was under sentence of death, should be secured. For this purpose she started from Philadelphia with two hired ruffians, armed to the teeth, and was making her way to Selinsgrove, on the Susquehanna, where the Governor's family resided. The Governor was secretly informed of their coming, and was prepared to receive them.... They were all apprehended, and after a trial and conviction were given a home in the penitentiary." William C. Armor, *Lives of the Governors of Pennsylvania with the Incidental History of the State from 1609 to 1873* (Philadelphia: James K. Simon, 1873), 320.

21. *Memoirs*, 1: 201.

22. Frederic A. Godcharles, *Chronicles of Central Pennsylvania* (New York: Lewis Historical Publishing Company, 1944), vol. 6, 322.

23. *Memoirs*, 1: 197–98. Carson gave no reason for the necessity of conveying the governor across the state line into Maryland. Possibly she assumed such action would delay pursuit by Pennsylvania authorities.

John Binns asserted that Carson was dressed in men's clothing, but Carson would have received a very different reception at the various inns they stopped at had she been dressing as a man. A *New Jersey Journal*, July 30, 1816, reprint from the *Democratic Press* (Philadelphia) reported, "She had a bundle with her in the gig, in which was tied up a sailor's roundabout, check shirt &c." Also see the *Columbian* (New York), August 8, 1816.

24. Letter to the editor, dated "Harrisburg, July 20" in the *Baltimore Patriot*, July 24, 1816.

25. *Memoirs*, 1: 199.

26. Ibid., 1: 201. Newspaper accounts differ from Carson's version of the sequence of events. According to a letter to the *Democratic Press*, Carson and her accomplices went to Harrisburg and sought an audience with Governor Snyder. Only after he refused to see them did Carson change her plan and head for Selinsgrove. *New Jersey Journal* (reprint of letter to Binns in the *Democratic Press*, dated "Harrisburg, July 20"), July 30, 1816. Unfortunately, no trial transcript or trial records of testimony exist to confirm which version is the more accurate one.

27. *Memoirs*, 1: 203.

28. *Recollections*, 275. According to Binns, Campbell communicated directly with him. He claimed she was also the person who warned Binns that Carson planned to kidnap his child.

29. *Memoirs*, 1: 204.

30. Ibid., 1: 203–4; *The Chronicle or Harrisburgh Visitor*, July 29, 1816.

31. *Memoirs*, 1: 204–5.

32. Ibid., 1: 205.

33. Ibid., 1: 206–7. In prison, Carson's companions were physically inspected. Bowen's tattoo was of interest to his jailors: "Mr. Justice Fahnestoch being extremely surprised by the appearance of Bowen's arm, on which he had, at some period, impressed, with India ink, the figure of a mermaid and some initials. At this sight that gentleman expressed his wonder, which Bowen archly increased by telling him he was born with the impression, consequently it was a natural mark;

this amazed him, and he gravely declared, he had never in all his born days before seen any thing so curious." *Memoirs*, 1: 205–6. The *Baltimore Patriot*, July 29, 1816, reported Bowen's various aliases and noted that he had been a sailor.

34. *Memoirs*, 1: 207.

35. Ibid., 1: 210. Carson's grand jury hearing was July 25. See The *Pennsylvania Republican* (Harrisburg), July 30, 1816, report of the hearing.

36. *Memoirs*, 1: 212. Attorneys Irvine and Maclean argued for the governor. *The Chronicle or Harrisburgh Visitor*, August 5, 1816; *American Watchman* (Wilmington, Delaware) August 10, 1816.

37. *Memoirs*, 1: 208. *United States Gazette*, July 29, 1816: "On Thursday last Mrs. Ann Carson, was called up on a writ of Habeas Corpus, before his Honour John Carson, Esq. for a hearing. Her attornies [*sic*] Messrs Fisher, Elder and Godwin, contended that the constitution and laws of Pennsylvania, entitled their client to the privileges of confronting her accusers, and that her commitment was illegal and oppressive, and moved for her enlargement. His honour the judge postponed his decision till this morning at 10 o'clock."

38. *Memoirs*, 1: 211.

39. Ibid., 1: 209.

40. Ibid., 1: 211.

41. Ibid., 1: 210.

42. Ibid., 1: 212. "This case has assumed great importance. Some, however, make light of the matter; which we are by no means disposed to do." *The Chronicle or Harrisburgh Visitor*, July 29, 1816.

43. *Washington City Weekly Gazette* (Washington, D.C.), July 27, 1816.

44. *United States Gazette*, August 5, 1816; *The Chronicle or Harrisburgh Visitor*, August 5, 1816. Carson said that two men offered to pay her bail, but she refused because they would not also bail out Bowen and Willis. One was a handsome young Irishman, the other an old German. According to Carson, the German rode "forty miles on horseback for the express purpose of seeing and conversing with the heroine of the famous conspiracy." *Memoirs*, 1: 213.

45. *Democratic Press* (Philadelphia), July 23, 1816; *Pennsylvania Republican* (Harrisburg) July 30, 1816.

46. Tilghman cited the Act of Assembly, February 21, 1814: "By which it is enacted that no verdict thereafter given, should be set aside, nor any judgment arrested or reversed, nor sentence stayed 'for any defect or error in the precept issued for any court, or in the venire issued for summoning and returning any juror or panels of jurors." Tilghman's final word on this case was, "Upon the whole it appears to us, that the provisions of the act of Assembly cure all the defects which have been shewn as cause for granting a writ of error, and therefore it cannot be granted, without running counter to the law, and establishing a precedent of dangerous example." *Relf's Philadelphia Gazette*, July 29, 1816; *United States Gazette*, July 29, 1816.

47. *Confession of Lieutenant Richard Smith, Who is Now under Sentence of Death for the Murder of Captain John Carson*. Broadside, Library Company of Philadelphia. The confession was initially published in the *Susquehanna Waterman* (Columbia, Pennsylvania) and reprinted in many newspapers around the country, including *The Reporter* (Brattleboro, Vermont), August 21, 1816; *Albany*

Daily Advertiser, August 9, 1816; *The Evening Post* (New York), July 30, 1816; *The Centinel of Freedom* (Newark, New Jersey), August 13, 1816; *The American Beacon and Commercial Diary* (Norfolk, Virginia), July 29, 1816; *Farmer's Repository* (Charlestown, West Virginia), August 14, 1816; *Carthage Gazette and Friend of the People* (Carthage, Tennessee), August 20, 1816.

48. Smith, *Confession*. Smith paraphrased from two verses in the book of Proverbs: "That they may keep thee from the strange woman, from the stranger which flattereth with her words" Proverbs 7:5; "Her house is the way to hell, going down to the chambers of death" Proverbs 7:27.

49. Several papers alleged that the confession was a fake. Counterfeit or not, the confession was part of the cultural productions associated with violent crimes in the early nineteenth century. Jason Fairbanks's murder trial in 1801 was among the first to supply the public with a long synopsis of trial proceedings, biographies of the condemned man, and extensive newspaper coverage. According to Daniel Cohen, Fisher Ames complained that media attention to such tragedies "frightened the timid, inspired the foolish, and corrupted the public's morals." Daniel A. Cohen, *Pillars of Salt, Monuments of Grace: New England Crime Literature and the Origins of American Popular Culture, 1674–1860* (New York: Oxford University Press, 1993), 191.

For reports that the confession was a fake, see *New York Evening Post*, August 8, 1816; *Albany Daily Advertiser*, August 9, 1816.

50. *The Chronicle or Harrisburgh Visitor*, August 5, 1816.

51. *New Jersey Journal*, July 30, 1816, the *Columbian* (New York), July 26, 1816. After the kidnapping attempt, Smith was put in leg irons until his execution. See the *Boston Daily Advertiser and Repertory*, July 30, 1816.

52. *Baltimore Patriot*, August 13, 1816. The newspaper estimated that 30,000 people attended the execution.

53. *The Chronicle or Harrisburgh Visitor*, August 19, 1816; *Baltimore American and Commercial Daily Advertiser* (from the *Democratic Press*), August 14, 1816.

54. Papers that carried this detailed account include the *Democratic Press* (Philadelphia), August 11, 1816; *Otsego* (New York) *Herald*, August 29, 1816; *The Union* (Washington, Kentucky), September 16, 1816; *American Beacon* (Norfolk, Virginia), August 20, 1816.

55. Smith's execution occurred at a pivotal moment in the history of punishment in America. Smith's was among the last of Philadelphia's public executions. Executions ceased to be spectacles and public demonstrations of authority. Although the state legislature called for privatization as a corrective to the perceived disorder and increased criminality that accompanied public hangings, two things were equally, if not more, important than social control in bringing an end to public executions: a growing emphasis on sentimentality, and the advent of a print culture that thrived on sensationalism and benefited from emotionalism and sentimental portrayals of executions. In fact, it may have been because of these two developments that authorities began to worry about crowd behavior at public executions. There may actually have been bigger crowds as a result of printed announcements than there had been previously. Smith's case illustrates how sentimentality and the new journalism worked in tandem.

56. *Memoirs*, 1: 216. "Mrs. Carson, we understand, strenuously opposed leaving Harrisburg, and made many efforts to prevent her associates from being put in irons." *New Jersey Journal*, September 17, 1816.

57. *New Jersey Journal*, September 24, 1816 (from the *Lancaster Journal*, September 9, 1816). Smith's confession was alleged to be a fake, but Carson's letter, was real. Years later, she wrote of the incident in detail, though with a somewhat different interpretation of the anonymous prisoner's motive. In her memoir, she says the cell's occupant left "odes, sonnets, madrigals, and a letter, all addressed to me by its late inhabitant, who, I suppose, fancying we were congenial spirits, adopted this method of mental communication between us, which I regret not having in my possession, or I would certainly present them to my readers, being a singular compound of curiosity, sympathy, and commiseration, but without merit to recommend them to attention." *Memoirs*, 1: 218-19.

58. *The Pennsylvania Republican* (Harrisburg), September 10, 1816; *New Jersey Journal*, September 17, 1816; *Memoirs*, 1: 219.

Hamilton Village, or Hamiltonville, was on property owned by the Hamilton family and was laid out by William Hamilton sometime between 1804 and 1809. It lay generally east of Forty-first Street, west of Thirty-third, from Filbert on the north to Woodland Avenue (or Darby Road) on the south. See http://uchs.net/Rosenthal/hamvil.html. Smith's tombstone says, "He was generous, noble, brave, A defender of Fort Erie, on the glorious 15th of August, 1814. He fell victim of his own errors, of bad advice, and the deep perfidy of others." *Democratic Republican* (Chambersburg, Pennsylvania), November 11, 1816.

59. The *True American* announcement was reprinted in the *New York Evening Post*, July 26, 1816.

60. *Democratic Press*, September 6, 1816; *Baltimore Patriot*, September 7, 1816; *New York Evening Post*, September 10, 1816.

61. "Extract of a letter from a gentleman in Harrisburg, to his friend in Washington, PA dated 20th July" was reprinted in several papers, including *The Union* (Washington, Kentucky), August 9, 1816.

62. *Baltimore American and Commercial Daily Advertiser*, August 17, 1816.

63. *Baltimore Patriot*, July 24, 1816; *Niles' Weekly Register* (Baltimore), July 27, 1816.

A few examples of "notorious" include *Baltimore Patriot*, July 25, 1816; *New York Evening Post*, December 13, 1816; *Maryland Gazette and Political Intelligencer*, December 19, 1816; *Portsmouth* (New Hampshire) *Oracle*, January 24, 1817. This term was still used to describe her in the early twentieth century: "Ann was the most captivating beauty of the underworld and the most notorious character in the state." Frederic A. Godcharles, *Pennsylvania, Political Governmental, Military and Civil* (New York: American Historical Society, 1933), 272-282.

64. Approximately 20 percent of all criminal court defendants were women. In late eighteenth-century Pennsylvania, one-third of all women accused had committed crimes involving property. Theft was especially common in urban centers. In Philadelphia, between 1783 and 1789, 53 of 84 cases involving women were theft (other categories were assault and fornication). G. S. Rowe, "Women's Crime and Criminal Administration in Pennsylvania, 1763-1790," *Pennsylvania*

Magazine of History and Biography 109 (1985): 335–424; Allen Steinberg, *The Transformation of Criminal Justice, Philadelphia, 1800–1880* (Chapel Hill: University of North Carolina Press, 1989), 43.

65. The most notorious Pennsylvania female criminal preceding Carson, Rachel Wall, was executed in 1789 for assaulting a woman on the public highway and stealing her bonnet. She was convicted of a capital offense because she was a habitual offender, having committed several other robberies, though none of them as violent as her last crime. Cohen, *Pillars of Salt*, 121, 132.

66. Isabelle Lehu, *Carnival on the Page: Popular Print Media in Antebellum America* (Chapel Hill: University of North Carolina Press, 2000), 7.

67. Binns later claimed that his actions foiled the kidnapping: "The public will remember that these nefarious schemes were defeated in consequence of information being timely given, by the editor of this paper, to Governor Snyder which led to the arrest of Ann Carson and her fellow conspirators beyond Harrisburg, whither they had proceeded to carry their plan into complete effect." *Democratic Press*, July 9, 1823.

68. Binns's testimony was reported in the *Commercial Advertiser* (New York), August 21, 1816.

69. Sanford W. Higginbotham, *The Keystone in the Democratic Arch: Pennsylvania Politics, 1800–1816* (Harrisburg: Pennsylvania Historical and Museum Commission, 1952), 155.

70. Ibid., 306.

71. A *Washington City Weekly Gazette* article was reprinted in the *Columbian* (New York), July 15, 1816. The *True American* (a Federalist paper) was the source of much of the criticism. The *United States Gazette* and the *Lancaster Journal* were also Federalist. Higginbotham, 20.

72. The *Columbian*, July 23, 1816. Curious readers could decide for themselves by purchasing the transcripts of Smith's and Carson's trials. The *United States Gazette* advertised the first part of Smith's trial in early June. The second part, with Carson's trial, a diagram of the room, and an appendix, was available a month later. *United States Gazette*, June 11; 1816, July 18, 1816.

73. "*Justice* is said to be even handed; yet Governor Snyder has been in the practice of granting pardons very liberally—and some six months ago he granted one, where the conviction was for the same crime as Smith's.—So there is no sense in vaunting of Governor Snyder's magnanimity on *this* occasion." *Chronicle or Harrisburgh Visitor*, August 26, 1816. My thanks to Katherine Elizabeth Thompson of Bucknell University for finding Harrisburg newspaper material for me.

74. *Columbian*, July 23, 1816.

75. Here is the formal charge against Carson: "Charged on oath with having within the said city combined together and entered into a conspiracy for the purpose of obstructing the justice of the country and of releasing by fraud and force from prison Richard Smith then in confinement under sentence of death in the gaol of the city and county of Philadelphia and further to compel the Governor of the Commonwealth to grant the said Richard Smith a pardon by seizing his person and restraining him of his liberty, and further by seizing a grandchild of the

Governor and a child of John Binns and holding them in duress, etc." Prisoners for Trial Docket, January 1816–January 1818, Philadelphia City Archives.

76. "The inconvenience of procuring the attendance of witnesses, and some other causes of less importance, induced the prosecuting officers at Harrisburg to believe, that it would be most expedient to have the trial of these persons take place in this city." *New Jersey Journal*, September 17, 1816.

77. Andrew Shankman, *Crucible of American Democracy: The Struggle to Fuse Egalitarianism & Capitalism in Jeffersonian Pennsylvania* (Lawrence: University Press of Kansas, 2004).

78. *Northern Whig* (Hudson, New York) (reprint from the *Binghamton Phoenix*), September 17, 1816.

79. Philip Shriver Klein, *Pennsylvania Politics, 1817–1832: A Game Without Rules* (Philadelphia: Historical Society of Pennsylvania, 1940), 45.

80. The terms "Old School" and "New School" described the split within the Democratic Republican party. Old School Democrats were strongest in the east. New School Democrats were "westerners primarily, and Scotch-Irishmen although supported as well by farsighted eastern politicians and by an active German minority." Klein, *Pennsylvania Politics*, 48.

81. *Memoirs*, 1: 210.

82. *The Chronicle or Harrisburgh Visitor*, August 12, 1816. Hugh Hamilton, editor of the *Chronicle* was an "erstwhile Quid" and Old School Democrat. Higginbotham, *The Keystone in the Democratic Arch*, 315. John Binns, Irish by birth, had been imprisoned in Ireland for involvement in revolutionary activities. After his release in 1801, he emigrated to the United States.

83. Heister rewarded Elder for his political efforts by appointing him state attorney general in 1820. Klein, *Pennsylvania Politics*, 86.

84. Higginbotham, *The Keystone in the Democratic Arch*, 20.

85. Klein, *Pennsylvania Politics*, 218.

86. In 1812, Ingersoll's father, Jared, was nominated as the vice presidential candidate by the Old School Democrats. In 1814, he ran for senator on the Federalist ticket (he was defeated by Democrat Jonathan Roberts). The younger Ingersoll was later elected as an anti-Jacksonian candidate to the Twenty-fourth Congress (March 4, 1835–March 3, 1837). Higginbotham, *The Keystone in the Democratic Arch*, 263, 306.

87. Antes may have been Snyder's brother-in-law. Catherine Antes was Snyder's second wife (she died in 1810) and mother of two of his children.

88. *Democratic Press*, November 9, 1816.

89. Ibid., October 31, 1816; *New Jersey Journal*, November 12, 1816. The prosecution may also have subpoenaed Snyder.

90. *Memoirs*, 2: 5.

91. Brown studied medicine under Benjamin Rush, but when Rush died he turned to law, apprenticing with William Rawle. Brown "soon attracted attention, and took a leading place at the bar, especially in criminal practice. He was remarkable for forensic eloquence and his skill in the examination of witnesses. It is said that at one time he appeared in almost every criminal case of importance." Frank

M. Eastman, *Courts and Lawyers of Pennsylvania: A History, 1623–1923*, 2 vols. (New York: American Historical Society, 1822), 2; 481–82.

92. Allen Steinberg, *The Transformation of Criminal Justice, Philadelphia, 1800–1880* (Chapel Hill: University of North Carolina Press, 1989), 18–20. Robert Bell says, "The entertainment of the courtroom action continued to be one of few shows in town, and citizens filled the courts and were familiar with the styles and reputations of various lawyers." Robert R. Bell, *The Philadelphia Lawyer: A History, 1735–1945* (London: Associated University Presses, 1992), 96–97.

93. *Memoirs*, 2: 5. Carson's lawyers were also not above portraying their client in a less-than-flattering way if it suited their purpose. According to Carson, "My counsel had asserted that my mental faculties were deranged."

94. *Memoirs*, 2: 7.

95. *Democratic Press*, November 11, 1816.

96. Steinberg, *The Transformation of Criminal Justice*, 84–85.

97. *Memoirs*, 2: 6.

98. Ibid., 2: 6.

99. Ibid., 1: 122; Binns, *Recollections of the Life of John Binns* (Philadelphia: The Author, 1864), 276.

Chapter 4. Courting Notoriety

1. *The Memoirs of the Celebrated and Beautiful Mrs. Ann Carson, Daughter of an Officer of the U.S. Navy, and Wife of Another, Whose Life Terminated in the Philadelphia Prison*. Second Edition, revised, enlarged, and continued till her death, by Mrs. M. Clarke, Anthoress of the *Fair American, Life of Thomas L. Hamblin, Edwin Forrest*, &c. &c., in Two Volumes (Philadelphia, 1838), 1: 83.

2. *Memoirs*, 1: 93.

3. The quotation on the title page reads, "I will nought extenuate nor set down aught in malice." But the content of Carson's memoir is distinctly at odds with this pronouncement.

4. *The History of the Celebrated Mrs. Ann Carson, widow of the late unfortunate Lieutenant Richard Smith, with a circumstantial account of her conspiracy against the late Governor of Pennsylvania, Simon Snyder; and of her sufferings in the several prisons in that state, interspersed with anecdotes of characters now living. Written by Herself* (Philadelphia: Published by the author [Robert Desilver], 1822).

5. *Memoirs*, 1: 10. With no extant trial transcripts, newspaper accounts, published letters, or other detailed documents, information about Carson's life between her acquittal on conspiracy charges in 1816 and publication of her memoir in early 1823 comes almost exclusively from the *Memoirs*.

6. *Memoirs*, 1: 21. This may have been John Montgomery. He is listed as "councillor at law," in *Matchett's Baltimore Directory for 1827* (Baltimore: R. J. Machett, 1827), 189. Montgomery was the Maryland state attorney general in 1811, and in 1820 he became mayor of Baltimore. See Index of Office Holders in

Edward C. Papenfuse et al., *Archives of Maryland, Historical List*, new series, vol. 1 (Annapolis: Maryland State Archives, 1990).

7. Carson was chagrined that Meredith revealed who she was: "Let not the lords of creation accuse our sex of tattling, when they are so deficient in discretion." *Memoirs*, 1: 21.

8. *Memoirs*, 1: 36.

9. Ibide, 1: 40. Orphans' Court File, Orphans' Court Records, Philadelphia County. Microfilm, Historical Society of Pennsylvania. Books 27–29, 1818–1824, pp. 69–70.

10. *Memoirs*, 1: 44. Mitchell was described as "alias WALPOLE, from New York, about 5 feet 9 or 10 inches high, dark eyes, well known in New York and Baltimore." *Poulson's American Daily Advertiser*, October 12, 1820.

11. This account is taken from the *History* and Mann's notice in *Poulson's American Daily Advertiser*, October 12, 1820.

12. *Memoirs*, 1: 58.

13. The *Philadelphia Directory and Register for 1821* (Philadelphia: M'Carty & Davis, 204 Market Street, 1821) lists "Mary Carr, widow of John, teacher Arch W Sch. 2nd [between 21st and 22nd Street]." These same listings are in the 1819, 1820, and 1822 directories *Memoirs*, 2: 84, 89.

14. *Memoirs*, 2: 34.

15. Ibid., 2: 92.

16. The *Sun*'s and the *Herald*'s coverage of the Helen Jewett and Mary Rogers murder cases exemplified this type of journalism. Andie Tucher, *Froth and Scum: Truth, Beauty, Goodness, and the Ax Murder in America's First Mass Medium* (Chapel Hill: University of North Carolina Press, 1994); Patricia Cline Cohen, *The Murder of Helen Jewett: The Life and Death of a Prostitute in Nineteenth-Century New York* (New York: Knopf, 1998); and Amy Gilman Srebnick, *The Mysterious Death of Mary Rogers: Sex and Culture in Nineteenth-Century New York* (Oxford: Oxford University Press, 1995). For earlier criminal accounts, see Daniel E. Williams, "Rogues, Rascals, and Scoundrels: The Underworld Literature of Early America," *American Studies* 24, no. 2 (Fall 1983): 5–19.

Daniel Cohen observes that the relationship between legal authority and the popular press grew increasingly antagonistic during the eighteenth and nineteenth centuries, as crime literature gradually shifted from the "contrite confessions appended to execution sermons" published in the early 1700s to criminal biographies and crime narratives alleging miscarriages of justice after 1800. According to Cohen, the shift reflected "a number of cultural insurgencies"—including sentimentalism—that challenged traditional authority after the Revolution. Cohen, *Pillars of Salt, Monuments of Grace: New England Crime Literature and the Origins of American Popular Culture, 1674–1860* (New York: Oxford University Press, 1993), 25.

17. One of the earliest of these American confessions is *The Vain Prodigal Life, and Tragical Penitent Death of Thomas Hellier* (London: Printed for Sam. Crouch, 1680). Hellier, a Virginia indentured servant, murdered his master and mistress.

18. *Memoirs of Stephen Burroughs* (Hanover, N.H., 1798; Boston, 1804; Philadelphia, 1812). Cohen, *Pillars of Salt*, 158–59; Daniel E. Williams, "In Defense

of Self: Author and Authority in the Memoirs of Stephen Burroughs," *Early American Literature* 25, no. 2 (1990), 96–122.

19. Cathy Davidson claims that almost half of the sentimental novels written in America before 1820 use the motif of protagonist who loves one man but is ordered by her father to marry another. Davidson, *Revolution and the Word: The Rise of the Novel in America* (New York: Oxford University Press, 1986).

20. See Rodney Hessinger, *Seduced, Abandoned, and Reborn: Visions of Youth in Middle-Class America, 1780–1850* (Philadelphia: University of Pennsylvania Press, 2005), chap. 1. Daniel Cohen has noted that early American sentimental fiction is much like modern "docudrama": *Pillars of Salt, Monuments of Grace*, 168.

21. *Memoirs*, 1: ix.

22. Murray argued for greater equality and independence for women in their private and public lives. Murray is best known for promoting these ideas in her *Gleaner* essays, published serially in Boston, and then published collectively, along with *The Traveller Returned* and another play, in 1798.

For a discussion of postrevolutionary prospects for American women in both their personal and public relationships, see Linda K. Kerber, "The Paradox of Women's Citizenship in the Early Republic," *American Historical Review* 97 (1992): 349–55.

Barbara Welter first described the new definition of gender roles that developed in the early nineteenth century, know as separate spheres ideology, in Welter, "The Cult of True Womanhood: 1820–1860," *American Quarterly* 18 (1966): 151–74. Also see Nancy F. Cott, *The Bonds of Womanhood: "Woman's Sphere" in New England, 1780–1835* (New Haven, Conn.: Yale University Press, 1977). For recent thoughts on how historians should move beyond this conceptual framework, see Linda Kerber et al., "Beyond Roles, Beyond Spheres: Thinking About Gender in the Early Republic," *William and Mary Quarterly* 3 (1989): 565–85.

23. Rosemarie Zagarri, "The Rights of Man and Woman in Post-Revolutionary America," *William and Mary Quarterly*, April 1998; Mary Ryan, *Women in Public: Between Banners and Ballots, 1825–1880* (Baltimore: Johns Hopkins University Press, 1990).

24. *Memoirs*, 1: 20. See Jay Fliegelman, *Prodigals and Pilgrims: The American Revolution Against Patriarchal Authority, 1750–1800* (Cambridge: Cambridge University Press, 1982); Linda K. Kerber, *Women of the Republic: Intellect and Ideology in Revolutionary America* (Chapel Hill: Published for the Institute of Early American History and culture by the University of North Carolina Press, 1980).

25. *Memoirs*, 1: 33–34. For a discussion of the affective family and companionate marriage in the early nineteenth century, see Anya Jabour, *Marriage in the Early Republic: Elizabeth and William Wirt and the Companionate Ideal* (Baltimore: Johns Hopkins University Press, 1998).

26. *Memoirs*, 1: 93.

27. Ibid., 1: 59.

28. Ibid., 1: 59.

29. Ibid., 1: 59.

30. Ibid., 1: 49. Ann Carson's understanding of marriage may have been influenced by changes in society's perspective on marriage. "Marital unions were

increasingly defined as private compacts with public ramifications rather than social institutions with roles and duties fixed by the place of the family in a hierarchical social order." Michael Grossberg, *Governing the Hearth: Law and the Family in Nineteenth-Century America* (Chapel Hill: University of North Carolina Press, 1985), 20.

    31. *Memoirs*, 1: 127.
    32. Ibid., 1:136, 142.
    33. Ibid., 1:142.
    34. Ibid., 1:143–44.
    35. Ibid., 1:144.
    36. Ibid., 1:144.
    37. Ibid., 1:145.
    38. Ibid., 1:112.
    39. Ibid., 1:146.

    40. Ibid., 1: 77. Carson's sentiments are suspiciously similar to those expressed by Constantia Dudley in Charles Brockden Brown's *Ormond* (1799), who Brown says was, "mistress of the product of her own labor." Dudley, like Carson, articulates ideals of independence, intelligence, and self-reliance for women. Ernest Earnest, *The American Eve in Fact and Fiction, 1775–1914* (Urbana: University of Illinois Press, 1974), 32–33; Steven Watts, *The Romance of Real Life: Charles Brockden Brown and the Origins of American Culture* (Baltimore: Johns Hopkins University Press, 1994), 89–100.

    41. One mode of social organization may be of more use than another depending on the time, place, and circumstances under investigation. The attributes associated with the middle class were not confined to the group of people who can be defined as such merely through either their wealth or their relationship to a means of production. As John Seed has said, "The specificity of context is crucial; which middle class, in what particular local or regional economy, shaped by what kinds of relations to other social classes, at what specific historical moment? Class, then, is not a matter only of this or that aspect of a group—size of income, type of occupation, life-style or whatever—but a shifting totality of social relations." John Seed, "From 'Middling Sort' to Middle Class in Late Eighteenth- and Early Nineteenth-Century England," in *Social Orders and Social Classes in Europe since 1500: Studies in Social Stratification*, ed. M. L. Bush, (London: Longman, 1992), 125.

    Burton J. Bledstein confirms these different paths to class identity: "One could enter the middle class piecemeal, through discriminating practices: in family activities, child-rearing procedures, gender relations, techniques of worship, work habits, labor relations, education and health methods, recreation routines, and personal as well as domestic consumption patterns." Burton J. Bledstein and Robert D. Johnson, eds., *The Middling Sorts: Explorations in the History of the American Middle Class* (New York: Routledge, 2001), 9.

    42. The term "middling interest" was in use (and in print) both as a political identification and as a social one by the 1820s. Lydia Maria Child believed the audience for her books was the "middling class." Preface to *The Mother's Book* (1831). Historians disagree about the timing of middle-class formation as well as the definition of this class. I am not concerned so much with its origins as with

identifying it in a time and place in which people began to consciously use the term "middling sorts" or "middling interests," and to identify them as such. Konstantin Dierks's essay, "Epistolary Culture and Middle-Class Formation in Eighteenth-Century Anglo-America," addresses the eighteenth-century development of this self-identification. Simon Middleton and Billy G. Smith, ed., *Class Matters: Early North America and the Atlantic World* (Philadelphia: University of Pennsylvania Press, 2008), 162–177.

43. *Memoirs*, 1: 19.

44. Ibid., 1: 89–90. Sean Wilentz, *Chants Democratic: New York City and the Rise of the American Working Class, 1788–1850* (New York: Oxford University Press, 1984); Gary J. Kornblith, "From Artisans to Businessmen: Master Mechanics in New England, 1789–1850" (Ph.D. dissertation., Princeton University, 1983); Lisa Lubow, "Artisans in Transition: Early Capitalist Development and the Carpenters of Boston, 1787–1837" (Ph.D. dissertation, University of California, Los Angeles, 1987).

45. Ann Carson to Stephen Girard, September 24, 1811. Girard Papers, Series 2, Reel 49, no 392, American Philosophical Society. Her imprisonment for debt was revealed during Richard Smith's murder trial in 1816. *The Trials of Richard Smith . . . as Princpal, and Ann Carson, alias Ann Smith, as accessory, for the Murder of Captain John Carson* (Philadelphia: Thomas Desilver, 1816), 44.

46. *Memoirs*, 2: 33.

47. Ibid., 1: 87. This notion harkens back to the idea of the eighteenth-century "competency"—the goal being to secure financial security rather than merely acquire wealth. See Susan Branson, "Women and the Family Economy in the Early Republic: The Case of Elizabeth Meredith," *Journal of the Early Republic* 16 (Spring 1996): 47–71.

48. *Memoirs*, 1: 185, 2:34.

49. Ibid., 2: 60. Steinberg points out that many aldermen and judges were "members of an emerging 'new' middle class, and many had backgrounds as workers." Allen Steinberg, *The Transformation of Criminal Justice, Philadelphia, 1800–1880* (Chapel Hill: University of North Carolina Press, 1989), 39.

50. Memoirs, 1: 180. Carson's dislike of these working-class men, of course, was intimately bound up with her trials. She not only found mechanics and tradesmen to be "ignorant, mean, and selfish" but also dangerous: "when invested with power, [they are] arbitrary, cruel, and vindictive." *Memoirs*, 1: 30.

51. *Memoirs*, 1: 215; 2: 33.

52. Ibid., 2: 11. The class origin of Carson's compatriots is not as unlikely as it might seem. They would have needed a certain level of education as well as skill to carry out counterfeiting and other illegal activities. Daniel A. Cohen has noted that members of flash gangs in Massachusetts also came from comfortable backgrounds. Cohen, "A Fellowship of Thieves: Property Criminals in Eighteenth-Century Massachusetts," *Journal of Social History* 22 (1988): 70.

53. "In the cities of early industrial America, the personal appearance of a stranger did not offer reliable clues to his identity." This was due in part to the Industrial Revolution, which had enabled "rising classes to imitate the dress and conduct of the older elites." Karen Halttunen, *Confidence Men and Painted Women: A*

Study of Middle-Class Culture in America (New Haven, Conn.: Yale University Press, 1982), 37; Claudia B. Kidwell and Margaret C. Christman, *Suiting Everyone: The Democratization of Clothing in America* (Washington, D.C.: Smithsonian Institution, 1974). See also Richard L. Bushman, *The Refinement of America: Persons, Houses, Cities* (New York: Knopf, 1993) for a discussion of the sharp line the middle class drew to separate themselves from the lower classes. The diffusion of gentility confused the issue of class because more people could afford the outward semblance of it.

54. C. Dallett Hemphill, *Bowing to Necessities: A History of manners in America, 1620–1860* (New York: Oxford University Press, 1999), 130–31. This behavior accompanied dress and consumption (both material and cultural). Concern with social and class distinctions burgeoned in the 1820s. Hemphill notes the growth in the number of conduct books offered for sale in the United States. Ninety percent of these new works were directed at (and written by) middle-class Americans. Hemphill, *Bowing to Necessity*, 131. Carson compared Madison rather unfavorably to herself: "I discovered that fame had, as usual, been very far from the truth, as Mrs. Madison is not so tall, much thicker, and inclining to *em bon point.*" *Memoirs*, 2: 26.

55. *Memoirs*, 2: 65, 66.

56. Black women, according to Carson, made up "a large majority in our female republic." Ibid., 2: 68.

57. *Memoirs*, 1: 177.

58. Ibid., 2: 67. Carson was also given a knife and fork.

59. *Memoirs*, 2: 68. She mentions this again a few pages later: "The cell was then filled with negroes, whose odour, added to the effluvia from the common sewer, formed a complication of stenches sufficient to create infectious and malignant distempers." *Memoirs*, 2: 71.

60. *Memoirs*, 1: 229.

61. Ibid., 1: 194. Carson also writes off a whole section of South Jersey: "That part of Jersey [around Burlington] was strongly prejudiced against me, being generally ignorant, consequently inquisitive, weak, credulous people." *Memoirs*, 1: 184.

62. *Memoirs*, 1: 205.

63. It is unclear if Carson succeeded in either of these ambitions. Mary Clarke recounted that "fifty copies were disposed of in a day for several days in succession" after it went on sale. She also claimed that "it was written for by the President, vice President, Gov. of Pennsylvania, and a great number of members of Congress, of both houses." *Memoirs*, 2: 103. However, under the terms of their contract with the printer, Carson and Clarke had to wait until his portion of the books was sold before they could make any profit. *Memoirs*, 2: 104.

64. *Democratic Press*, January 25, 1823.

65. Carson's sister Eliza was engaged to be married to the *Pickering*'s commander, Captain Hillyard. *Memoirs*, 1: 30.

66. Jeffrey M. Dorwart, with Jean K. Wolf, *The Philadelphia Navy Yard from the Birth of the U.S. Navy to the Nuclear Age* (Philadelphia: University of Pennsylvania Press, 2001), 30.

67. It was also Mrs. Hutton's wish that her son marry Ann. She went so far as to attempt to persuade the Bakers not to allow Ann to marry John Carson. *Memoirs*, 1: 38.

68. *Memoirs*, 1: 46.

69. Ibid., 1: 75.

70. Ibid., 1: 73.

71. Ibid., 1: 73.

72. Ibid., 1: 84. Carson's store is listed for the first time in the 1811 city directory at 184 South Second Street. The next listing is 1814, when the shop is in Thomas Baker's name at the Southwest corner of Dock and Second streets.

73. *Memoirs*, 1: 87.

74. Ibid., 1: 85. A Ciscebo is the declared lover of a married woman.

75. *Memoirs*, 1: 98.

76. Ibid., 1: 98.

77. Ibid., 1: 112–13.

78. This may have been Isaac Hull. See *List of Officers of the Navy of the United States and of the Marine Corps, from 1775 to 1900*, ed. Edward W. Callahan (New York: Haskell House, 1969), 282.

79. *Memoirs*, 1: 123.

80. Ibid., 1: 131.

81. Ibid., 1: 133.

82. Ibid., 2: 38.

83. Ibid., 2: 47.

84. Ibid., 2: 12–13.

85. Ibid., 2: 38.

86. Ibid., 1: xi.

87. A healthy market existed for sexually explicit books in the early republic—many of them, like Edward Ward's *Female Policy Detected; or, The Arts of a Designing Woman Laid Open* (Philadelphia, Printed for D. Hogan, 1807), were reprints of books that were over one hundred years old. See Clare A. Lyons, *Sex Among the Rabble: An Intimate History of Gender and Power in the Age of Revolution, Philadelphia, 1730–1830* (Chapel Hill: University of North Carolina Press, 2006), 298–99.

88. *Memoirs*, 2: 103.

Chapter 5. An Unsuitable Job for a Woman

1. *A Compendious Trial of the Rev. William Hogan* (Philadelphia: 1822). See Kathleen Kennedy, "A Charge Never Easily Made: The Meaning of Respectability and Women's Work in the Trial of the Reverend William Hogan, 1822," *American Nineteenth Century History* 7, no. 1 (March 2006): 29–62.

2. *Letter to Henry, Bishop of Philadelphia* [by a lady], (Philadelphia: Printed for the author, 1821). The difference of opinion between Hogan and Philadelphia's bishop became known as the "Hogan Schism." Francis E. Tourscher, *The Hogan Schism and Trustee Troubles in St. Mary's Church Philadelphia, 1820–1829*

(Philadelphia: Peter Reilly Company, 1930). Dale Light, *Rome and the New Republic: Conflict and Community in Philadelphia Catholicism Between the Revolution and the Civil War* (Notre Dame, Ind.: University of Notre Dame Press, 1996). Another pamphlet might also be by Clarke: *A Summary of the Persecutions of the Rev. William Hogan, from Bishop Conwell, by an Episcopalian* (1822).

3. "Ha, ha, ha, said Mr. D. did not you sell one thousand copies of Hogan's trial and clear a thousand dollars by it, while I sunk money on my edition?" *Memoirs*, 2: 109. Desilver published a transcript written by Joseph A. Dowling, *The trial of the Rev. William Hogan: Pastor of St. Mary's Church, for an assault and battery on Mary Connell; tried before the Mayor's court in and for the city of Philadelphia* (Philadelphia: R. Desilver, 1822).

4. Isabelle Lehu, *Carnival on the Page: Popular Print Media in Antebellum America* (Chapel Hill: University of North Carolina Press, 2000), 7.

5. Her husband (presumably Mr. Carr) died sometime in 1816. No information is available on the Carr family to confirm this. Whether Clarke remarried afterward is not certain. She was not married in 1822 when Ann Carson lived with her. She does not mention a second husband in any of her writings. Apparently her name change confused people, including the mayor of Philadelphia. In 1823, he referred to her as Mrs. Carr. She corrected him: "'Mr. W,' replied I, 'my name is not Carr but Clarke, and there are persons here who may report I go by two names, as you know.'" *The Memoirs of the Celebrated and Beautiful Mrs. Ann Carson, Daughter of an officer of the U.S. Navy, and Wife of Another, whose life Terminator in the Philadelphia prison*. Second Edition, revised, enlarged, and continued till her death, by Mrs. M. Clarke, Authoress of the *Fair American, Life of Thomas L. Hamblin, Edwin Forrest*, &c. &c., in two volumes, (Philadelphia, 1838) 165.

6. In her preface to volume 2 of the *Tea Tray*, Clarke says that she was living in New York City prior to starting the magazine.

7. *Sarah Maria Cornell, or, The Fall River Murder, a Domestic Drama in Three Acts* (New York, 1833) "By Mrs. M. Clarke, authoress of the Fair Americans, Benevolent Lawyers, &c."

8. *New-York Mirror, A Weekly Journal Devoted to Literature and the Fine Arts*, September 21, 1833, 40, no. 12.

9. *New-York Mirror*, October 19, 1833, 40, no. 16. Quoted in George C. D. Odell, *Annals of the New York Stage* (New York: Columbia University Press), vol. 3, 688–89.

10. Catherine Williams was divorced and forty-six years old when she began her writing career to support herself. David R. Kasserman, *Fall River Outrage: Life, Murder, and Justice in Early Industrial New England* (Philadelphia: University of Pennsylvania Press, 1986), 119. Patricia Caldwell, ed., *Fall River: An Authentic Narrative* (New York: Oxford University Press, 1993.)

11. Caldwell, *Fall River*, 127. In the appendix, Williams describes her personal experience of a camp meeting in Connecticut.

12. Williams blamed Cornell's religious practices and "idolatrous regard for ministers, for preachers of the gospel, which at the present day is a scandal to the cause of Christianity." Caldwell, *Fall River*, 4.

13. Frances Trollope, *Domestic Manners of the Americans* (1832; repr. Richard Mullen, Oxford: Oxford University Press, 1984), 143.

14. Clarke, *Sarah Maria Cornell*, 47. Clarke signed her name to the published version of the play, but she did not mention this play on the title page of her subsequent writings.

15. It was advertised as "a new comick [*sic*] piece, written by a lady of this city." *United States Gazette*, January 5 and January 6, 1815. Clarke may have changed the title and published it as *The Fair Americans*. See Amelia Howe Kritzer's introduction to The *Fair Americans* in *Plays by Early American Women, 1775–1850* (Ann Arbor: University of Michigan Press, 1995), 16.

16. *Lake Champlain* was published in *Tea Tray* 3, nos. 2 and 3 (January 13, and January 20, 1816). *Venture It* was published in *Tea Tray* 3, nos. 11–21 (March–April 1816).

17. If she did so when Forrest was a boy, this would not have been before about 1812. Clarke never mentions the name of this theater. One possibility is the Apollo Street Theater. "In 1811 a small house on Apollo Street, between South and Shippen Streets, was fitted up and opened as the Apollo Street Theatre, but the venture proved a failure, and the theatre soon closed its doors." M. Antonia Lynch, *The Old District of Southwark in the County of Philadelphia* (Philadelphia: Printed for the City History Society, 1909), 110.

18. *The History of Edwin Forrest, The celebrated American Tragedian, from his Childhood to His present elevated station as a performer. Written by an individual who has known him from his boyhood* (New York: Printed and published for the author, 1837), 7. Philadelphia City Archives, Common Please Court, Insolvency petitions. The list of subscribers, to the *Intellectual Regale, or Ladies' Tea Tray*, is bound at the back of volume 2.

19. Richard Moody, *Edwin Forrest: First Star of the American Stage* (New Year: Alfred A. Knopf, 1960).

20. Clarke did not name the book, but it is probably *The Biography of Edwin Forrest: The Distinguished American Tragedian* (Philadelphia: Turner & Fisher, 1835). The author is listed as "E.T.W."

21. Clarke met with William Forrest sometime before his death in 1833. She recalled "after a separation of seven years, we met frequently in the green room of the Chatham Street Theater, where we conversed confidentially of that early period in Edwin's debut; and, from him, I learned many of the facts here related as well as others from travelers who accompanied them on their western circuit." *The History of Edwin Forrest*, 24.

22. *The History of Edwin Forrest*, 5.

23. *The History of Edwin Forrest*, 11. This would have been 1826, after Forrest returned from touring. He performed (playing Othello) at the new Bowery Theater in November 1826. Clarke did not mention where her favorable notice of Forrest appeared, but it may have been in the *New-York Mirror*. Most theater reviews were unsigned. Clarke also claimed to have helped settle a salary dispute for Forrest. In 1831, he sued the manager of the Chestnut Street Theater, Mr. Lamb, for his $200 nightly salary. Clarke says she was "the confidential person who proposed the terms of suspension to Mr. Lamb." *The History of Edwin Forrest*, 12.

24. *The History of Edwin Forrest*, 10.
25. Trollope, *Domestic Manners*, 300. Trollope visited New York City from April to May 1831.
26. Faye E. Dudden, *Women in the American Theater: Actresses and Audiences, 1790–1870* (New Haven, Conn.: Yale University Press, 1994), 24.
27. Soliciting in a theater was not a crime. Rosemarie K. Bank, *Theater Culture in America, 1825–1860* (Cambridge: Cambridge University Press, 1997), 135.
28. David Grimstead, *Melodrama Unveiled: American Theater and Culture, 1800–1850* (Chicago: University of Chicago Press, 1968), 56. Rosemarie K. Bank disputes Grimstead's claim that theaters had this class-based identity. See Bank, *Theater Culture in America*.
29. Dudden, *Women in the American Theater*, 45.
30. Ibid., 28. Another actress with literary aspirations was Charlotte Cushman. She wrote a short story, "The Actress," for *Godey's Lady's Book* (February 1837). Kemble was part of the star system that arose in the American theater in the first quarter of the nineteenth century. Traditionally, theater companies relied on stock players to entertain audiences. Beginning in the 1810s, managers began promoting specific talents and importing them from Britain. Kemble was one of these imports.
31. Bank, *Theater Culture in America*, 136; Timothy J. Gilfoyle, *City of Eros: New York City, Prostitution, and the Commercialization of Sex, 1790–1920* (New York: Norton, 1992), 31. Claudia D. Johnson, *American Actress: Perspective on the Nineteenth Century* (Chicago: Nelson-Hall, 1984), 3–35.
32. Joe Cowell, *Thirty Years Passed Among the Players in England and America*, 2 vols. (New York: Harper & Bros., 1844). Quoted in Bank, *Theater Culture in America*, 137. Claudia Johnson, "That Guilty Third Tier: Prostitution in Nineteenth-Century American Theater," *American Quarterly* 27, no. 5 (December 1975): 575–84.
33. William Dunlap's novel of theatrical life, *Memoirs of a Water Drinker*, depicts this unsavory aspect of the theater: a nonactress who frequents backstage is pursued and almost sexually molested by a man who assumes she is available.
34. Clarke advertised the Hamblin biography in the Forrest biography "like Mr. Hamblin [Forrest] traded in talent; though not like him altogether, as Mr. Forrest scorned to speculate on females as Mr. H did. (But more of this is in another work that will appear soon.)" Clarke, *The History of Edwin Forrest*, 13.
35. *A Concise History of the Life and Amours of Thomas S. Hamblin, Late Manager of the Bowery Theatre. As communicated by his legal wife, Mrs. Elizabeth Hamblin, to Mrs. M. Clarke* (Philadelphia, 1838), 3. Clarke refers to Medina's article "Our Actors" in *The Ladies' Companion, a Monthly Magazine; Devoted to Literature and the Arts* (June 1837): 95.
36. *A Concise History*, 32.
37. Ibid., 8. An article by "Oily Attree," which appeared in the *Sunday Flash*, suggested that Gallagher was the mother of Hamblin's daughter, Missouri Miller. *Sunday Flash*, September 19, 1841. Cited in Patricia Cline Cohen, *The Murder of Helen Jewett* (New York: Random House, 1998), 459, n. 7.
38. *A Concise History*, 15. The Stanford University Library copy of *A Concise History* has "This is a damnd lie" handwritten in the margin next to this claim on page 25.

39. *A Concise History*, 22.
40. Dudden, *Women in the American Theater*, 61.
41. Ibid., 59.
42. *A Concise History*, 8.
43. Ibid., 21.
44. Ibid., 20–21.
45. Ibid., 18.
46. Ibid., 15.
47. *New York Sun*, April 2, 1834. Quoted in Bank, *Theater Culture in America*, 135.
48. Cohen, *The Murder of Helen Jewett*, 78.
49. Ibid, 251.
50. Ibid., 249.
51. Ibid., 37.
52. *Spirit of the Times*, June 23, 1838. Medina died shortly afterward, in November 1838. questions were raised about her death as well. Dudden, *Women in the American Theater*, 70. *Attack on Thomas S. Hamblin, following the death of actress Louisa Missouri in 1838*, American Antiquarian Society.
53. Bank, *Theater Culture in America*, 116.
54. Ibid., 156. New York City mayor Philip Hone's account of the riot is in his published diary, *The Diary of Philip Hone, 1828–1851*, ed. Bayard Tuckerman (New York: Dodd, Mead, 1910).
55. *A Concise History*, 19.
56. Ibid., 19–20.
57. Several other women were writing at the same time as Mary Clarke, including Sarah Pogson, *The Female Enthusiast* (1807); and Frances Wright, *Altorf* (1819). Charlotte Barnes (b. 1818), the daughter of actors at the Park Theater, performed in her own plays as well as in others (including the lead in *Hamlet*). Her best-known play, *Octavia Bragaldi*, debuted at the Park Theater on November 8, 1837. Kritzer, *Plays by Early American Women*, 19–24.
58. *A Concise History*, 35–36.
59. The *Spirit of the Times* praised Medina's talent in its notice of the debut of her play, *Earnest Maltravers*: "A new drama from the pen of his [Hamblin's] accomplished lady, Louisa Medina Hamblin, and said to be one of her best efforts in a line wherein she has already been preeminently successful." *Spirit of the Times*, March 17, 1838. *Earnest Maltravers* was also Missouri Miller's debut performance.
60. *A Concise History*, 4.
61. Ibid., 4.

Chapter 6. Betrayal and Revenge

1. *The Memoirs of the Celebrated and Beautiful Mrs. Ann Carson, Daughter of an Officer of the U.S. Navy, and Wife of Another, Whose Life Terminated in the Philadelphia Prison*, second edition, revised, enlarged, and continued till her death, by Mrs. M. Clarke, authoress of The *Fair American, Life of Thomas L.*

Hamblin, Edwin Forrest, &c. &c., in Two Volumes (Philadelphia, 1838). In the preface, dated November 28, 1838, Clarke says she is living in New York City.

2. Convict Docket 1819–1824, p. 101, Philadelphia City Archives; *Memoirs*, 2: 79. My reconstruction of Carson's activities after 1820 is taken from newspaper accounts, trial and convict dockets, and the *Memoirs*.

3. One of Clarke's two pamphlets is *Letter to Henry, Bishop of Philadelphia. By a Lady* (Philadelphia: Printed for the author, 1821). The other pamphlet, which Clarke says is titled *The Cause of the Catholics*, has not been located. Butler was probably also selling her trial transcript at this time. Hogan's trial for assaulting his servant concluded in early April 1822. Clarke would have issued the transcript as soon afterward as possible. *A Compendious Trial of the Rev. William Hogan, Pastor of the Roman Catholic Church of St. Mary's, on an Indictment for an Assault and Battery, on the Person of Mary Connell. By a Listener* (Philadelphia, 1822).

4. *Memoirs*, 2: 83.

5. Ibid., 2: 93.

6. Carson went to live with Clarke on July 3, 1822, at 1 Bryan's Court. 2: 84.

7. Clarke remarked that her son was small enough to sit on Carson's knee. If Clarke's husband died in 1816, this boy could have been as young as 6 in 1822. Clarke also had at least two daughters, who lived with her mother in another part of the city. Memoirs, 2: 103.

8. Joseph's guardian (Adam Henchman) had stopped paying for his board. Memoirs, 2: 92; Orphans' Court Records, Philadelphia County, Books 27–29, 1818–1824, 69. Carson's oldest son, John, was 20 in 1822. Carson told Clarke that John worked in a countinghouse "somewhere south." Her son William (about eighteen) was apprenticed to a cabinetmaker somewhere in the city. Carson also had a daughter, Jeannette, who Clarke does not mention in the *Memoirs*. Jeannette may have been with Jane Baker, who had moved to Pensacola, Florida, sometime after Thomas Baker died in 1820. Jeannette is described at Smith's trial as the youngest child. If she was conceived before John Carson left in 1812, then she was at least ten years old in 1822.

9. Clarke may have had Carson make a fair copy of the manuscript: the copy the printer worked from was in Carson's handwriting. Clarke commented on the trouble the printer had with typesetting because Carson was such a poor speller. *Memoirs*, 2: 92.

10. Clarke told her readers that Desilver was also a Freemason and therefore duty-bound to "succour the distressed and oppressed." Ibid., 2: 94.

11. The *Lancaster Journal* advertised the book in late October. The ad was reprinted in the *Baltimore Patriot*, October 31, 1822: "In press, and will immediately be published the life of the celebrated Mrs. Ann Carson, and widow of the late unfortunate Lieutenant Richard Smyth, with anecdotes of various persons now living, and a circumstantial account of the conspiracy against the late Governor, Simon Snyder, and her sufferings in the different prisons of Pennsylvania, written by herself."

12. *Memoirs*, 2: 97. According to Clarke, two of Carson's enemies, one an unnamed lawyer and the other "TB" (Thomas Bradford—see *Memoirs*, xii), threatened to prosecute Desilver for libel. *Memoirs*, 2: 97–98.

13. That Clarke only published her lawyer's names by initials is an indication of her libel worries, even in 1838. Memoirs, 2: 102.

14. *Memoirs*, 2: 102.

15. Ibid., 2: 95.

16. Ibid., 2: 97.

17. *Democratic Press*, January 25, 1823. Despite his outrage, Binns printed an unnamed bookshop's advertisement for the book the same day as his review. "Book Shop, 121 S. 5th Street 6th door above Spruce St." And he printed Desilver's advertisement three days later.

18. *Memoirs*, 2: 104.

19. Ibid., 2: 108. Clarke's rented house was on Chestnut Street "2nd door above Schuylkill." *Memoirs*, 2: 139.

20. New York City was a key distribution center for counterfeit money in the United States. The money was printed in Canada, in the township of Durham, where manufacturers clustered along a road called "Cogniac Street." In New York, a handful of families specialized in both the wholesale and retail end of the process, selling money to "shovers" such as Ferras. Stephen Mihm," Making Money, Creating Confidence: Counterfeiting and Capitalism in the United States, 1789–1877" (Ph.D. dissertation, New York University, 2003), 79, 130–31.

21. *Memoirs*, 2: 106.

22. She also left Clarke's plays with a Mr. Wurden. Ibid., 2: 106.

23. *Memoirs*, 2: 107.

24. Ibid., 2: 113.

25. Ibid., 2: 111.

26. Ibid., 2: 111.

27. Ibid., 2: 110.

28. Ibid., 2: 108–9. "But counterfeits on banks with a good reputation could sometimes pass even if the person receiving it suspected a counterfeit. After all, as one person later recalled, 'it was a popular remark among men of business . . . that they preferred a good counterfeit on a solid bank to any genuine bill upon the "shyster" institution.'" Mihm, "Making Money," 152–54. This uncertainty among tradesmen as to the authenticity of a banknote is not surprising given the large number of banks in this era that circulated their own notes. By 1819, 341 banks printed their own notes. With several denominations for each bank, as many as seventeen hundred different kinds of notes were circulating in the United States. Mihm, "Making Money," p. 153, n. 38.

29. Ibid., 2:109. Clarke was resigned to parting ways with Carson, despite her affection for her. She told Desilver, "What an ill-fated, unfortunate woman she is; I am afraid there is a dark destiny suspended over her." Ibid., 2: 110.

30. Ibid., 2: 115–16.

31. Ibid., 2: 113–14.

32. Ibid., 2: 21.

33. Ibid., 2: 133. It is puzzling that Clarke did not sue Carson for loss of earnings on the *History*.

34. *Memoirs*, 2: 133–34.

35. Ibid., 2: 134.

36. Mark Kurlansky, *The Big Oyster: History on the Half Shell* (New York: Ballantine, 2006): 159.

37. Mihm, "Making Money," 127–28. "Shoving the queer" was slang for passing a counterfeit note. Charles Sutton, *The New York Tombs: Its Secrets and Its Mysteries* (New York: United States Publishing Company, 1874), 597. Cited in Mihm, "Making Money," 127, n. 2.

38. *Memoirs*, 2: 134. A barouche was a four-wheel open carriage with a collapsing hood. Jane Austen readers will recall that Mrs. Elton, in *Emma*, brags of her wealthy brother's barouche-landau. "My brother and sister have promised us a visit in the spring, or summer at farthest," continued Mrs. Elton; "and that will be our time for exploring. While they are with us, we shall explore a great deal, I dare say. They will have their barouche-landau, of course, which holds four perfectly." *Emma* (1816), chap. 32.

39. *Memoirs*, 2: 135. One of Carson's shovers was Kitty O'Brien. O'Brien was the wife of Charles Mitchell, who gave Carson the banknote from the Mann robbery.

40. *Memoirs*, 2: 136–37.

41. Ibid., 2: 139–40. Clarke went back to the New York Mail stage office on Third Street and got Carson's money ($3.50) refunded for the part of the New York journey she did not take (from Trenton to Manhattan). Clarke says she bought Carson, by now in prison, "several necessities" with the money.

42. McLean had monetary incentive for his resourcefulness. The reward for capturing Carson was $40 and "all expenses paid." Ibid., 2: 140.

43. *Memoirs*, 2: 141.

44. Ibid., 2: 144.

45. Alderman (and newspaper editor) William Duane wrote the extradition letter McLean carried with him. Duane's letter urges haste: "Be so good as to send me the requisite requisition [*sic*] as soon as possible, as an effort is made to get Ann Carson released from the prison in Trenton, in which she is confined." June 9, 1823. Pennsylvania State Archives, Records of Department of State Record Group 26, File September 1821–December 1827, Box no. 3. See also Gertrude MacKinney, ed., Executive Minutes of Governor Joseph Heister, *Pennsylvania Archives*, ninth series, vol. 8 (1822–Oct. 24, 1826), (1934), 5944–45.

46. *Baltimore Patriot*, June 14, 1823.

47. Ibid., June 17, 1823—reporting from Trenton *True American*.

48. *City Gazette and Commerical Daily Advertiser* (Charleston, South Carolina), June 23, 1823.

49. *Democratic Press* (reprint from *Freeman's Journal*), June 16, 1823.

50. *Democratic Press*, June 7 and June 9, 1823.

51. Ibid., June 19, 1823.

52. Details of the conspiracy and testimony from the hearing at the mayor's court come from Binns's transcript in the *Democratic Press*, June 20, 1823.

53. "Charged on oath of Sarah H. Willis with having entered into a combination and conspiracy to pass and utter false forged and counterfeited notes purporting to be good and genuine notes of sundry incorporated Banks as well as those of Steven Gerard's [*sic*] Bank they well knowing they were forged and

counterfeited." Prisoners for Trial Docket (September 1822–December 1824), Philadelphia City Archives, 255.

"Charged on oath of James Brady with having passed to James Brady and Hugh Brady trading under the firm of J & H Brady for a valuable consideration . . . note purporting to be a good and genuine note of the Bank of Stephen Gerard [*sic*] for five dollars she well knowing at the same time it was forged and counterfeited." Prisoners for Trial Docket (September 1822–December 1824), Philadelphia City Archives, 256.

54. The grand jury and petit jury members are listed in Mary Clarke's anonymously authored *Mrs. Carson's Last Adventure: The trial by jury at the Mayor's Court of Philadelphia, held July 2, 1823, of Ann Carson, Sarah Maland, Sarah Willis, alias Kelly, alias Whiticar, alias Hewes, of Cape May, New Jersey, William Butler, & Dr. Loring, for passing counterfeit notes on Girard's Bank, value five dollars, for which they were all convicted: also, the trial of Elizabeth Shepperd, Jeremiah Moore and William Schaffer, for a conspiracy to pass them* (Philadelphia, 1823).

55. *Memoirs*, 2: 158.
56. Ibid.
57. Ibid., 2: 159.
58. Ibid., 2: 161.
59. Ibid., 2: 160.
60. Ibid., 2: 164.
61. "Mr. Phillips stated that Ann Carson . . . is sick, lame and unable to come to court. The Trial of the prisoners was in consequence postponed until Monday morning next at 10 o'clock, and the prisoners remanded to Jail." *Democratic Press*, June 25, 1823.

62. "The defendant being sworn saith in addition to her former affidavit for postponement of her trial, That she verily believes she cannot at this time procure a fair and impartial trial in consequence of the excitement of the public mind, which as she verily believes has been occasioned by certain publications in the newspaper called the Democratic Press, edited by John Binns one of the Alderman of the City of Philadelphia, and as such one of the Judges of this Court. . . . That one of the pieces is headed 'As we expected:'—That by their publication the public mind has been enflamed and sufficient time has not elapsed for the fervor to have abated, so as to afford her a fair and impartial trial." *Democratic Press*, July 3, 1823.

63. *Salem* (Massachusetts) *Gazette*, June 20, 1823; *City Gazette and Commercial Daily Advertiser* (Charleston, South Carolina), June 23, 1823.

64. *Democratic Press*, July 9, 1823.
65. *Memoirs*, 2: 163.
66. Ibid., 2: 157; *Mrs. Carson's Last Adventure*, 7.
67. *Memoirs*, 2: 164, 165.
68. Ibid., 2: 165.
69. *Mrs. Carson's Last Adventure*, 8.

70. Convict Docket, 1819–1824, Mayor's Court, Philadelphia City Archives, 270; "This woman was also stated by the Recorder, to be an old convict, but in consideration of the feebleness of her intellect, and her having been made the

dupe of others, her term of imprisonment was abridged." *Democratic Press*, July 8, 1823; *Mrs. Carson's Last Adventure*, 9.

Mayor Wharton wrote to Girard after the trial to assure him that the counterfeit money had been destroyed and the "daring gang of counterfeiters who have been engaged in the above nefarious work" were all in prison. Robert Wharton, Mayor to Stephen Girard, August 8, 1823. Girard Papers, Series II, reel 85, no. 648 (Letters Received 1823), American Philosophical Society.

71. "The public will remember that these nefarious schemes were defeated in consequence of information being timely given, by the editor of this paper." *Democratic Press*, July 9, 1823.

Other papers that carried news of her sentencing include the *Essex Register* (Salem, Massachusetts) and the *Saratoga* (New York) *Sentinel*. Both July 29, 1823. A few weeks later, the *Haverhill* (New Hampshire) *Gazette* ran an article titled "Villains Vade Mecum," which advertised a book that revealed the trade secrets of successful criminals. The paper suggested that if Carson had used this book she would not have been caught. August 9, 1823.

72. Carson shared this quality with her contemporary, Lord Byron (1788–April 1824). Lady Caroline Lamb said of him after their first meeting in 1813 that he was "mad, bad, and dangerous to know." Quoted in Elizabeth Longford, *The Life of Byron* (Boston: Little, Brown, 1976), 50.

73. *Democratic Press*, July 9, 1823.

74. Ibid., July 9, 1823.

75. *Mrs. Carson's Last Adventure*, 12.

76. *Memoirs*, 2: 167.

77. Ibid., 2: 167.

78. Ann Carson to Stephen Girard, December 1, 1823. Girard Papers, Series II, reel 86, no. 982 (Letters Received 1823–1824), American Philosophical Society. There is no record of a reply to Carson's letter.

79. Overn was described as a thirty-five-year-old white woman, "5′1 ½, born at sea, a house servant, palid face, blue eyes, black hair." Convict Docket 1819–1824, Philadelphia City Archives, 333.

80. The coroner listed the cause of death as "typhus fever." Death Register for Philadelphia Prisons, 1819–1830. Convict Philadelphia County Folio 270, Philadelphia City Archives. Clarke said that because of rumors that Carson died of her wounds, the prison had a coroner and jury give verdict of typhus fever. *Memoirs*, 2: 172.

81. *Memoirs*, 2: 173.

82. Ibid., 2: 175. Staughton was the minister for the Second Presbyterian Church. The Hutton family connection made sense: two of Carson's sisters were married to Huttons.

83. *Memoirs*, 2: 175.

84. *Saratoga* (New York) *Sentinel*, May 11, 1824, reprint of the announcement in the *Philadelphia Gazette*.

85. *Baltimore Patriot*, April 29, 1824.

86. Rosanna Overn was discharged from prison in July 1829. Convict Docket 1819–1824, Philadelphia City Archives, 333. I found no discharge record for O'Brien.

87. Convict Docket 1819–1824, Mayor's Court, Philadelphia City Archives, 270.

88. Loring was released in October 1829. He was described at the time of his sentencing as age "40 white man 5'10" born in Mass. Light complexion light blue eyes gray hair on his breast an MD." Convict Docket 1819–1824, Mayor's Court, Philadelphia City Archives, 270.

89. "Take care of my books, said she, I have money to print a second edition, if I live to get out; if I die it is yours, and you can get it out. Yes, replied I, with additions, just as you say, replied she laughing." *Memoirs*, 2: 166.

90. *Memoirs*, 2: 93.

91. Ibid., 2: 132.

92. Ibid., 2: 109. Clarke also had Mayor Wharton mention her transcript of Carson's counterfeiting trial. *Mrs. Carson's Last Adventure* "by a listener" (1823) used the same pseudonym as her Hogan trial transcript.

93. *Memoirs*, 2: 131.

94. Ibid., 2: 157.

95. Ibid., 2: 154–55.

96. Ibid., 2: 173.

97. Ibid., 2: 151. "The Petition of Ann Carson relict of John Carson praying the Court, to appoint a Gaurdian [*sic*] for the persons and estates of her minor children William, Joseph, and Jeannette. The Court took no order thereon, but vacated the appointment of Thomas Newlin as Guardian of said Children." Orphan's Court Records, Philadelphia County, Books 27–29, 1818–1824, 383. The petition is dated June 14, 1820.

98. When Willis was not in a position to send Carson money, she turned to another male admirer for support. Carson lived "under the protection" of Thomas Newlin. (This was probably in 1818, the year that Newlin became guardian of the Carson children.) He rented a house near the hospital for Carson and her children. Once Carson met Mitchell, however, she had a falling out with Newlin, and he withdrew his financial support and resigned as guardian of her children.

99. *Memoirs*, 2: 151. Lear committed suicide in Washington, D.C., in October 1816. Because Willis, along with Carson, was in prison awaiting trial from July until November of that year, if this story is true, Willis stole the jewels sometime before he met Carson.

100. Willis was still in jail when Carson was arrested for counterfeiting. *Memoirs*, 2: 148–51.

101. Ibid., 2: 153.

102. Ibid., 2: 122.

Index

Abbott, Mary (Baker), 25
Abbott, Thomas, 5, 24, 25, 29, 33, 41, 45
Alcuin, 75
Anderson riot, 102
Antes, Henry, 51, 65
Armstrong, Thomas, Judge, 25; defense attorney for Ann Carson, 63
Armstrong's Ferry, 51
Aurora (Philadelphia), 123
Avery, Reverend Ephraim K., 92

Badger, Samuel, alderman and judge of the Court of Common Pleas, 29, 112
Baker, Ann. *See* Ann Baker Carson
Baker, Eliza, engagement to Captain Hillyard, 5; engagement to John Hutton, 5
Baker, James, 136
Baker, Jane: arrested for conspiracy, 57; boarders, 5; conspiracy trial, 67; death in Pensacola, 136; lends money to Carson, 9, 36; letter to Girard, 135; opposes Carson's shop, 8; runs Carson's shop, 46; sews for Quartermaster Corps, 12; testimony at Smith's trial, 33, 34, 35, 36; witnesses shooting, 24
Baker, Sarah: school, 9
Baker, Thomas Captain, captain of *Delaware*, 4; in debtor's prison, 135; detained in France, 3; lives with Abbotts, 25; moves family to New Castle, 5; prisoner on the *Jersey*, 1; witnesses shooting, 24; and yellow fever, 4
Baltimore Patriot, 118, 130
Barkley, Temperance, 10; testimony at Smith's trial, 38, 41, 43
Beissel, Frederick, owner of Golden Fleece Inn, 65
Beissel, Miss, 54
The Benevolent Lawyers, 91, 110
Binns, John: and Bank of Pennsylvania, 64; editor of *Democratic Press*, 46, 49–50, 62, 123; political ties to Snyder, 65; review of the *History*, 83, 109
Black, Ferman, keeper of Walnut Street prison, 49
Bowen, Elijah, 48, 50, 54
Brady, James, shopkeeper, 116, 119
Broadhead, Daniel, 62
Brown, David Paul, defense attorney for Ann Carson, 66
Browne, Peter A., defense attorney for Smith, 34, 47
Burroughs, Stephen, 73
Butler, William, 106, 111, 118, 125

Campbell, Sarah Jane, 48; testifies at conspiracy trial, 65, 66
Carr, Mary. *See* Mary Clarke
Carson, Ann Baker: accessory to murder, 41–43; admirers, 86; alias, 51, 117; arrested for conspiracy, 51; arrested in New Jersey, 117; attacked, 128; in Baltimore courtroom, 70; bigamy charge, 46; and black prisoners, 81; boards with Mrs. Ferras, 110; china shop, 9, 10, 23; asks Clarke to write memoir, 69; conspiracy trial, 63; counterfeiting trial, 121; cross-examines Sarah Willis, 125; in debtor's prison, 36, 79; dies, 128; elopement, 85; escape from Trenton jail, 117; *feme sole* trader, 36; before grand jury, 118; requests loan from Girard, 10, 79; marriage, ideas on, 76, 77, 83, 88; marriage proposals, 84, 87, 88; marriage to Smith, 26, 77; middle-class status, 80; moves to New York, 115; needlework, 9, 71, 110; and opiates, 46; passes counterfeit bank note, 116; petitions Stephen Girard, 127–128; plan to liberate Smith, 48–49; and politics, 64; publicity, 60–61; purchases counterfeit money, 111; racism, 81–82; receives letter in Lancaster jail, 60; relationship with

Carson, Ann Baker (*Cont.*)
Mr. M—n, 86; relationship with Charles Mitchell, 88; returns to Philadelphia, 116; sentenced for robbery, 72; sews for Quartermaster Corps, 12; trial as accessory to murder, 44, 67

Carson, Jeanette, 136

Carson, John, ix; in Charleston, South Carolina, 8; Chief Officer of the *China*, 7; chinaware, 9; commission for *Wasp*, 11; drinking, 8, 12; duel, 85, 86; funeral, 30; jealousy of Hutton, 85; marriage to Ann, 7; master of *Pennsylvania Packet*, 7; *Pennsylvania Packet* seized in Whampoa, 7; petition for divorce, 27; rumors about his death, 25, 149; sails on *Phoenix*, 11; service under Captain Baker, 6; shot by Smith, 24, 29; attempt to stab Smith, 28

Carson, John H., son of Ann, 136

Carson, Joseph, son of Ann, 26, 136

Carson, Joseph, Harrisburg judge, 53

Carson, William, son of Ann, 129

Cassin, Lieutenant, 11

Charlotte Temple, 16, 73

Chatham Street Theater (also Chatham Garden Theater), 95, 96

Chew, Benjamin, Carson's defense attorney, 63

Child, Lydia Maria, 15

City Gazette and Commercial Daily Advertiser (Charleston, S.C.), 118

Clark, Daniel, 34, 35

Clarke, Mary, admiration for Dr. Franklin, 135; arrested for debt, 19; *The Benevolent Lawyers*, 91; and Carson's body, 129; changes name, 91; class identity, 134; *Concise History of the Life and Amours of Thomas S. Hamblin*, 97; at counterfeiting trial, 121–122, 124; editor of *Intellectual Regale, or Ladies Tea Tray*, 13; editorial identity, 18; family circumstances, 14; *Fair Americans*, 17, 103; fear of grave robbers, 129; friendship with Joseph Hutton, 94; and gender conventions, 22; ghostwrites *History of the Celebrated Mrs. Ann Carson*, 72; *History of Edwin Forrest*, 95; Hogan trial transcript, 91, 106; *Lake Champlain, or The American Tars on the Borders of Canada*, 17, 94; manages theater, 94; *Memoirs of the Celebrated and Beautiful Mrs. Ann Carson*, 131–134; nativism, 101; pamphlet on Catholic schism, 106; *Parterre*, 22, 90; *The Return from Camp*, 17, 90, 94; *Sarah Maria Cornell, or, The Fall River Murder*, 91, 92; sues Carson, 114; writes plays for *Tea Tray*, 17; *Venture It, A Comedy in Five Acts*, 17, 94; and Naomi Vincent, 100; visits Carson in prison, 127

Clifton, Josephine, 99, 100

Cohen, Patricia Cline, 101

Columbian (New York), 63

Concise History of the Life and Amours of Thomas S. Hamblin, 97

Connell, Mary, 90

Connellin, Mary, 51; testifies at conspiracy trial, 65

Coquette, The, 16, 73

Davis, Captain, 4

Democratic Press (Philadelphia): coverage of Carson's activities, 62, 118, 125

Dennie, Joseph, 18

Desilver, Robert, printer, agrees to publish *History of the Celebrated Mrs. Ann Carson*, 72; and *History*'s brisk sales, 109, 110; Hogan trial transcript, 91; libel worries, 108; publishes Smith trial transcript, 31, 40; refuses to print second edition of *History*, 110; rents house to Clarke, 110; service under Captain Baker, 106

dime novels, 73

divorce law, in Pennsylvania, 32

Duane, William, Alderman, 121

Dudden, Faye, 96

Dunlap, William, 96

Elder, Thomas, Harrisburg attorney, 54, 65

Embargo Act, 9

Fahnstoch, Harrisburg justice of the peace, 51

The Fair Americans, 17, 103

Farren riot, 102

Febiger, Elizabeth Carson, 136

feme covert, 9

feme sole, 14, 36

Fermor, Mrs., 99

Index

Ferras, Mrs., boardinghousekeeper in New York City, 110
Fisher, Redwood, 37
Forrest, Edwin, 94
Forrest, William, 95, 97

Gaines, General, 34
Gale, Major Anthony, 87
Gallagher, Mary, 181, 182
Geise, keeper of Walnut Street prison, 49
Gilpin, Joshua and Thomas, 7
Girard, Stephen, 10; Jane Baker's letter to, 135; Ann Carson requests loan, 10, 79; John Carson hired for India voyage, 11; counterfeit bank notes, 111, 116, 119, 120; petition from Ann Carson, 127
Golden Fleece Inn, Harrisburg, 51, 54

Hale, Sarah J.: and *American Ladies' Magazine*, 15, 22
Hamblin, Elizabeth Blanchard: manager of Richmond Hill Theater, 98; marriage to Thomas Hamblin, 97–98
Hamblin, Thomas: and Anderson riot, 102; and brothels, 101; and Josephine Clifton, 99–100; divorce, 98; and *Fair Americans*, 103; Farren riot, 102; and Helen Jewett, 101; manager of Bowery Theater, 99; marriage to Elizabeth Hamblin, 97–98; and Louisa Medina, 98; and death of Louisa Missouri Miller, 101; and Naomi Vincent, 99–100
Harris, Captain, 84
Harrisburg Chronicle (Harrisburg), 65
Hart, John, constable, 30, 59
Heartt, Dennis, printer, 19
Hemphill, C. Dallett, 81
Hillyard, Captain of the *Pickering*, 5
History of Edwin Forrest, 95
History of the Celebrated Mrs. Ann Carson, 70–75; and class, 78–82; and nativism, 82; reviewed by Binns, 83
Hogan, Rev. William, 90
Hurley, Rev. Michael Hurly, 51, 58
Hutton, John, 5
Hutton, Joseph, 5; association with Mary Clarke, 94; marriage to Sarah Baker, 136; thespian, 94
Hutton, Nathaniel, 84–85
Hutton, Sarah (Baker), 82, 136

Ingersoll, Edward, prosecuting attorney, 43
Ingersoll, Jared, attorney general of Pennsylvania, 31, 45
Ingersoll, Joseph R., defense attorney for Ann Carson, 63, 65
Intellectual Regale, or Ladies Tea Tray. See *Tea Tray*

Jay Treaty, 3
Jewett, Helen, 101
jurors, in Smith's trial, 45

Kelker, keeper of Harrisburg jail, 54
Kelker, Mary, 54, 59
Kelley, Mary, 15
Kemble, Frances (Fanny), 96, 97
Kittera, Thomas, deputy attorney general, defense attorney for Ann Carson, 65, 66

Lady's Magazine (London), 13
Lake Champlain, or The American Tars on the Borders of Canada, 17, 94
Lear, Tobias, 133
Levy, Sampson, Smith's defense attorney, 41
Lewis, H. C., editor, 15
Logan, Deborah, 59
Loring, Dr. Charles, 71, 118, 125
Loyd, Joseph, defense attorney for Ann Carson, 63

Madison, Dolly, 81
Mann, Thomas, 71
marriage, 31, 44; Carson's attitude toward, 76, 77, 83, 88
Mason, Priscilla, 75
Mayland, Sarah, 118, 125, 129
McKibbin, Captain, 11
McLean, John, constable, 116
Medina, Louisa, 98; adaptation of Bulwer-Lytton's *Earnest Maltravers*, 101; governess to Hamblin's daughter, 103; Hamblin's mistress, 98; *Wacousta*, 103
Memoirs of Stephen Burroughs, 73
Memoirs of the Celebrated and Beautiful Mrs. Ann Carson, x, 105
Meredith, Elizabeth, 4
Meredith, William, Philadelphia attorney, 70
middle class: construction of identity, 70, 78–79
Mihm, Stephen, 116

Miller, Louisa Missouri, 101
Mitchell, Charles, friend of Richard Smith, 71; and Mann robbery, 71; relationship with Carson, 88
Montgomery, John, Baltimore prosecutor, 70
Mullany, Colonel James R., 34
Murray, Judith Sargent, 5, 75, 139

nativism: in *Concise History of the Life and Amours of Thomas S. Hamblin*, 101; in *History of the Celebrated Mrs. Ann Carson*, 82
New York Herald, 73, 99
New-York Mirror, 92, 96
New York Sun, 73, 101
Newlin, Thomas, Carson children's court-appointed guardian, 71, 132, 136
newspapers, changes in reporting, 61
Niles' Weekly Register, 61
Nonimportation Act, 9

O'Brian, Kitty, 128
Overn, Rosanna, 111, 125, 128

Parrish, Captain, ix, 105
Parrish, Sarah, 118, 125
Parterre, 22, 90
Pennsylvania Supreme Court, 47, 48, 57, 124
Philadelphia, Catholic community, 90; Court of Common Pleas, 30; geography and population, 16; map, 2
Philadelphia Gazette, 130
Philadelphia Ledger, 137
Philips, Zaligman, Carson defense attorney, 63, 71, 123–124
Poe, Edgar Allan, 96
Port Folio, 18
Poulson's American Daily Advertiser (Philadelphia): John Carson's funeral announcement, 30
Power of Sympathy, The, 16, 73
print culture, 91
Prune Street debtor's prison, 20, 36

Quartermaster Corps, 12

Rawle, William: Carson's defense attorney, 65; Smith's defense attorney, 31
Reed, Jacob, judge: conspiracy trial, 105; speech at counterfeiting trial, 126–127

Relf's Philadelphia Gazette and Daily Advertiser: John Carson's funeral announcement, 30; report on Smith's trial, 40
Republican Argus (Northumberland, Pa.), 64
republicanism, 76
Return from Camp, The, 17, 90, 94
Richmond Hill Theater, 92, 98
Riley, Isaac, printer, 113
Risley, Jacob, demands Clarke's arrest, 19
Roberts, cashier of Girard bank, 124
Rush, Jacob: instructions to murder trial jury, 39–40; judge at Carson's accessory to murder trial, 41; judge at Smith's trial, 30

Sarah Maria Cornell, or, The Fall River Murder, 91–93
Saville, John, shopkeeper, 116, 119
Sedgwick, Catharine Maria, 15
Shaw, George, lawyer, 108, 112
Shepherd, Elizabeth, 118, 120, 125
Smith, Jonathan B., lawyer, 29, 45
Smith, Richard, Battle of Sacketts Harbor, 25; charged with first-degree murder, 31; *Confession*, 57; denied pardon, 47; execution, 58–59; marriage to Ann Carson, 26, 77; shoots John Carson, 24, 29; trial for murder, 24, 30–40; trial transcript, 67; writ of error petition, 47
Smith, Thomas, printer, 20
Snyder, Simon, governor of Pennsylvania, 46; denies Smith a pardon, 47; subpoenaed to testify in Philadelphia, 66; testifies against Carson, 55,
Snyder, Mrs. Simon, 54
Spirit of the Times, 96, 101
Staughton, Dr., burying ground, 129
Stoops, Mrs., ix, 105

Tea Tray: demise of, 15; employees, 19; proposal for, 13; style of, 90; subscribers, 13, 19
theaters: and brothels, 97; and class, 96; and women, 94, 96
Tilghman, William, chief justice of Pennsylvania Supreme Court, 57, 62
trials, as entertainment, 66
Trollope, Frances, 93
True American (Trenton, N.J.), 60, 123

Ulrich, Laurel Thatcher, 139
United States Gazette (Philadelphia): John Carson's funeral announcement, 30; Clarke's advertisement, 13

Venture It, A Comedy in Five Acts, 17, 94
Vincent, Naomi, 99–100

Wallingford, Mary, 75
Walnut Street jail, ix, 36, 63, 110; black prisoners in, 81
Walnut Street Theater, 94, 102
Washington City Weekly Gazette, 55, 63
Way, Henry, 50
Weekly Visitor or Ladies' Miscellany, 13
Wharton, Robert, mayor of Philadelphia, 99, 114, 116, 120

White, Sarah, 10
Williams, Catherine, 92
Willis, Henry, 48, 50, 108; alias John Ryde, 67; in Baltimore with Carson, 70; robs Tobias Lear, 133
Willis, Sarah, 118, 119, 120, 125
Willock, Mr., purser of the *Pickering*, 5
Wollstonecraft, Mary, 139
women, criminals, 61; and education, 1, 3–4, 75; and prison clothing, 81; and racism, 82; sexuality, 89; wage-earners, 8–9, 13, 22–23; writers, 15

yellow fever, 6
Yellow Springs, 36
Young Ladies Academy of Philadelphia, 3, 4, 75

Acknowledgments

The National Endowment for the Humanities, the School of Arts and Humanities at the University of Texas at Dallas, and the Library Company of Philadelphia provided financial assistance for this project. Syracuse University generously allowed me to begin my new job by taking a year's leave to complete the book.

Over the years, I have presented parts of this book at several venues. Thank you to the people at the University of Texas at Dallas Gender Studies group, the Dallas Social History seminar, the British Association for American Studies, and the Class Conference in Big Sky, Montana. A special thanks to the folks in the University of Georgia History department, especially Allan Kulikoff, Greg Nobles, and Stephen Mihm. Frank Cogliano, Robert Mason, and Rhodri Jeffreys-Jones of the University of Edinburgh Modern History seminar gave me useful comments on chapter revisions.

Portions of a few chapters began life as articles: "Sex and Other Middle-Class Pastimes in the Life of Ann Carson," in *Class Matters: Early North America and the Atlantic World*, ed. Simon Middleton and Billy G. Smith (Philadelphia: University of Pennsylvania Press, 2008); "Gendered Strategies for Success in the Early Nineteenth-Century Literary Marketplace: Mary Carr and the *Ladies' Tea Tray*," *Journal of American Studies* 40, no. 1 (April 2006): 35–51; "'He Swore His Life Was in Danger from Me': The Attempted Kidnapping of Governor Simon Snyder," *Pennsylvania History* 67, no. 3 (Summer 2000): 349–60. I thank the journals and their publishers for allowing me to include material in this book.

Research was carried out at several Philadelphia institutions, including the Philadelphia City Archives where most of the evidence of Carson's crimes resides. A good part of my work was done at the Library Company of Philadelphia; James Green, Cornelia King, and Philip Lapsansky continue to be the dream team of the scholar's world. Thank you also to Valerie-Anne Lutz and Librarian Roy Goodman at the American Philosophical Society, Elizabeth Laurent at Girard College, Megan Hahn Fraser at the Independence Seaport Museum, and Andrea Ashby Leraris at Independence National Historical Park. I also had generous help at the Pennsylvania Hospital.

Many people encouraged and advised me on this project. My thanks to Billy Smith, Simon Middleton, Bruce Mann, Alison Games, Leslie Patrick, Laura Edwards, Sherri Gesin, Michael Wilson, Erin Smith, David Edmunds, Martha Selby, Simon Newman, Marina Moskowitz, Leeyanne and Eric Moore, Kris McDaniel, and Nina Stoeckel. Stephen Mihm did his darndest to find me a counterfeit Girard banknote. And out of the blue one day a few years ago I received an email from Nicole Ruediger, a direct descendant of Thomas Baker. I owe her thanks for sharing her family's genealogy records with me.

Susan Klepp, Dallett Hemphill, Thomas Humphrey, and Kathleen Wellman read and commented on the entire manuscript in its various versions. Tom not only read the book; he also listened patiently to hours of descriptions, speculations, and complaints.

Once again, my editor at the University of Pennsylvania press, Robert Lockhart, his assistant Chris Hu, project editor Noreen O'Connor-Abel, and copyeditor Kathy McQueen all made the publishing process a pleasure rather than a chore.

I have come to realize how important locations and atmosphere are to the writing process. Many people and places contributed to my ability to actually put words on a page. Dan and Sally Gordon at Wissahickon-Wanderers HQ are wonderful friends and the best of hosts—even offering a choice of dogs to sleep with. Bundle provided me with time everyday to leave the computer, walk around the block, and let things sink in. And the commentary and wit of Phil Liggett and Paul Sherwen during the month of July 2007 eased my final tinkerings on the chapters.

Susan Klepp introduced me to Ann Carson. Susan has at times been my coauthor, mentor, and critic. She has always been a good friend. Though I frequently cursed the day that Carson (or "that piece of work," as Leslie Patrick rightly refers to her) came into my life, this project was entertaining and challenging. At moments, it was even fun. Thank you, Susan.

Mark and Kaitlin know far more about Ann Carson and Mary Clarke than they ever wanted to. Thank you for your patience and encouragement. And, finally, to absent friends: Bundle and Fuzz.